Aside from her work for the NMOA and her community, over the years Margaret mothered nine children—Bonnie, Sandra, Thomas, Robert, Dale, Mary, Timothy, Jeffrey, and Janette; periodically held jobs to supplement her family's income; and was involved with other organizations. She was a communicant and catechism teacher at St. Bernard's Church in Irons, Michigan, and active in the Spirit of the Woods Music Association. From the mid-1970s through the 1980s, Margaret was chairperson of the local Indian Education (Title IV) Program, which serviced tribal children in the Manistee County area. After her work was done, she enjoyed mushroom hunting and beadwork, and her family and friends remember that she loved to spend her free time picking blueberries, gardening, baking, canning preserves, and cooking for all of the people who knew and loved her.

In 1970, while still a regional unit of the NMOA, the members of Unit Seven formed a new organization called the Thornapple River Band of Ottawa Indians. They created the organization to help preserve and promote Ottawa culture, and to serve as an official tribal government for their community. Due to some internal conflicts, the Thornapple Band divided. Meanwhile, Margaret stayed active in the NMOA. When one faction of the former Thornapple Band reorganized as Little River Band of Ottawa Indians, Inc., Margaret continued to serve her community as a member of the Little River Board of Directors, motivated by her vision of a strong tribal government and sovereignty for her people.

Margaret served on the Little River Band's Enrollment Committee for many years, in addition to her seat on the board of directors. In fact, she had already been compiling genealogies for nearly a decade, which were used to determine the eligibility of tribal members for a number of federal payments, benefits, and treaty-based rights. The genealogical data Margaret gathered entitled many tribe members to cash payments awarded to the Ottawas as a result of a successful suit filed with the Indian Claims Commission (Docket 40-K), federal education monies, and, for a short time, guaranteed hunting and fishing rights for tribe members.

But these successes alone were not enough for Margaret. During her years of service with the NMOA, Unit Seven, and its successor organizations of the Thornapple Band and the Little River Band, Margaret—like many others—became frustrated with the response of federal officials to the legitimate needs and rights of Ottawa people. The members and leaders of the NMOA focused most of their attention and effort on payment of "Indian money." Margaret wanted more than that, and over the years, she continued to raise the issue of tribal sovereignty.

After reaffirmation of the Little River Band in 1994, Margaret continued to work for her tribe as a member of the Tribal Council. She continued to pursue the causes most important to her. Having grown up at and around Indian Village, Margaret wanted the Tribe to reacquire this parcel of land, which was so important to preserving its history. She sponsored resolutions for research on the history and title of the property, and positioned the Tribe to reassert ownership when the opportunity to do so arose. As a result of a legal settlement, Indian Village was returned to the Little River Ottawas on June 19, 1996.

Margaret served her people until the final days of her life, and the Little River community lost one of its most respected, hard-working, and dedicated elders when she passed, on January 2, 1997. Margaret had been diagnosed with kidney failure during her time as a councilperson. With the exception of short, health-related absences from her seat on the Tribal Council, she served her community continually, even attending a Tribal Council meeting just weeks before her death. Many Little River Ottawas remember that she would come to meetings or work immediately after completing dialysis, and if she was too weak to leave her home, she still conducted what business she could by phone. When concerned colleagues asked why she was working while in ill health, she replied that the work she did for her people was simply "more important."

Margaret Bailey Chandler always wanted to be known for her honesty. She believed that the only way to separate fact from fiction was to participate in the events that were shaping her tribe's future. For more than fifty years, she actively represented her people and fought for federal reaffirmation and political sovereignty for her tribe. Because of her meticulous notes of meeting agendas, minutes, and events between 1950 and 1970, she helped to preserve an important part of Little River Ottawa history. Her records are irreplaceable, and without them, the Tribe might have never been federally reaffirmed. Margaret believed that reaffirmation of her tribe's sovereignty was the most important issue that she pursued in her lifetime, and she had lived to see it happen.

On a sunny September day in 1996, more than 150 Little River Ottawas gathered at the site of Indian Village for a special picnic, held to commemorate the second anniversary of their federal reaffirmation and the return of the Indian Village property to the Tribe. Gathered under a large canopy tent—while their children played nearby, and men tended to a Sacred Fire and a pig roasted over glowing embers—Tribe members formed a Talking Circle, visiting with one another, sharing stories about Indian Village, and discussing their visions of what the Tribe would accomplish in the years to come. After most people had arrived, one tribal member called for everyone's attention. He recited a short history of Indian Village and then invited Tribe members to share their memories of this place. Several members expressed their respect for, and gratitude towards, the elders who had worked so tirelessly and passionately for their tribe.

In the midst of these reminiscences, tribal member Bill Memberto called out, announcing that he had a special presentation to make to one of the elders, who "needed to be recognized for her work and dedication." He asked Margaret Chandler to step forward. Bill held up an eagle feather, and while Margaret made her way to the spotlight, he explained that the feather had come from the eagle's breast, plucked from the area that covered its heart. When he handed the feather to Margaret, he explained that he and the Little River Ottawas wanted to honor her "for all of the work and dedication she gave from her heart to protect and preserve the Tribe." When she took the eagle feather, she said that she would always honor this gift. But in the minds of the Little River Ottawas, she already had.

In January 1997, the Little River Ottawas lost one of their most respected and devoted elders. Now, a decade later, her strength of spirit continues to permeate and motivate the tribal community: "She gave her all to this Tribe and then some. . . . She was an inspiration to us all back then and she still is today." Margaret lived to see her vision of a better world for the Little River Ottawas—a cause for which she selflessly and tirelessly worked and fought all of her life to achieve—slowly take shape and become reality. For this, she will always be honored and remembered by her tribe, and for her determination and commitment to her people, the Little River Ottawas say *kchi-miigwech!*

Preface

This manuscript has been a work in progress for nearly twenty years. It has existed in many forms, and has kept evolving as the Little River Band of Ottawa Indians' story continues. The original manuscript is based on a 1979 ethnohistorical study written by Dr. Richard White. During their pursuit of federal recognition, the Little River Ottawas commissioned me to revise and add to Dr. White's study, a task that I accepted with his gracious permission. A draft of this manuscript was submitted to the United States Congress Select Committee on Indian Affairs in 1993 to support the Little River Band's bid for a legislative restoration of the trust relationship severed by the United States nearly a century before. Subsequent to the Little River Ottawas' federal recognition in 1994, the manuscript was again revised and supplemented at the request of the Little River Band Tribal Council and used to educate band members about the history of the Ottawas' relationship with the United States.

All of the earlier drafts focused necessarily upon the political survival and cultural continuity of the Little River Ottawas from treaty times to the present. I wrote the text as a series of direct responses either to issues raised during the legislative process, or to show that the Little River Ottawas' documented history would allow them to meet the mandatory criteria of the Bureau of Indian Affairs' federal acknowledgment process. Leah C. Vetne oversaw the final transformation of this manuscript. She reorganized and edited the original manuscript to address a more general readership, retaining a focus on Little River Ottawa political and cultural survival while minimizing the historical arguments addressed to readers holding federal offices. The text is supplemented with images and depictions of the people who lived through the events discussed in historical documents. Captions accompanying this revision add a new dimension to the manuscript, portraying Ottawa life as the Little River Ottawas themselves lived it.

I collected many of the images in this manuscript in 1990 and 1991 for a project funded by the Public Museum of Grand Rapids (Michigan). The Grand Rapids museum, then in the process of constructing a new building and designing new exhibits, commissioned me to travel throughout western Michigan and make photocopy images of photographs in the private collections of people whose ancestors had lived on the Grand River. These images can be seen throughout the museum's permanent exhibit *Anishinabek: The People of This Place*. The Public Museum of Grand Rapids houses the original collection and has generously allowed the Little River Band to duplicate these published images.

Documentary research for the project was carried out at the National Archives in Washington, D.C.; the Bureau of Indian Affairs Field Office in Sault Ste. Marie, Michigan; the Federal Records Center in Chicago, Illinois; the Clarke Historical Library at Central Michigan University in Mount Pleasant; the Burton Historical Collection in the Detroit Public Library; the Bentley Historical Library at the University of Michigan in Ann Arbor; Michigan State University Library in East Lansing; the Archives of Michigan; the Michigan Room Collections of the Grand Rapids (Michigan) Public Library; the Manistee (Michigan) County Museum; the Rose Hawley Museum at Ludington, Michigan; the Loutit District Library in Grand Haven, Michigan; and in the homes of Tribe members.

My sincere appreciation for making this project possible are due to tribal elders Percy Campeau, Margaret (née Bailey) Chandler, Jim Koon Jr., Katherine (née Sam) Glocheski, Steve and Dorothy Medacco, Alex and Rose Sams, Ruth (née Koon) Dean, Elizabeth (née Theodore) Bailey, Doris (née Bailey) Wabsis, George and Lucille Pego, and Marcella (née Moore) Leusby—all of whom enriched this story with their recollections, papers, and photographs. Members of the Little River Band tribal councils, past and present, read and discussed drafts. Former Tribal Council chairpersons Bonnie (née Lempke) Kenny and Daniel Bailey, as well as Robert Guenthardt and councilpersons Anne Guenthardt Avery and Margaret (née Bailey) Chandler made the valuable contributions of their collected historical documents, personal insights, and encouragement.

Anna Mae (née Sams) Lempke, Anna Jean (née Sams) Guenthardt, Lavern (née Wahr) Oren, and Katherine (née Sam) Glocheski shared with me their experiences of living at Indian Village.

Leah C. Vetne and Tribe member Melissa Zelenak-Rubis coordinated the Tribe's review of the manuscript, images, and captions—work that took place over several months of regular meetings of the Little River Band Book Review Committee. Appointed to the book-review committee by the Tribal Council were Tribe members Valerie Chandler and Connie (née Lempke) Waitner. Mark Dougher, tribal employee and longtime friend of the Little River Ottawas, as well as Tribe members Elaine Porter and Jonnie J. Sam II also regularly attended book-review committee meetings. All of these individuals contributed their insight and input, as well as their extensive and detailed knowledge of the Tribe's recent history, particularly from 1988 to the present. Special thanks go to Valerie Chandler, who collected and cataloged many of the photographs; Mark Dougher and Valerie Chandler, whose organized and detailed notes were invaluable to composing the final chapters; Jonnie J. Sam II, Connie Waitner, and Elaine Porter for sharing their historical and cultural knowledge; and Melissa Zelenak-Rubis, who contributed photographs from her personal collection, took many of the photographs that appear in the final chapters, and restored old and damaged photographs. My thanks also go to Joseph C. Quick II, who created the maps appearing in the early chapters of this book.

My sincere thanks to everyone involved in the production of this book and the telling of the Little River Ottawas' story.

Land beneath the Trees

"Naaminitigong ndojeba" translates from the Anishinaabemowin to "I am from the land beneath the trees." For a long time this is how the people known today as Gaaching Zibii Daawaa Anishinaabek would have identified where there were from—home.

Although it has specifically come to mean the area of Michigan now called Manistee, it was used for the entire region from Pakweyaashking (Land of the Cattails, now known as Arcadia) south to Bowting (Grand Rapids) and the Mishiiminikaaning (Land of Apples, Portland). Go east from the lakeshore, moving inland to the middle area of the state.

Many of the place names were different; Onagamaa (Singing Waters) became Onekama. The place known as Negwedoonhkaa (It is sandy) is called Hamlin in Mason County. Even Lugington had a different name, as did the Pere Marquette River—called Niindibekagoning (or Notipekego by some), meaning Place of Skulls. One can no longer find Waabgankiishkbogong (Place of the Clay) unless you look for Montague, although Mashkigong (Place of Marsh) may be easy to locate.

Although there are other names in use, today the descendants who are known as Little River Band Ottawas can say with pride, "Naaminitigong ndojeba," secure in the knowledge they can still call home the Land beneath the Trees.

Introduction: The Analytical Paradigm

The Indians of lower Michigan have gone far on the way to effective assimilation. They all understand and speak English; they are not distinguishable from their white neighbors in dress, except when they dress for show in supposedly traditional costume; they share on equal terms with other citizens in all school and other social agencies. They no longer maintain any tribal organizations or traditional ceremonies, except for the benefit of tourists. Their ancient arts and crafts survive only in half-forgotten imitations, or newer adaptations for tourist trade. They are in the transitional stage in that they have abandoned their old laws and customs while they have not learned to use the civic and social instruments that they have tacitly accepted. Archie Phinney says: "The culture, racial integrity and native genius of the Michigan Indians have degenerated beyond all hope of revival."[1]

Too often, the history and culture of Native peoples is regarded as Bureau of Indian Affairs investigator John Holst viewed that of the Michigan Ottawas in 1939—as static, as if immutable culture extended back to some mysterious, primordial beginning. In such a view, only the coming of Europeans to North America caused change in American Indian cultures, and this change was almost uniformly destructive. Cultural evolution in the larger American society is taken for granted and seen as natural, but change in American Indian societies is inevitably described as a loss of culture. This erroneous, mythological view of culture change has been socially, politically, and economically damaging to the Michigan Ottawas. The myth of cultural disintegration is simply that: a myth.

Federal officials, historians, and the broader American public have assumed that culture change, or whatever has replaced old customs or organizations in Indian life, is somehow "un-Indian." Social-science scholarship and a substantial body of historical analysis challenge that view. Studies of colonialism and its effects on indigenous band and tribal cultures now correctly assert that change in Native societies can be a successful response to altered conditions and just as "Indian" as what preceded it.[2] Anthropologists who study the phenomena of culture change in hunter-gatherer societies throughout the world are currently seeking new theoretical perspectives—not to interpret the cultural disintegration of these peoples, but to adequately explore their continuity and transformation.[3]

Like many other former hunter-gatherers, the Ottawas who historically occupied villages throughout Michigan's Grand River Valley—at one time collectively called the Grand River Bands—have adapted and changed over time in response to the demands of industrialized societies upon their lands, resources, and cultures. This change is a sign of their vitality as a people. If they had not changed, they would have vanished long ago, as nineteenth-century American politicians and writers so often predicted they would. The Ottawas have not vanished. Instead, they have survived into modern times, and they continue to thrive as a culturally and politically distinct group.

The Ottawas had known centuries of cultural, social, and political change before the United States claimed jurisdiction over their territory and American settlers came among them.

This book traces prehistoric and early historic Ottawa migrations from Georgian Bay into Michigan's Lower Peninsula, and their settlement in the Grand River Valley. It documents the relationship between the Ottawas and the United States through the first occupation of the Grand River Valley by Americans, the process and effects of treaty making, and the Ottawas' eventual abandonment of their Grand River villages and settlements on reservations in Mason, Muskegon, and Oceana counties during the mid-nineteenth century. This book records the story of how Ottawas who moved to these reservations lost title to their land, but managed to survive as a distinct people in the face of dispossession by American settlers during the 1860s, 1870s, and 1880s.

Although the nineteenth century was a time of severe economic and demographic disruption for the Ottawas, their cultural emphasis on the structures of kinship facilitated evolution of social and political structures according to Indian—not American—precedents. Even during the twentieth century, long after Ottawas were thought to be fully acculturated members of Michigan society, their leaders continued to exercise the culturally prescribed skills of consensus building among family members and extended kin, to pursue social and political agendas that emphasize the continuing distinction between themselves and their west Michigan neighbors. This book traces the work of twentieth-century Ottawa leaders, and documents the lives of the Ottawas who supported these leaders during the difficult years of the Great Depression, the post–World War II fluorescence of Michigan Indian politics, and the events that led to the restoration of the government-to-government relationship between the Little River Band of Ottawa Indians and the United States in 1994.

The Little River Band of Ottawa Indians evolved from Ottawa people who lived in a number of historical communities throughout the nineteenth and twentieth centuries. Their ancestors have been known variously as the Grand River Bands, the Manistee Ottawas, the Indian Town and Pere Marquette reservation communities, members of Northern Michigan Ottawa Association Unit Seven, and the Thornapple Band of Ottawa Indians. Regardless of title, their community was, and is, tied together by bonds of recognized kinship, consensus building by leaders around issues critical to the continuity of their community, and a continuing sense of their distinctness from the people who settled around them. These features of Ottawa society allowed ancestors of the Little River Ottawas to thwart the efforts of the United States to forcibly remove them to lands west of the Mississippi River, and to build lives for themselves and their descendants on lands they occupied when Europeans first entered the Great Lakes.

The Little River Ottawas have not been "assimilated," as John Holst reported in 1939. Today, many band members still reside within or nearby their treaty-reserved lands, and their community still operates based upon Ottawa customs and sociopolitical structures. In an ever-changing environment, the Little River Ottawas have maintained a vital, living society, defined by their own culture and values, adapting and changing as they always have.

CHAPTER 1

When the Europeans Came

The earliest written Ottawa history was recorded in 1615 when Samuel de Champlain, as he canoed on the French River, met the first Ottawa people the French encountered. These Ottawas lived along the shores of Lake Huron's Georgian Bay, on the Bruce Peninsula, on Manitoulin Island in present-day Ontario, and per-haps in Michigan's northern Lower Peninsula. On that day, Champlain met only a few members of the large and influential Ottawa Tribe.

As a large tribe spread over a vast area, the Ottawas became well-known purveyors of foods and items of indigenous manufacture throughout the entire Great Lakes region. The Ottawas obtained meat from the northern Lake Superior tribes, who enjoyed an abundance of large game, in exchange for *wampum* (beads), fishing nets, woven-reed mats, fish, berries, and other goods. When the French arrived, the Ottawas sold them birch-bark canoes and manufactured items in exchange for pots, shells, paints, and other things. Long before they met the French, however, the Ottawas had established a reputation for their trading excursions throughout the Great Lakes region: their very name translated from Algonquian means "traders." They were the only

■ There are no contemporary images of the Ottawa trading brigades that once traveled the northern Great Lakes. This painting is a realistic portrayal of the canoes in which the Ottawas traveled. These lake-worthy vessels could be powered by oar or sail, and could carry as much as five tons. The artist also accurately depicts the style of Ottawa men's clothing and adornments, as well as the range of articles the Ottawas traded during the years of the European fur trade, between 1615 and the late 1700s. *We Dined in a Cottonwood Tree*, painting by Robert Griffing. Courtesy of Paramount Press, Inc.

aboriginal people known to paddle their long birch-bark canoes—called *wiigwaas jiimaanan*—across the open waters of the Great Lakes, "out of sight of land."[1] By traveling so extensively, the Ottawas facilitated, and at times controlled, trade in the Great Lakes region. They also helped to maintain good relationships among the Great Lakes tribes, as the reciprocal exchange of goods and knowledge between the region's Native peoples created and sustained friendships and diplomacy.

The Ottawas' lifestyle was similar to, but distinct from, that of their tribal neighbors. Unlike the highly mobile Chippewas, who accessed a broad area to harvest diverse resources and did not inhabit their villages year round, the Ottawas maintained semipermanent villages. In their villages, the Ottawas practiced swidden agriculture to grow their own corn, beans, squash, sunflowers, and other crops, which they harvested for their own subsistence, for storage, and for trade.[2] Their villages were located along the Great Lakes shoreline, at places where abundant fisheries provided a plentiful source of protein. These villages were never

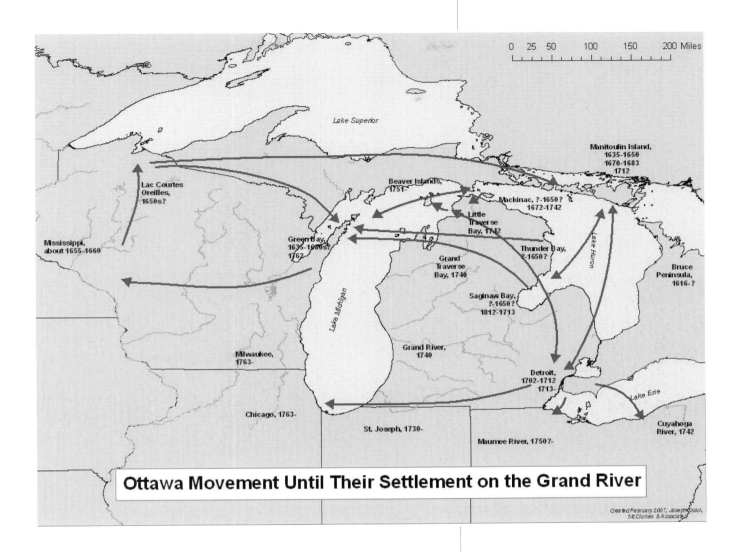

Ottawa Movement Until Their Settlement on the Grand River

completely abandoned during the winter hunting season, as were those of the Chippewas. Some families stayed in these villages year round, subsisting on stored food and fish, while hunting and trapping parties traveled away from settlements in the winter. Families traveled widely throughout the Great Lakes during the summer months to visit with neighboring tribes and to trade. When Ottawa gardens had exhausted the soil at village sites, the Ottawas packed up and moved entire villages to new locations where the soil was fertile.

Ottawa life changed radically when the New York Iroquois invaded Ontario and Michigan. The Iroquois destroyed Huron-Petun towns that neighbored Ottawa settlements, triggering a series of Huron and Ottawa migrations that came to be known as the Diaspora. The Ottawas, along

■ During the late 1500s, Europeans supplied the Iroquois with firearms. Iroquois warriors used these (and other) weapons to fight their way through southern Ontario, eventually driving the Ottawas from their homes. Between 1615 and their return to the Straits of Mackinac in 1671, the Ottawas moved their villages as far west as the Mississippi River and as far north as Bayfield, Wisconsin, and many lived for long periods of time on Wisconsin's Door Peninsula. When the Iroquois threat ended, Ottawas occupied villages along the northern shores of Lakes Huron and Michigan, and spread throughout Michigan's Lower Peninsula.

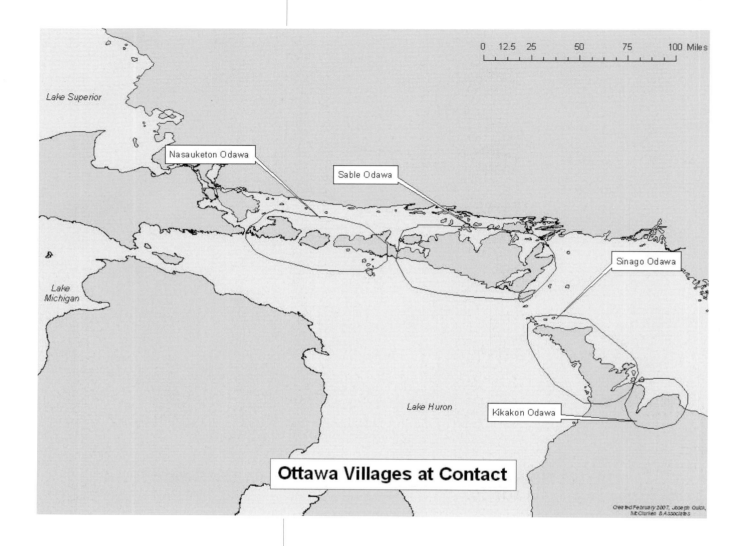

Ottawa Villages at Contact

Created February 2007, Joseph Quick,
McClurken & Associates

■ When French missionaries and explorers first came to the Great Lakes, ancestors of the modern Ottawa Tribe lived in four groups—the Kiskakon, Sinago, Sauble, and Nasaukeuton. Ottawa villages stretched along the northern shore of Lake Huron, from Georgian Bay to the Straits of Mackinac.

with the remaining Huron-Petuns, fled westward—first to the Straits of Mackinac and Saginaw and Thunder bays before they moved yet further west. Ottawa people joined with the Hurons and other Algonquins around Green Bay, and then moved to a nearby Potawatomi village called Mechingan on the shores of Lake Michigan. Some Ottawas stayed at Green Bay for several decades, and others fled as far west as the Mississippi River in the mid-1650s. Hostilities with the Sioux, however, pushed the westernmost Ottawas east into the Great Lakes region again.

The desperate circumstances of the Diaspora brought Great Lakes tribes that had once lived in tribally defined territories together at refugee centers in the western Great Lakes region. The Ottawas built settlements alongside those of other tribes and often shared villages

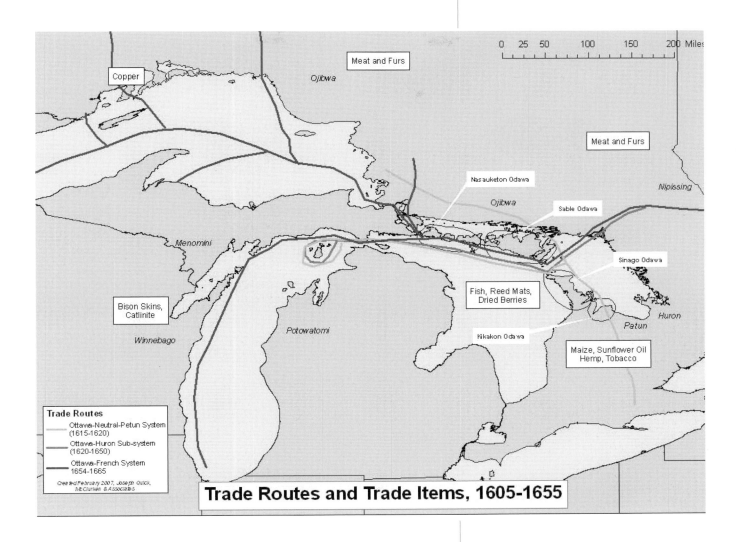

Trade Routes and Trade Items, 1605-1655

with members of these tribes. Living in crowded villages in restricted territories where there were not enough natural resources to support communities, the Ottawas and other displaced tribes lost many people to hunger and disease. The survivors of the Diaspora intermarried and formed new alliances and trading partnerships that helped reshape Ottawa life, a change that paved the way for even greater social change and migrations during the eighteenth century.

During this time—the 1650s and 1660s—the Ottawas became famous in the Great Lakes fur trade as "middlemen," carrying furs from the western Great Lakes to Montreal trade fairs.[3] By the early 1670s, Iroquois invasions ended, and the Ottawas returned to their historic villages on the Straits of Mackinac. Their four distinct bands—the Sable,

■ The name Ottawa is most often translated as "The Traders." Ottawa cultural identity, since the earliest recorded history, has rested upon the Ottawas' extensive travel from their villages on Lake Huron throughout the Great Lakes in large, lake-worthy birch-bark canoes. Ottawa people were known for their woven mats and finely made fur robes, and for trading crops from the southern Great Lakes in exchange for northern furs.

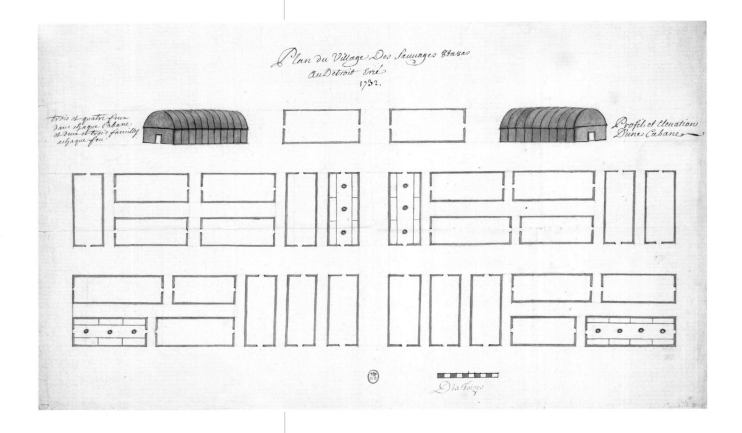

■ Ottawas built substantial villages comprised of longhouses, which they occupied for much of the year. As this 1732 drawing shows, each longhouse provided shelter to three or four families, represented in the drawing by three or four fire pits or hearths in a single longhouse. Villages were located near gardens and fisheries, which provided reliable sources of food. Ottawa families would travel from their villages to hunt, fish, trade, make war, or to visit friends and relatives in other places. "Plan of the Ottawa Village at Detroit drawn in 1732" (in Feest and Feest, "Ottawa," 1978). Bibliothèque nationale de France—Estampes et photographie.

Sinago, Kiskakon, and the Nassauaketon—settled in separate villages on Michigan's Upper Peninsula, on Manitoulin Island, on Keweenaw and Chaquamegon bays on the south shore of Lake Superior, and in northern Michigan, the point from which they began their permanent entry into Michigan's Lower Peninsula.

These Ottawa villages were prime sites for the Ottawas to continue their historic patterns of practicing horticulture, fishing, and trade. From 1670 to 1700, Ottawas lived on both sides of the Straits of Mackinac, and they enhanced their prestige as fur traders by transporting furs along the Ottawa River to Montreal and back. The Ottawas helped Europeans who entered their territories, supplying the French Fort Du Baud (established at St. Ignace in 1689) and the *coureurs de bois* traveling through en route to the western country with food and other goods.[4] Ottawas lived beside, and at times under the tutelage of, Jesuit priests who influenced Ottawa culture and customs. When the French moved their military post to Michilimackinac in 1715, the Ottawas went with them, building a new village and clearing fields to help supply food for the Europeans who entered the northern Great Lakes region.

The Ottawas' historic economy marked by travel and trade helped them to adapt when the French presence increased in northern Michigan. The Ottawas followed the newcomers into the Lower Peninsula, where Europeans established trading and military posts. Between 1700 and 1730, the Ottawas built villages at Detroit, Saginaw Bay, and St. Joseph. Ottawas at Fort Michilimackinac exhausted their swidden gardens by 1740, and in 1742, moved to the Lake Michigan shoreline, in the region called Waganagisi (It Is Bent) or L'Arbre Croche (Crooked Tree), the French name for the area. This village was later called Middle Village, and the name L'Arbre Croche was applied to the entire Lake Michigan shoreline between Mackinac and Shingwaksibing (Pine River), near modern-day Charlevoix. By 1765, more than one thousand Ottawas lived in the L'Arbre Croche region, and another two hundred of their relatives lived at Beaver Island. The Ottawas used the rich fisheries and reliable growing season at L'Arbre Croche to build a stable economy that would sustain them throughout the next two centuries of social and political change.

Ottawa demographic patterns continued to change throughout the eighteenth century as Ottawas from northern Michigan moved into the southern Lower Peninsula. By the 1750s, Ottawa bands had settled in horticultural villages on the Grand River. Charles Langlade, son of a French man and an Ottawa woman, who was the sister of the powerful L'Arbre Croche leader Nissawakwat, received a license from the British Crown to serve as the only legal fur trader on the Grand River and its tributaries in 1755. Ten years later, the Ottawas' numbers had swelled to 600 on the St. Joseph River, 400 at Saginaw Bay, and 1,200 at Detroit—places all easily accessible to Grand River Ottawas by connecting water routes.

When the British military arrived in southern Michigan during the 1760s, Ottawas had moved from L'Arbre Croche, St. Joseph, Saginaw Bay, and Detroit to build villages on the Grand River, and by the 1780s, about 1,200 Ottawas lived in these villages.[5] Originally, the Ottawas who had expanded across the Lower Peninsula built settlements close to Lake Michigan's shores where fish were plentiful; but fertile corn lands and marshes rich with wildlife drew them inland. Since the Kalamazoo and Grand rivers were easy to navigate in canoes, the shore and inland

■ The British took control of former French forts in 1761, including Fort Michilimackinac, which became Fort Mackinac. British officers challenged the regional political order and assumed that the Ottawas would willingly surrender to British rules for trade. In 1763, Ottawa warriors responded by entering and capturing Fort Mackinac. This painting envisions the Ottawas who led the attack. *The Conspiracy,* painting by Robert Griffing. Courtesy of Paramount Press, Inc.

Ottawas were able to communicate, cooperate, and share access to the lake. Ottawas on the Grand River also enjoyed abundant fall sturgeon (*nme*) harvests, and their villages flourished in this well-provisioned environment. By the eve of the War of 1812, the Grand River Ottawa villages were supported by fields that produced crops sufficient to feed warriors on the field of battle against Americans. These Grand River Bands maintained close ties with the Ottawas on the Muskegon, White, Pentwater, Pere Marquette, and Manistee rivers throughout the nineteenth century—connections that were, and still are, characteristic among Ottawa communities.

By the time American settlers began entering the Michigan Territory after the War of 1812, Ottawas lived at the mouths of all major rivers (*ziibiin*) flowing into Lake Michigan between the Kalamazoo River and the Straits of Mackinac. In the first formal count of Michigan Ottawas conducted by the United States in 1839, Ottawa numbers were split almost evenly between the Grand River settlements and those at Little Traverse Bay. The Ottawas' expansions were altered again by American settlement between 1821 and 1855, when they ceded title to their Michigan lands to the United States. By 1858 and 1859, the Grand River Ottawas would move north to a reservation, where they joined other related Ottawas on the Pere Marquette and Manistee rivers—a merger of bands that eventually evolved into the modern-day Little River Band of Ottawa Indians.

Although the Ottawas historically occupied their villages more permanently than did other neighboring bands and tribes, the Ottawas migrated extensively between the mid-seventeenth through the mid-nineteenth centuries in response to changed conditions. They were allies of both French and British trading partners. They moved furs along well-traversed water routes, supplied European forts and settlements with food, and at times accepted, or even embraced, Jesuit teaching and ritual. For a time, the Ottawas prospered as they integrated their own economic and cultural practices with those of Europeans, forming new relationships based on intermarriage and kinship, trade and reciprocity. This pattern of coexistence and cooperation would persist in Ottawa society for generations to come, and sustain them as they endured the hardships that accompanied American settlement in Michigan.

■ Here, artist Paul Kane depicts an Indian family at a summer camp on Georgian Bay—a place that Ottawas called home when the French first came to the Great Lakes. The image features realistic details, such as the two men fishing from their birch-bark canoe in the water, and the women standing in front of a *tipi*. Tipis, which were easy to construct and strike, were used by travelers as temporary shelters.

Ojibwa Camp, painting by Paul Kane. With permission of the Royal Ontario Museum.

CHAPTER 2

Kinsmen and Confederates

Ottawa society was based on interconnecting family relationships. The Ottawas regarded familial—or kinship—
connections differently than Americans think about family
relationships. In Ottawa society, a person had several mothers
(*gashina*) and fathers (*oosna*): a biological mother and all her sisters,
and, likewise, a biological father and all his brothers. All of the children
of an individual's mothers and fathers, cousins by the Euro-American
definition, were his or her brothers and sisters. When a couple married,
their respective families also became kin to one another. These kinship
protocols created intricate family webs; in fact, every person in a village
might be related to one another by Ottawa reckoning. According to Ottawa ethics, every individual was responsible for providing and caring for
family members in some way, and these responsibilities were delegated
according to age, sex, and relationships between individuals.

Cooperation and mobility among kin were essential to Ottawa
economic practices. Horticulture allowed the Ottawas to live a relatively
sedentary life in comparison to mobile Chippewa bands (as noted in
chapter 1). Until the late 1830s, Ottawa villages consisted entirely of

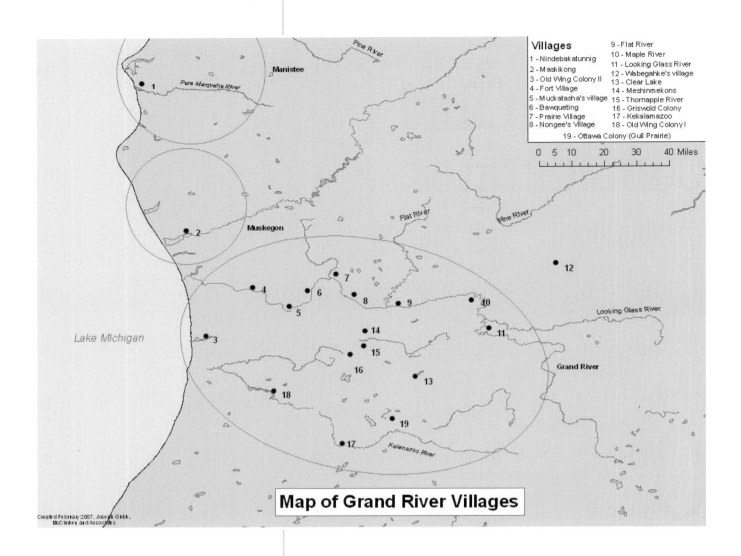

Villages

1 - Nindebakatunnig	9 - Flat River
2 - Maskikong	10 - Maple River
3 - Old Wing Colony II	11 - Looking Glass River
4 - Fort Village	12 - Wabegahke's village
5 - Muckatasha's village	13 - Clear Lake
6 - Bawqueting	14 - Meshinmekons
7 - Prairie Village	15 - Thornapple River
8 - Nongee's Village	16 - Griswold Colony
	17 - Kekalamazoo
	18 - Old Wing Colony I

19 - Ottawa Colony (Gull Prairie)

0   5 10   20   30   40 Miles

Map of Grand River Villages

Created February 2007, Joseph Oulok,
McClurken and Associates

■ The Grand River Ottawa ancestors of the Little River Ottawas lived in villages located on the Grand River and its tributaries, and along the Kalamazoo River and its tributaries. The earliest careful tally of these villages was conducted in 1838, when the Ottawas lived in the settlements shown on this map.

bark lodges, longhouses, and garden plots. Ottawa bands stayed in their villages for most of the year, where they cultivated swidden gardens and fished the nearby streams and lakes. In their villages, Ottawa women, children, and elders were responsible for planting, protecting, harvesting, and storing crops. Extended-family bands traveled to distant hunting and trapping grounds in the winter, where women set up temporary camps of dome-shaped structures called *wagenogans*, or cone-shaped tipis. During their stay in these camps, men were primarily responsible for hunting, fishing, and trapping, while women tended to their families' needs, preserved the meat and hides, and gathered wood for fires. In the spring, families traveled to their band's maple grove to tap trees for sap, which they boiled to produce maple syrup (*ziiwaagimide*) and sugar (*ziisibaakwat*) for subsistence and sale. For every person in a village, the work of raising corn and vegetables; fishing, hunting, and trapping wild game; and manufacturing sugar was a full-time occupation.

The Ottawas on the Grand River, in southwestern Michigan, and on the more northern Muskegon, Pentwater, Pere Marquette, White, and Manistee rivers lived in small villages—unlike the Ottawas on Little Traverse Bay, who lived in large settlements composed of several extended-family bands. Riverside Ottawa villages were home to anywhere between 30 and 160 people, while villages at Little Traverse Bay at times supported more than 300 inhabitants. In 1839, the Ottawa summer village on the Pere Marquette River housed about 30 people compared to the 317 people at the Little Traverse Bay Ottawa settlement of Weqwetonsing or "Bay Place" (modern-day Harbor Springs). For the Ottawas south of Little Traverse Bay, the terms "village" and "band" were virtually synonymous. The various Ottawa bands were widely interconnected by kinship ties—established through intermarriages—which stretched across and transcended great distances and created friendships among bands and villages.

Ottawa life was governed, in part, by the ethic of coexistence of kinsmen and a desire for the well-being of the band. The Ottawa band, not the individuals who constituted it, controlled the necessities of life. Each band claimed a territory, land, and resources, which they could permit other individuals or bands to access. Whether or not a band allowed others to use these territories depended as much upon Ottawa rules of reciprocal giving and hospitality as economic need. If a band's lands could not sustain its members, in-laws and relatives in other villages might be called on for permission to hunt, fish, or gather plant resources in their territories. This ideal made mobility and adaptability important parts of Ottawa life: bands sought the help of others in times of need and shortage, as well as received those in need. The Ottawas also cooperated to produce the food and tools they needed, and traded specialized products and skills with one another. They gave gifts, married one another, and fostered friendships. They celebrated, mourned, and feasted together. In short, Ottawas depended on their kin for survival.

Kinship was so important to Ottawas that they counted another kind of relationship—*ododem*—that drew even more people into the family web. Ododem is a clan system; in the Ottawa language, "ododem" translates as "of my family." Each Ottawa belonged to an ododem—a

■ Between 1846 and 1848, Canadian artist Paul Kane traveled from Ontario to Vancouver, British Columbia. En route to the west, Kane sketched and painted the local families he encountered, including those living along the shores of Lake Huron, at Sault Ste. Marie, and at the Straits of Mackinac. Kane's paintings are the only contemporary images that depict indigenous family life during the nineteenth century. This painting dates between 1848 and 1856.

This is an image of a summer camp on the shore of The St. Mary's River. Kane shows men and women together, but performing their separate tasks. The woman in the background carries wood, while another holds a child in a cradleboard. Five people sit around a cook fire. One man peers into a container made of birch bark, and two other men look toward their *wagenogan* lodge, made of bulrushes and birch bark. Blankets the family obtained by trading furs and food dries in the sun. *Ojibwa Village*, painting by Paul Kane. With permission of the Royal Ontario Museum.

family clan founded by an ancestral spirit embodied in an animal—which children inherited from their fathers. Some of the prominent Grand River Ottawa clans were the Moose, Raccoon, Fox, Beaver, Bear, Otter, Sturgeon, Pike, and Crane, among others. In this kinship system, an Ottawa would be welcomed and given food and shelter by members of his or her clan who lived in other villages throughout a wide geographic range.

At each Ottawa settlement, an *ogema*—a wise and well-spoken leader who was often the head of a large family—presided over the village or band. The ogema was responsible for helping his band members reach consensus decisions, and for carrying out the wishes of his band members within the band and through the interactions of band members with others outside of the community. The authority of an ogema was granted to him by his band members, but it was not absolute. If an ogema overstepped his limited authority—an especially grievous offense—he faced the contempt of the offended band as well as his own people, and

he could be punished, sometimes even by death. Throughout their history, Ottawa bands have been connected by kinship, yet have remained politically independent and self-governing, making important decisions through discussion in councils. Ottawa ethics called for respect of the autonomy of other bands, and one band could not impose its political positions on others.

Although each Ottawa band regarded itself and other bands as sovereign entities, the Ottawas would come together in regional confederacies to face problems affecting many bands. Regional confederacies were made up of all the bands in a general geographic area, such as the Grand Traverse, Little Traverse, and Grand River confederacies. At gatherings of regional confederacies, Ottawa bands held formal councils to discuss and reach decisions in the best interest of all the bands. When the Ottawas faced issues affecting an even greater number of bands, they gathered in larger confederacies; for example, all of the bands between the Kalamazoo and Manistee rivers became known as the Grand River

■ Kane shows Ottawa life in a larger encampment in this painting. The camp is comprised of seven *tipis* made of birch-bark and bulrushes. Children sit inside one tipi, while one woman grinds corn in a hollow log pestle called a *potagon* and another carries an infant on her back. In the background, two men fish at the edge of the water, while three other men talk together in the foreground as their dog plays nearby. This image suggests the intimacy in which Ottawa people lived, the division of labor between men and women, and the leisure of summer life in the Great Lakes. *Indian Encampment on Lake Huron,* c. 1845, oil on canvas by Paul Kane. Art Gallery of Ontario, Toronto. Purchase, 1932

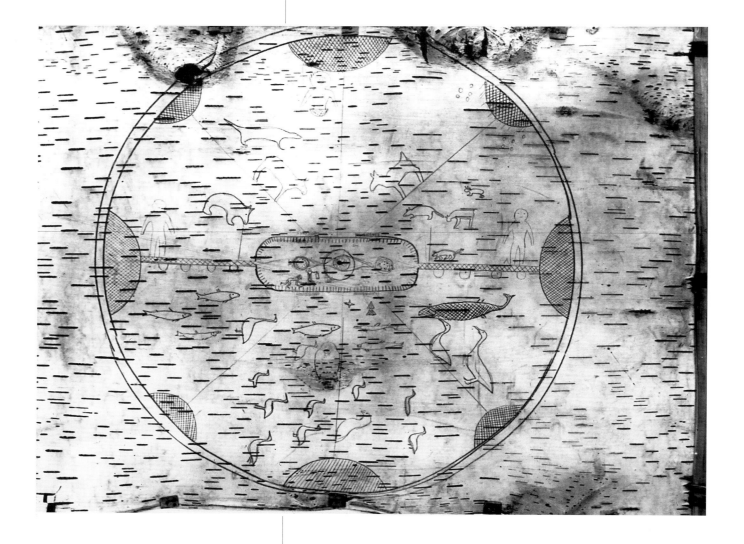

■ This image was carved in birch bark at a Grand River Ottawa village some time in the early nineteenth century. The story it tells is complex. A man who is ill looks for a cure for his complaint. In order to be healed, he calls upon the Grand River Ottawas' clan spirits for aid and assistance. Among the Grand River Ottawa clans depicted in this image are Bear, Moose, Otter, Beaver, Sturgeon, Rabbit, Raccoon, Pike, Heron, Crane, and several unidentifiable water birds. Ottawa healing scroll. The original scroll no longer exists. This image was printed from a glass lantern image housed at the Public Museum of Grand Rapids.

Bands, and all of the bands between the Manistee River and the Straits of Mackinac as the Traverse Bands. When matters of national interest demanded the attention of all Ottawas, regional confederacies could join together to act as the united Ottawa Tribe. When the Ottawas negotiated with the United States in 1836 (discussed in chapter 4), the Ottawa bands in northern and southern Michigan joined together and acted as a single tribal entity. Confederacies, regional or tribal, were built on common interest, language, identity, culture, and kin relationships established through intermarriage. However, just as one band could not speak for another, confederacies could not impose decisions on others; consensus was required before any action could be carried out. These band and confederacy structures are features of Ottawa political life that reach back hundreds, if not thousands, of years, and still exist today.

Ottawa bands and confederacies were shifting political structures. Band members came together to ensure the well-being of their community, and they could choose to leave their band and join another for the same reasons. If, for instance, a large village depleted the natural resources within the home area to the point that they could not support the whole band, a group of members might move elsewhere and begin a new settlement so that everyone would be provided for. At other times, infighting between family members could cause enough social tension for one party to move away, or for a band to divide into one or more parts. Between 1837 and 1839, social tension caused the Ottawa band at Bowting Village (now the site of downtown Grand Rapids) to divide. The Bowting band split when the community affiliated with two different Christian denominations. Noahquageshik became a Baptist, and he and his followers built a new village at a Christian mission in Barry County, while Noahquageshik's son-in-law, Megisinini, stayed with the unconverted and Catholic Ottawas at Bowting. Such changing band structures and movement of band populations were patterns of Ottawa village life that helped to maintain peace and the well-being of all Ottawas.

Ottawa society is best thought of as a matrix of kin relationships created by both genealogical descendancy and the joining of entire families through marriages. Social and political relationships operated within the bounds of kinship; kin-based bands controlled territories and rights to harvest resources; and the primary processes of production and distribution of food and goods were governed by ethics that defined the roles of men, women, and children. *Ogemuk* and family heads, often called "headmen" in historical documents, oversaw day-to-day life in Ottawa villages and represented their bands in regional and tribal confederacies, but they did not have the right to impose their will on others. The tradition of intermarriage between families and bands bound the Ottawas together, as did their pursuit of collective well-being. The family structure of historic Ottawa bands as independent and autonomous units, as well as the practice of coming together as confederacies or as a tribe, are foundations upon which Ottawa communities still stand today.

■ The Ottawas, under provisions of the 1821 Treaty of Chicago, were to receive the benefit of a blacksmith and instruction in farming. The United States delegated delivery of these services to the Baptist Missionary Society. Ogema Noquageshik invited the Baptists to build their new mission station at his village of Bowting. Baptist missionaries used money that the Ottawas obtained from the sale (to the United States) of their land between the Kalamazoo and Grand rivers to clear land and build a farm, school, sawmill, and several houses for leading Ottawas. This contemporary sketch is drawn from the east side of the Grand River, the site of modern-day downtown Grand Rapids. The artist shows the Baptist mission in the background, which stood near what is now Bridge Street on the west side of the City of Grand Rapids. Ottawa men ride the rapids of the Grand River in sleek dugout canoes while they spear fish. Drawing of the Baptist mission. Grand Rapids Public Library Collection (#54) Neg. #100, Grand Rapids view, 1831.

CHAPTER 3

Coexistence and Conquest

After the War of 1812, the Ottawas living between the Kalamazoo and Grand rivers, known collectively as the Grand River Bands, were on the front line of American settlement. Fur traders were the first to arrive on the Grand River Ottawas' homelands, and settlers entered next, their travel to the Michigan Territory facilitated by the opening of the Erie Canal in 1826. Americans flooded onto Ottawa lands—particularly during the 1830s, when Michigan's population was the fastest growing in the country. They reached Ottawa villages by boat on the Grand River, and by traveling the well-worn footpaths that linked Ottawa villages to each other and to the resources of the Ottawas' historic estate.[1] By 1831, Americans already lived throughout Grand River Ottawa lands along the Kalamazoo and Grand rivers. The growing American presence altered the patterns of Ottawa life, particularly in the Ottawas' southern territories, where fur traders built posts along the Grand River and its tributaries, and Catholic and Protestant missionaries established schools and churches. It was not long before Americans would demand that the Ottawas surrender title

■ Gardens tended by women and elders provided a substantial part of the Ottawa diet. The Ottawas created their gardens by girdling trees, burning the trunks and branches, and planting crops between the tree's remains. This form of planting in soil enriched with wood ash is called swidden agriculture. Ottawas grew large crops of corn, squash, pumpkins, and sunflowers.

Each spring, Ottawa families would gather at the sites of their large villages, where they planted their gardens. While many Ottawas traveled to visit relatives and friends during the summer, some stayed in the villages to guard the crops. This image, painted during the 1830s, shows women standing on a platform at the edge of a cornfield, protecting the crops from birds. *Guarding the Cornfields*, painting by Seth Eastman. Courtesy of W. Duncan and Nivin MacMillan and Afton Historical Society Press.

to their southern Michigan lands and move away from their homes to build new villages in the north.

In the wake of settlement, the Ottawas' economic practices continued relatively unchanged as they hunted and trapped furs for sale to Euro-Americans throughout the 1820s and 1830s. The Grand River Valley was particularly rich in fur-bearing animals, and the Ottawas harvested enough fur to earn the American Fur Company—then Michigan's largest corporate interest—substantial profit. Independent fur traders soon set up posts at Grand River Ottawa villages to compete directly with the American Fur Company, and the rivalry between fur companies accelerated the harvest of furs, depleting many fur-bearing species in southern Michigan by the 1830s. Just as the Ottawas moved their villages when they exhausted the soil, they too sought out more lucrative hunting and trapping sites by traveling to lands along the Pentwater, Pere Marquette, and Manistee rivers, and even farther north.

■ Ottawas had lived in villages along the Grand River and its tributaries for nearly 150 years when Americans claimed the lands for settlement. Trails branched out from these villages in all directions, which the Ottawas used to visit relatives and friends in other villages, to travel to hunting and gathering grounds and fisheries, and for trade. Many of the trails created by the Grand River Ottawas became roads that are still traveled today. Map of trails along the Grand River, Wilbert B. Hinsdale. *Archaeological Atlas of Michigan* (Ann Arbor: University of Michigan Press, 1931).

■ Ottawa women, children, and elders made maple sugar each spring. The tons of sugar the Ottawas produced provided many families with the cash they needed to buy food and tools. This image is rich in cultural detail. It shows women cutting wood and carrying maple sap, and the process by which the sap was boiled into maple sugar. The birch-bark and bulrush-mat covered *wagenogan* provided shelter from the cool spring weather. *Indian Sugar Camp*, painting by Seth Eastman. Courtesy of W. Duncan and Nivin MacMillan and Afton Historical Society Press.

For a time, the Grand River Ottawas comfortably coexisted with settlers and traders. Traders often married Ottawa women and fathered children with them. Some of these children, who were raised by their mothers' families, grew up to become the next generation of influential Ottawa ogemuk. The names Bailey, Campeau, DeVerney, Robinson, and Genereau—carried by Little River Ottawas today—can be traced to these unions. John Robinson, who became an influential preacher and political leader among Ottawas, was the son of Rix Robinson, a supervisor of the American Fur Company's Grand River operations who married two Ottawa women. The independent traders, brothers Louis and Antoine Campeau, were Rix Robinson's leading competitors. Antoine fathered William Campeau, also known as Cobmoosa (The Great Walker), who became one of the most recognized nineteenth-century Grand River Ottawa leaders.

During the 1820s, Catholic and Protestant missionaries also moved to Ottawa villages, where they began the work of "civilizing" the Ottawas by attempting to turn them into Christian farmers. In 1821, Ogema Keeway-cooshcum ceded Ottawa land between the Kalamazoo and Grand rivers in exchange for a mission school (among other things) without the approval of the other Ottawa bands who lived on the land—a breach of political protocol that eventually led to his death. The Ottawas who opposed this intrusion prevented missionaries from building any churches or schools until 1825, when Ogema Noahquageshik invited a Baptist missionary to construct a blacksmith shop and mission at Bowting (modern-day Grand Rapids). In addition, McCoy and his successor, Leonard Slater, opened a farm, a sawmill, and a school there. These events caused religious, economic, and social tensions within and among the Grand River Ottawa bands that survived almost the entire nineteenth century.

■ Ottawas were masters of spear fishing. The rapids of the Grand River were known particularly for their sturgeon fisheries. Each fall, hundreds of Ottawas would gather to spear the large fish. To do this, two men in a canoe would paddle out on the water, and one would handle the canoe while the other speared fish. When the men brought their catch to shore, the Ottawas would feast. Ottawa fishermen would collect enough fish in just a few days to feed their entire village for most of the winter. Women preserved the stockpiled fish by smoking and storing the meat. *Spearing Fish*, painting by Seth Eastman. Courtesy of W. Duncan and Nivin MacMillan and Afton Historical Society Press.

■ Fishing was an essential element of the Ottawa economy. In this sketch, Paul Kane depicts two men in a canoe on the St. Mary's River, one using a pole to maneuver the vessel upriver. Notice the dip net, which was used for catching fish close to the water's surface, resting over the bow of the canoe. *Spear Fishing*, sketch by Paul Kane. With permission of the Royal Ontario Museum.

As Catholic and Protestant endeavors to convert and "civilize" the Grand River Ottawas intensified during the 1820s and early 1830s, Ottawa opinions divided over the issue of religion—traditional versus Christian, Catholic versus Protestant—as they weighed the material benefits of the missionary presence. French Catholic traders who married into Ottawa bands disapproved of Protestants who converted their Indian relatives, and Protestants complained about traders' commercial practices, social lives, and sexual liaisons.[2] Ottawas themselves objected when Baptist missionaries unfairly dispensed treaty funds intended for all Ottawas solely to Noahquageshik's band, the only Baptist band on the Grand River. While many Ottawas who lived in the eastern villages of the Grand River remained unconverted "traditionalists" throughout the nineteenth century, others became Catholics or joined Protestant sects. Most Grand River Ottawa ancestors of the Little River Band who converted to Christianity became Catholics. Ogema Naokequabee's band, whose

home was likely Fort Village, were Catholic converts whose descendants became one of the core kin groups constituting the modern-day Little River Ottawas. Although missionaries created circumstances over which the Ottawas differed, the processes of dividing and reforming band populations based on issues of importance and ideology had long been a hallmark of Ottawa life.

Settlers' hospitality towards the Ottawas dwindled as American numbers increased and their farms became productive on the Ottawas' most fertile riparian lands. Settlers understood little about Ottawa life, and most had less desire to know or respect Ottawa culture.[3] At present-day Ionia, settlers took over Ottawa lands so rapidly that they actually bought Indian lodges and lived in them until their own log houses were built. Politicians saw Ottawa lands as cheap real estate and pressured the Ottawas to sell all of their Michigan territories to the United States, paving the way for Michigan to achieve statehood. What would happen

■ Each band claimed its own trapping territories. Friends, relatives, and visitors could ask to share a territory, but trapping in another band's territory without prior permission was a grievous offense, punishable by a beating or even death.

Muskrat furs were a standard medium of trade for the Ottawas. Here, two men spear muskrats from their lodges. Men carried the kill back to their family camp, where women skinned the animals, cooked the meat, and stretched the hides for sale. *Trapping Muskrat,* painting by Seth Eastman. Courtesy of W. Duncan and Nivin MacMillan and Afton Historical Society Press.

to the Ottawas after they sold the land was a matter of debate: some envisioned Ottawa assimilation into American society, while others wanted the Ottawas removed from Michigan altogether. The Ottawas sold almost all of their land to the United States at the 1821 Treaty of Chicago and the 1836 Treaty of Washington, but they refused to leave Michigan. When American intentions to coexist became attempts to conquer and dispel the Ottawas, the Ottawas relied on ancient political strategies and processes to thwart American efforts. Ottawas relied on the skills of their leaders to negotiate for their permanent homes in Michigan, despite the increasingly hostile circumstances caused by settlement.

CHAPTER 4

The Will of the Grand Council

A merican pressure for an Ottawa land cession mounted throughout the 1830s as local, territorial, and federal politicians sought to oblige land speculators and settlers alike with cheap, ready-to-claim real estate. Ottawa bands responded to plans by gathering in council, first as regional confederacies and then as a tribe. Despite more than two hundred years of political dealings with Europeans and their North American descendants, Ottawas reached decisions in much the same way they always had. In June 1834—two years before the Ottawas would enter into negotiations with the United States—the Grand River Bands hosted their northern relatives, the Little Traverse Bands (otherwise called the L'Arbre Croche Indians), in formal council at Grand Rapids. Catholic missionary Father Frederick Baraga observed the proceedings—an all-day "grand council"—in which the bands of the Ottawa Tribe discussed whether they would retreat or stay put in the face of "the threatening danger" of forced removal from their homelands.[1] That day, the chiefs and headmen of the Ottawa Tribe resolved to neither cede nor leave their Michigan lands.

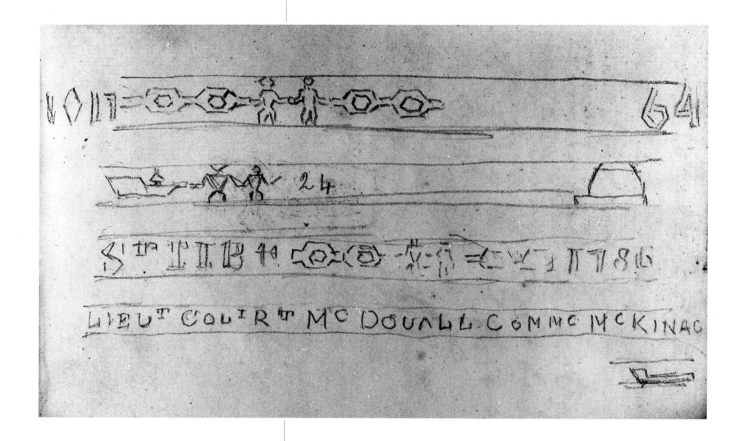

■ *Wampum* belts were woven using beads that were handmade from clam shells found only on the eastern seaboard of the United States. These purple and white beads were used to create patterns that recalled special events and agreements to the minds of the Ottawas.

This sketch shows the patterns Paul Kane saw on wampum belts at Mackinac in 1842. Although Kane did not record the stories represented on the belts, the designs suggest the nature of the Ottawas' relationship with the British. On the first belt, which likely dates to 1864, two men hold hands, joining two ends of a chain. This design appears often on artifacts found in other parts of the United States, and is often called a "friendship chain." The friendship-chain design is also incorporated in the third belt in the drawing. The fourth belt incorporates the name of Lieutenant Colonel Robert McDounll [McDougal], the commander at Fort Mackinac. *Wampum Belts*, sketch by Paul Kane. Stark Museum of Art, Orange, Texas.

According to Father Baraga, the grand council began when the leaders of the Grand River Bands and Traverse Bands "assembled out in the open, and chose a small round valley," where they built fires, laid out tobacco (*sema*), and mounted a flag. The proceedings were a solemn affair: the ogemuk and headmen prepared themselves for council in silence, and then "a sign was given, and the Indians came here from all sides, slowly and seriously. Women and children were not to be seen. Silently they laid themselves prone in the circle, and each one lit his tobacco pipe. Thus they remained for a very long time, without speaking a word." The silence—intended for offering prayers to sanctify the proceedings—ended when one ogema finally declared: "Well, my brothers! Why have you come here? What is your intention? Do explain yourselves!" One speaker for the Little Traverse Ottawas rose and walked around the circle, shaking each man's hand before speaking, after which each *ogemagigido*—leaders chosen for their rhetorical elegance—did the same until every band leader had stated his people's position. At the end of their discussion, the leaders of the combined confederacies "firmly resolved never to cede their lands . . . [so as] not to make themselves or their children unhappy." They sealed the pact by silently passing a *wampum*—a string of white and purple shell beads that was "a sign of their unity and their united sentiment"—around the circle. A Grand River ogemagigido then shook the hands of each of the "Indians of Arbre Croche" and again declared aloud the Ottawas' agreement "never to sell their land." After the leaders reached an agreement, they made "several reciprocal speeches" until they adjourned the council at the end of the day.[2]

That day in June 1834, Father Baraga observed centuries-old traditions of Ottawa decision making through ritual, open discussion, and consensus resolution. Further, although many Ottawas had become Christians, Baraga's description shows that they had not abandoned the ceremonial and symbolic expressions that guided and governed their councils. Father Baraga witnessed the united front of the Ottawa Tribe, and how the Ottawas determined a course of action on issues that affected all of the Ottawa bands. "It is remarkable," he wrote, "how the Indians. . . . are earnest and deliberate in their councils; and it is admirable how much natural eloquence and power of expression some of these simple inhabitants of the forest possess."[3] A Baptist missionary who was also present among the Grand River Ottawas commented on the Ottawas' stated resolve regarding a land cession. Recalling the events of 1834, he wrote: "The main body of the Ottawas was on the Grand River and its vicinity, and these strongly objected to selling any of their country. Twice they met in council . . . and each time resolved that their country should not be sold."[4]

Following the grand council in June 1834, politicians, traders, and missionaries attempted to convince the Ottawas to send delegations to Washington to discuss a land cession. The Grand River Bands—although divided along Protestant, Catholic, and traditionalist lines—still refused to sell their lands and objected strongly to Americans' wish to "civilize" them. Some Ottawas from Little Traverse Bay had already visited the nation's capital, but had only offered to sell their rights to Upper Peninsula lands and some islands in northern Lake Huron. They were reluctant to visit again and unwilling to turn over as much land as the United States wanted them to sell. The Grand River Ottawas flatly refused to negotiate any agreements away from the view of their people. In a petition to President Andrew Jackson, they made their will clear:

Now we take a pen to communicate our thoughts. Not only what is in our mouths, but that which comes from our whole hearts we shall speak. We are afraid & the reason is, because you already would take our land. We think not to shoulder this our land & carry it where you are, it is too heavy. We hear that you would make a treaty for our land. We refuse to go, it is too hard for us. We think to remain on our land here & not sell it. . . . Were we desirous to make a treaty for your land, you would refuse us, you would say "I cannot sell the graves of my relation." We have not a mind to remove to a distant land our children would suffer. You say we shall see prosperity, & be in health, if we remove. We have knowledge of the country you offer us, our eyes have seen it, & our feet have trode on it. . . . You might think we would sell should you come here but our mind would be the same.[5]

This document was signed by several factions of the Grand River Bands, including Noahquageshik, the leader of the Baptist band at Grand Rapids; leaders of the Catholic bands, Muccatosha and Megisinini; and Cobmoosa, who represented the traditionalist community at Lowell.

The Grand River Bands held firm to the agreement made in the 1834 tribe-wide council at Grand Rapids, and they withstood pressure from American agents until the United States threatened to move the entire Ottawa Tribe from Michigan to Kansas. As Michigan prepared for statehood in 1835, the Ottawas continued to suffer the ills of settlement. Many Ottawas died from smallpox that year, and in these uncertain times their resolution to refuse a land cession slowly disintegrated. During this time, two federal agents—savvy politicians who had spent many years in Michigan and were familiar with Ottawa political life—attempted to persuade Ottawa delegations to visit Washington. Convincing the Ottawas to travel to Washington was a difficult task: The agents knew that the Ottawas had voiced united opposition to a land cession, and they knew that if negotiations were held in the Ottawas' home territory, no treaty could be made without band consensus reached in open council. If the Ottawas held such a council, the agents knew that band unity against a sale could prevail. To prevent this, the agents wanted to bring Ottawa ogemuk to Washington, where band leaders would be separated from their people and could more easily be persuaded to cede their Michigan lands.

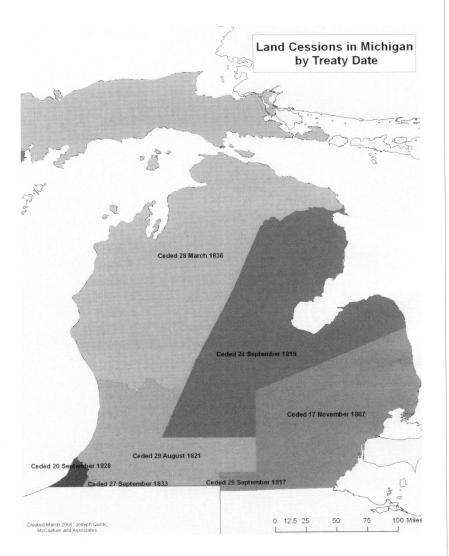

Land Cessions in Michigan by Treaty Date

Ceded 28 March 1836

Ceded 24 September 1819

Ceded 17 November 1807

Ceded 29 August 1821

Ceded 20 September 1828

Ceded 27 September 1833   Ceded 29 September 1817

Created March 2008, Joseph Quick, McClurken and Associates

0   12.5 25   50   75   100 Miles

■ Ottawas participated in negotiating more than twenty treaties with the United States. The core of the Ottawa homeland, as it was recognized from 1700 forward, was sold to the United States in the 1821 Treaty of Chicago and 1836 Treaty of Washington.

By 1836, the two federal agents managed to convince the Grand River Ottawas to send delegations to Washington to negotiate a treaty with the United States. As one observer recalled, the Grand River Bands, "upon being informed that the delegation from La Arbacroche would probably cede away the whole without the consent of the nation, they resolved to send a delegation to Washington to prevent it." Wanting to "appear as aloof as far as possible," the Grand River Bands sent a delegation of young men who had no authority to make binding decisions for their bands, and one trusted ogema who remained opposed to a treaty. However, the influence of federal treaty negotiators, fur traders, missionaries, and others who had much to gain from a large Ottawa land cession in the end convinced the delegates to negotiate a treaty.[6]

The resulting document—the 1836 Treaty of Washington—permitted the Ottawas to stay in Michigan, although not indefinitely. It created a number of reservations, including one 70,000-acre reservation on the Manistee River for the Grand River Ottawas, and several others located in such a way that Ottawa bands could continue living in the villages they had occupied for most of the eighteenth and nineteenth centuries. The Grand River Bands—those living on the Grand, Muskegon, White, Pentwater, and Pere Marquette rivers—were to leave their horticultural villages and move north to the Manistee Reservation, lands that the Grand River Bands had used as hunting grounds for many years. In addition to creating reservations, the 1836 treaty also preserved the Ottawas' hunting and fishing rights on the lands they had sold throughout western Michigan. Finally, the United States agreed to provide the tools and funds the Ottawas would need to make farms and transition from an economy based on hunting, fishing, and gardening to one based on animal-powered agriculture. Faced with a prospect of being forcefully driven from Michigan by the United States Army, these treaty provisions were the best for which Ottawas leaders could hope.

However, the letter and intent of the 1836 Treaty of Washington simply did not materialize in Michigan. After the treaty negotiations, the United States Senate amended the original treaty language in such a way that, upon its ratification, the Ottawas were promised only five years of secure tenure on their Michigan reserves. After five years, they could decide to move west, or the United States could allow them to remain on their reservations for a longer time. The Ottawas had to agree to these amendments before the treaty could be ratified by Congress. In July 1836, one of the agents who had initiated the treaty traveled to Mackinac to meet with representatives of five Ottawa confederacies—the Grand Traverse, Little Traverse, Mackinac, Sault Ste. Marie, and Grand River bands. Before the delegation of Grand River ogemuk had arrived at Mackinac, the agent presented the amended treaty conspicuously and with an undertone of threat to the gathering of Ottawa representatives. When the Grand River ogemuk arrived, they were too late to voice their objection and decline assent to the treaty amendments before the document was finalized. The 1836 treaty did not turn out as the Ottawas intended, but they believed that they had entered into a mutually binding agreement with the United States and expected the federal government to fulfill its promises. In the years following 1836, the Ottawas continually pressed federal officers to carry out and enforce treaty stipulations, as federal agents inconsistently delivered the educational funds, tools, and services the Ottawas had been promised.

Ottawa leaders wrote many letters and petitions complaining about federal lapses and were especially tenacious of their right to live on reservations in Michigan. The reservations—the provision most important to the Ottawas if they were to have protected, permanent homes where they could continue to support themselves and their families—were never secured. Federal surveyors marked the boundaries for only two of the fourteen 1836 reservations: the Grand River Ottawa reservation at Manistee and a second reservation at Grand Traverse Bay. Except when Christian missionaries joined Ottawa leaders to demand that they do so, federal officers did not protect the Ottawas' surveyed or unsurveyed reservations from intruders. In exchange for title to almost their entire Michigan estate, the Ottawas received erratic delivery of economic aid, uncertain tenure of their reservations, and a continuing threat of being removed from Michigan.

The Ottawas had agreed in council in 1834 not to cede land to the United States, but the will of their grand council eroded as they contended with the possibility of forced removal from their Michigan homes. Nonetheless, the Ottawas stood together as a tribe at the 1836 treaty negotiations and refused to leave their lands, and even as the federal government continually failed to fulfill its treaty-stipulated promises, the Ottawas demonstrated their resolve to remain on their ancestral homelands after 1836. With the threat of removal still impending, most Grand River Ottawas refused to leave their historic villages on the Grand River and move north to the Manistee Reservation, which, if removal became a reality, they would soon have to vacate. In this context of uncertainty, Ottawa leaders continued to guide their bands through the changed and changing conditions in Michigan by creating consensus among their people and winning support for a united course of action. Less than twenty years after they negotiated the 1836 Treaty of Washington, Ottawa leaders would again be called on to determine, assert, and defend the will of the Ottawas to remain in Michigan, and to ensure the survival and happiness of their people.

■ Augustin Hamlin Jr., grandson of the famous Ottawa war leader Nissawakwat, was born near St. Ignace, Michigan, shortly after the turn of the nineteenth century. He was selected by his village *ogemuk* to be educated in Catholic schools, first at Cincinnati, Ohio, and then at the College of the Propaganda Fide in Rome, Italy. In 1834, while studying in Rome, Hamlin learned that the Ottawas were being pressured to sell all of their Michigan lands and move to Kansas—knowledge that prompted him to return to the United States at once.

When Hamlin returned to his home, he advised his relatives against removal. He was among the Ottawas from Little Traverse Bay who participated in the tribe-wide council held at Grand Rapids in 1834. Hamlin traveled with the Ottawa delegation to Washington, D.C., in 1836, where he translated the treaty negotiations from English to Ottawa. The 1836 Treaty of Washington, which Hamlin helped to make, protected the Ottawas' right to remain in Michigan, made land reservations, and preserved the Ottawas' rights to hunt, fish, and gather on lands they sold to the United States. Bass Otis painted this image of Hamlin at the time of the 1836 treaty negotiations. Ottawa chief Augustin Hamlin Jr. (aka Kanapima, Ka-Na-Pi-Ma). Portrait by Bass Otis, ca. 1835; print obtained from McKinney & Hall Indian Portrait Gallery.

CHAPTER 5

"Civilizing" the Ottawas

The federal government had two major goals for the 1836 Treaty of Washington: to secure a large land cession, and to develop a plan to "civilize" the Ottawas. Foremost, federal and state officials wanted the Grand River Ottawas to move north of land that Americans valued for farming. On land reservations in northern Michigan, representatives of the federal and state governments hoped that the Ottawas would clear land, plant crops, raise livestock, and work for wages, like their American neighbors; in short, government agents envisioned that the Ottawas would assimilate into American society by becoming "civilized," Christian farmers. However, amendments made to the 1836 treaty all but guaranteed the failure of this plan. Since the treaty assured the Ottawas only five years of tenure over their reservation lands, moving north to resettle, build homes, and develop farms only to be forced to remove from Michigan and leave their hard work behind made little sense to the Ottawas.

The 1836 treaty did not provide the Grand River Ottawas with much incentive to move to their 70,000-acre reservation on the Manistee River, even though the United States opened a model farm and a

35

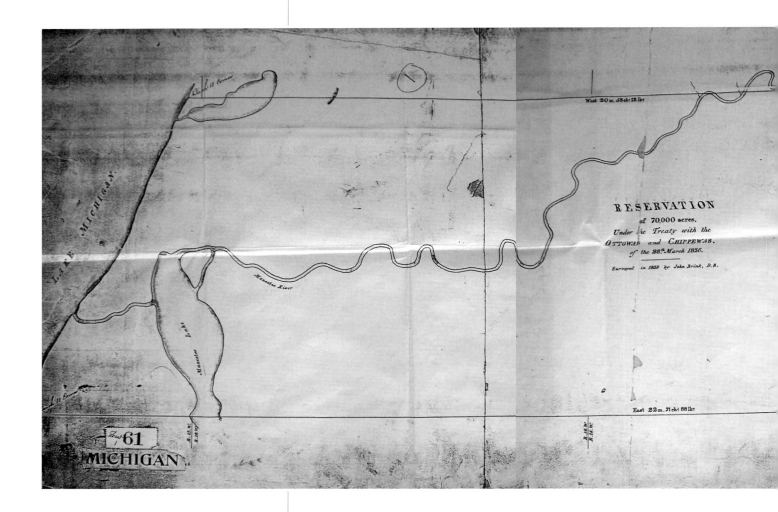

RESERVATION
of 70,000 acres.
Under the Treaty with the
OTTOWAS and CHIPPEWAS,
of the 28th March 1836.

Surveyed in 1839 by John Brink, D.S.

■ The 1836 Treaty of Washington set aside a 70,000-acre reservation on the Manistee River. This official survey map, made by the U.S. government, shows the boundaries of the Manistee Reservation. The federal government built an agency station on the reservation in 1838, complete with a blacksmith shop, farm, and trading post. Lumbermen who knew that the Ottawas only held secure title to their reservations for five years quickly moved onto the reservation, where they cut trees and built a

continued opposite

blacksmith shop and allowed traders to visit there. Instead, most Grand River Ottawas opted to remain on their homelands along the Grand River and its tributaries, where they continued to subsist by historic practices of hunting, fishing, gathering wild plant foods, and raising garden crops. To protect the sites of their gardens and villages, several bands bought the lands they lived upon as the United States offered them for sale. Grand River Ottawas began buying land where their villages stood as early as 1837 or 1838. The Ottawas who lived in villages where Christian denominations had built churches attempted to adopt animal-powered agriculture, using horses and plows to prepare fields for planting, and raising livestock for meat. These Ottawas became a part of Michigan's evolving society, yet remained distinct from their American neighbors.

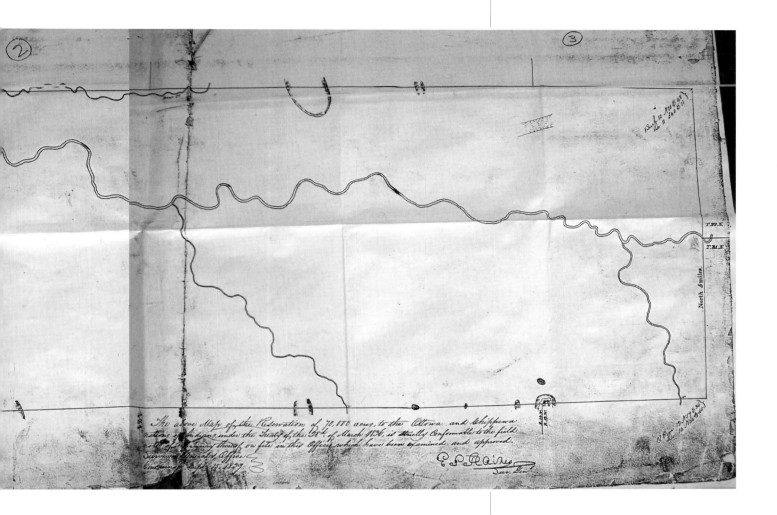

Despite the Ottawas' best efforts, many Michigan officials believed that the Ottawas were a public nuisance and an impediment to American settlement of the rich farmlands in southwestern Michigan. The United States continued to receive letters from Americans asking that the federal government remove the Ottawas from the state. Newspapers frequently voiced the opinion that Michigan and its American population would be better off if the Indians moved away; these calls for removal circulated into the 1840s. The Ottawas who wanted to remain in their historic territories had three choices: flee north to Canada, continue to buy title to their ceded lands in Michigan, or press the United States to enter into a new treaty that would make their homes in Michigan permanent and protect their reservations, confirming their right to remain on their historic homelands.

sawmill at modern-day Stronach. These lumbermen and others who squatted on the reservation believed that the lands they claimed and the "improvements" (cleared fields, houses, outbuildings, etc.) they made would soon legally belong to them. The United States offered the reservation land for sale in 1841, largely to facilitate the cutting of its virgin forests and satisfy Americans who squatted there. Survey map of the Manistee Reservation, 1841, surveyed in 1839 by John Brink, D.S. NARA-College Park, Cartographic and Architectural Records, RG 49, Michigan Map #32.

Few Ottawas went to Canada, although some traveled to the homes of kinsmen at Walpole and Manitoulin islands, just beyond the American border.[1] Other Grand River Ottawas joined their relatives in the Little Traverse Bay Ottawa communities. However, the majority of Grand River Ottawas stayed in their historic villages during the 1840s. The Grand River Ottawas' decision to remain in their historic villages demanded that they adapt to the rapidly evolving social, economic, political, and environmental conditions in Michigan—just as their ancestors had when the French and British arrived in earlier centuries. Grand River Ottawas adopted some elements of American customs and culture, but the direction and pace of these changes remained under Ottawa control.

The Ottawas who tried to buy land in the Grand River Valley and elsewhere in southwestern Michigan faced large and persistent obstacles. Federal agents in Michigan and in Washington debated the Ottawas' right to purchase lands on the open market, bound as they were to move to reservations. While these debates went on, Christian and traditionalist Ottawa bands enlisted the aid of friendly Americans to help them make land purchases. Ogemainini Wawkazoo from Little Traverse Bay, for example, bought land near the modern-day city of Holland in 1839, and the members of his band built a new village there for themselves and their extended family members from the Little Traverse and Grand River bands. On the Grand River, Cobmoosa's father, Antoine Campeau, bought the Ottawas title to their village lands at Lowell. Muccatosha and Megisinini's people pooled nearly $1,200 of their own money and purchased land in the name of a fur trader named Richard Godfroy. Rix Robinson, husband to two Ottawa women, bought hundreds of acres at and around Nebawnaygezhick's village at the mouth of the Thornapple River, and welcomed Ottawas to continue using it. Paquodush, in a rare instance, purchased land at Fort Village in his own name, where he and his band peeled hemlock bark for tanning, and continued trapping along the Grand River bayous of Ottawa County.[2]

Protestant Grand River bands moved away from the influences of traditionalism and Catholicism. Baptists had built a mission settlement on the Grand River at Grand Rapids in 1825, and by 1836 the compound consisted of a parsonage, a church/school, a government-sponsored farm, a blacksmith shop, and a sawmill. Noahquageshik and his Baptist converts moved from this settlement, which was the most successful

Protestant mission in southern Michigan, to their winter trapping grounds at Gun Lake in Barry County, and bought land there in the name of their missionary. A few other Ottawas from the Grand River Bands joined a second nearby Protestant mission called Griswold Colony. These Protestant Ottawas adopted American-style agriculture more extensively than the Ottawas who stayed in their villages on the Grand River.

Throughout the 1830s and 1840s, American settlers destroyed the natural resources that the Ottawas of southern Michigan relied upon for hunting, trapping, fishing, and foraging. This depopulation of Native plant and animal species exacerbated the difficulties that the Ottawas were experiencing, and bands were forced to move widely throughout Michigan in order to find enough food. For a time, the southern Ottawas traveled to their nearby territories at the Kankakee Marsh in northern Indiana, and to northern Michigan to hunt and fish in their relatives' territories. Village populations began to dwindle as families moved

■ Shortly after Rix Robinson began his career as a trader with the American Fur Company, he became head of the company's operation on the Grand River. Robinson built relationships with his clients just as generations of Ottawas had done—by establishing kinship relations by marrying into a prominent Ottawa family. Robinson's family associations and access to the tools of trade placed him at the center of regional politics. He married twice, though only images of his second wife, Ziibiqua ("River Woman"), survive. Without the support of men like Rix Robinson, Americans who wished to have the Ottawas moved away from Michigan might have succeeded in their efforts. Americans who married into Ottawa families often proved to be important political allies. Rix Robinson and wife Ziibiqua.

north to unclaimed land that was closer to undisturbed resources and beyond the line of American settlement. Some Grand River Ottawas joined the more isolated and secure Grand Traverse and Little Traverse Ottawa villages.

Some Ottawas who chose to remain on the Grand River joined together and formed new communities along the river and its tributaries at places where they might still adequately support themselves and their families. By 1846, for example, Ogema Wawbegaykake's followers moved upstream from Kookoosh's village at the mouth of the Maple River to land bordering on the Saginaw River drainage. A small group of Catholic-affiliated Grand River Ottawas built a new village on the Muskegon River near present-day Newaygo. Ogema Louis Genereau and his family left Maple River Village and sought refuge at Ottawa Colony in Barry County before moving to the Old Wing settlement in Allegan County, and then to the Manistee River area. Only in 1858 and 1859 would the remaining Grand River Ottawas finally move north to build new settlements or join those of their relatives on the Manistee River. Like their ancestors who fled Iroquois invasions and Sioux hostilities, Ottawas migrated in search of land where they could live in peace and security, and in these new places they formed new alliances and bands.

Ottawas who lived in villages along the Muskegon, White, Pentwater, Pere Marquette, and Manistee rivers also continued to subsist by hunting, fishing, trapping, and foraging. The Ottawas in these settlements, located where soils were sandy and not readily demanded by American farmers, remained relatively isolated, safe from the influence of settlers who were then rapidly streaming into the new state of Michigan. Missionaries never established stations at these villages. Although Father Baraga held Mass at Muskegon and visiting priests ministered to the Ottawas, when Protestant missionaries approached Ogema Misshewatik and his headman Payshawsegay about building a mission at Muskegon, the band spoke with one voice to oppose it.

Federal officials had hoped in 1836 that the mission on the Manistee Reservation would become a model settlement where Ottawas would learn the skills to become "civilized," Christian farmers. Neither the wishes of government officials nor the best efforts of missionaries made this vision a reality. Despite large infusions of federal money, the Manistee mission failed in 1838. The Ottawas of Kewaycushcum's village at Manistee did not want to participate in the mission activities, and the

Grand River Bands could not be convinced to move north. The mission never contained more than forty-four "permanent" Ottawa residents—individuals who merely skipped the trapping season to remain on the grounds during the winter.

As American settlement spread west of the Mississippi in the 1840s, the federal government's efforts to remove the Ottawas from Michigan waned. The Ottawas had become landowners. They had formed alliances with influential Americans, many of whom had become the Ottawas' customers or even family members, who used well-placed political pressure to stop efforts to export the Ottawas. Although efforts to remove them to land west of the Mississippi eventually ceased, the Ottawas pressed the federal government for a new treaty that would guarantee their right to remain in Michigan on reservations that were surveyed and protected from encroachment by settlers—permanent homes where they could live as distinct people on their ancestral lands.

By the 1850s it was clear that two primary aims of the 1836 treaty had not been reached: the Ottawas had not resettled on reservations, and they certainly had not assimilated into American society. Some bought land, became Christians, or adopted agricultural technologies; but the Ottawas, for the most part, continued to live according to historic practices of hunting, gathering, and gardening. Their communities were still led by ogemuk and headmen who were the heads of families. Kin connections continued to facilitate the Ottawas' migrations and the allocation of resources that remained available for harvest by Ottawa bands. The Ottawas had not abandoned their culture to become "civilized" Americans; instead, their culture changed only so much as was necessary to preserve their identity in an unstable world—a process that would continue and carry the Ottawas through the nineteenth and twentieth centuries

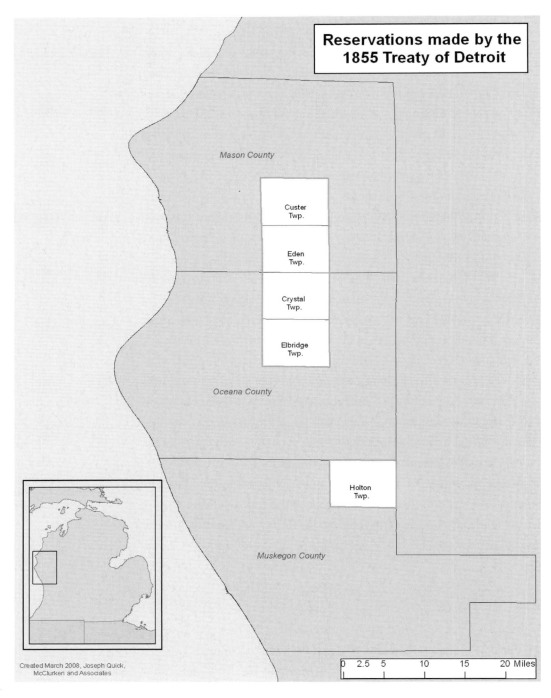

Reservations made by the
1855 Treaty of Detroit

Mason County

Custer
Twp.

Eden
Twp.

Crystal
Twp.

Elbridge
Twp.

Oceana County

Holton
Twp.

Muskegon County

Created March 2008, Joseph Quick,
McClurken and Associates

0 2.5 5   10   15   20 Miles

■ Ancestors of the Little River Ottawas made new land reservations by the 1855 Treaty of Detroit, comprised of Custer and Eden townships in Mason County, Crystal and Elbridge townships in Oceana County, and Holton Township in Muskegon County.

CHAPTER 6

"Strong Titles" and the Government "Swan"

By the mid-1850s, the Ottawas' efforts to end the imminent threat of their removal from Michigan had been successful. Although most Americans no longer wanted to rid the state of its Indian inhabitants, the Ottawas' knew that they remained vulnerable without an official promise that they would not be removed from their ancestral lands. Ottawa ogemuk and headmen continuously wrote letters to federal officials asking for a new treaty that would once and for all end the removal threat inherent in the provisions of the 1836 Treaty of Washington and secure Michigan as their legal, permanent home. Ogemuk from the northern and southern communities traveled to Washington and met with high-ranking officials to demand a new treaty. By 1853, the Ottawas convinced a newly appointed commissioner of Indian Affairs to consider their request, and in 1854 he made plans for renewed negotiations between the Ottawas and the United States.

With a new treaty on the horizon, Ottawa leaders mobilized their communities to win consensus support and approval for the demands they would make at the upcoming negotiations. Ogemuk and headmen of the various Ottawa bands identified and agreed upon their most important concerns when they met in regional confederacies, and then in a tribe-wide council, to discuss the challenges ahead—just as they had at Grand Rapids twenty years earlier. In January 1855, the Ottawas, who wished to "make known our unanimous wish and mind," expressed their desires in a petition to the commissioner of Indian Affairs:

> We love the spot where our Forefathers bones are laid, and we desire that our bones may rest beside theirs also. . . .
>
> You white people are laboring for your children when you accumulate property you lay it aside that they may have the benefit when you are gone—So even do we desire to the same for our children.
>
> Our children are reaching forth their hands to you and desire you to keep the money for them which is our due. . . .
>
> We want to learn about our reservations—about the fields and the payment for our improvements.
>
> We desire you to inform us fully in regard to all our rights under the different Treaties that we and our people may know and understand.
>
> We have purchased land to make us homes—where we can bring up our children, and from this spot we have risen up to go to Washington—hoping that our wish and desire may be granted.[1]

To this, the Grand River Bands added:

> We the indians (undersigned) residing upon the Grand River with one mind agree with our friends & connexions and desire that this our united request may be granted. . . . We have the consent and names of the chiefs who are absent and all are anxious that our wish may be truly granted to us. Our old men & young men are agreed and we desire of our Father to inform us all about the old Treaties made with our ancestors; that we can know and understand what belongs to us.[2]

Eighty-three ogemuk and headmen signed this petition, thirty-four of whom were leaders of the Grand River Bands. A month later, sixteen Ottawa delegates carried this message directly to the commissioner of Indian Affairs in Washington. The Ottawas had decided on two simple goals for their new treaty: to secure definite tenure over their lands, and to settle their outstanding financial affairs with the United States.

Federal officials had their own agenda for the new treaty. Having failed to convince the Ottawas to leave the state, the commissioner who represented the United States in the treaty negotiations also wanted to secure the Ottawas' tenure in Michigan and to sort out their financial entanglements. With no desire for another land cession, the federal government instead wanted to provide the Ottawas with permanent homes on reservations that, unlike those created by the 1836 treaty, would be protected from encroachment and theft. The commissioner also planned to provide the Ottawas with the tools and training that would help them become valuable workers and better farmers. He hoped that this plan would help the Ottawas to become more like other Americans, eventually ending the need for federal guardianship over their property and affairs. In short, the commissioner wanted to develop a strategy that would eventually make Americans out of Ottawas and destroy their tribal identity.

Unlike his predecessors, the commissioner of Indian Affairs was perceptive enough to know that assimilating the Ottawas would be a long process. The commissioner of Indian Affairs and the Michigan Indian agent believed that the Ottawas needed land reservations and assistance to make the treaty objectives reality; for the Ottawas to successfully assimilate, they needed to be "colonized & have a permanent home with an interest in the soil."[3] As Americans were already settling on the reservation lands set aside in the 1836 Treaty of Washington, establishing firm boundaries around the Ottawas' legal homes was critical. The two treaty commissioners knew that if the Ottawas were to relocate on their reservations and transform themselves into farmers, the federal government also had to provide the tools, materials, and services they would need to move north, build homes, and clear the land. In the months preceding treaty negotiations, the two federal agents worked to create the basis of an agreement that would accomplish their goals to concentrate the Michigan Ottawas on a few clearly bounded and protected reservations, and to supervise them so that Ottawa culture could be transformed.

The ogemuk did not want to repeat the Ottawas' mistakes of 1836. This time, they agreed and demanded that treaty negotiations take place in Michigan, in view of their constituents. In 1854 and 1855, the Ottawas sent various delegations to Washington to ask the commissioner to come to Michigan to treat with them. The Grand River Ottawas sent

Articles of Agreement and Convention made and concluded at the City of Detroit in the State of Michigan this Thirty First day of July, one thousand eight hundred and fifty five between George W Manypenny and Henry C Gilbert Commissioners on the part of the United States and the Ottawa and Chippewa Indians of Michigan parties to the treaty of March 28th 1836.

In view of the existing condition of the Ottawas and Chippewas and of their legal and equitable claims against the United States it is agreed between the contracting parties as following.

Article 1.

The United States will withdraw from sale for the benefit of said Indians as hereinafter provided all the unsold public lands in the state of Michigan embraced in the following descriptions to wit; First,— For the use of the said Bands residing at & near Sault Ste Marie, Sections 13.14.23.24.25.26.27. and 28. in Township 47. North, Range 5. West — Sections 18. 19. and 30 in Township 47. North, Range 4 West — Sections 11. 12. 13.14. 10. 22. 23. 25 and 26. in Township 47. North, Range 3. West and Section 29. in Township 47. North, Range 2. West — Sections 2. 3. 4. 11. 14. and 15 in Township 47. North, Range 2. East and Section 34. in Township 48. North Range 2. East. — Sections. 6. 7. 18. 19. 20. 28. 29. and 33.

Sault Ste Marie Bands.

A Shaw, waw, no, Ke wain, ge Chief, his + Mark, seal.
Waw, bo, jieg, Chief. his + Mark, seal.
Kay, bay, no, din, Chief. his + Mark, seal.
O maw no mawne. Chief. his + Mark, seal.
Shaw, waw, Chief. his + Mark, seal.
Pi, aw, be, daw, sing, Chief. his + Mark, seal.
Waw, iwe gun, Headman. his + Mark, seal.
Pay, ne, gwon, Headman. his + Mark, seal.
Bwan, Headman. his + Mark, seal.
Taw, meace, Headman. his + Mark, seal.
Shaw o, ge, ghick Headman. his + Mark, seal.
Saw gaw, gien, Headman. his + Mark, seal.

Grand River Bands.

Ne, baw nay ge ghick Chief his + Mark, seal
Shaw gwaw bawno Chief his + Mark, seal.
Aish Ke baw gosh 2d Chief his + Mark, seal.
Nay, waw, goo Chief his + Mark, seal.
Ne, be, ne, Seh, Chief. his + Mark, seal.
Waw be gay Kake Chief. his + Mark, seal.
Ke, ne, we, ge ghick Chief. his + Mark, seal.
Men, daw, waw, be, Chief his + Mark, seal.
Maish Ke aw she Chief. his + Mark, seal.

Nabunegezick, Nebenesee, Chingwash, Pabawme, Eshcomongee, and the Protestant Ottawa preacher Joseph Elliott. This delegation was accompanied by a former Indian agent whom the Ottawas trusted, and the Grand River Ottawas' relative and friend Louis Campeau, the French trader and uncle to Ottawa ogema Cobmoosa. Other Ottawa bands also sent delegations to Washington to make the same request. The Ottawas' efforts and persistence at last convinced the commissioner of Indian Affairs to come to Michigan, and in the summer of 1855, the Ottawas and the United States made a treaty at Detroit.

The Ottawas again prepared for treaty negotiations by coming together in formal council. According to ancient protocol, the Ottawas chose a representative—an *ogemagigido*—to speak for each band, regional confederacy, and the whole tribe. Five regional confederacies representing

Pay Shaw se, gay, Chief.   his + Mark, seal,
Pay, baw, me,   Headman.   his + Mark seal
Pe, go. Chief.   his + Mark, seal,
Ching, gwosh, Chief   his + Mark, seal.
Shaw be quo, ung. Chief   his + Mark, seal
Andrew J. Blackbird, Headman,   his + Mark seal,
Ke, sis swaw bay Headman   his + Mark seal.
Naw te, naish, cum, Headman.   his + Mark, seal,
                Grand Traverse Bands.
Aish quay, go nay, be, Chief.   his + Mark, seal,
Ah, Ko, say, Chief.   his + Mark, seal,
Kay, quay to say, Chief.   his + Mark seal,
Onaw, maw, nince, Chief.   his + Mark, seal,
Shaw bu aw quug, Chief   his + Mark, seal,
Louis, Mick saw bay Headman   his + Mark, seal.
May, dway, aw, she, Headman,   his + Mark seal,
Me, tay, o, neig, Chief.   his + Mark, seal,
Me, naw, quot Headman,   his + Mark, seal,
                Little Traverse Bands.
Waw, so, Chief   his + Mark, seal.
Mwaw ke we naw Chief,   his + Mark, seal,
Pe, taw, se, gay, Headman,   his + Mark, seal,
Ke, ne me chaw gun Chief,   his + Mark seal,
May, tway, on daw gaw she, Headman   his + Mark seal,
Me, ge, se, mong, Headman,   his + Mark, seal,
Pi, a, quick, way, me, dong, Headman   his + Mark, seal,
Kay, way, Kew do, Headman,   his + Mark, seal,

■ Pictured here is the signature page of the 1855 Treaty of Detroit. The following *ogemuk* signed the treaty on behalf of the Grand River Ottawas: Ne-baw-nay-ge-zhick, Shaw-gwaw-baw-no, Aish-ke-baw-gosh, Nay-waw-goo, Ne-be-ne-seh, Waw-be-gay-kake, Ke-ne-we-ge-zhick, Men-daw-waw-be, Maish-ke-aw-she, Pay-shaw-se-gay, Pay-baw-me, Pe-go, Ching-gwosh, Shaw-be-quo-ung, Ke-sis-swaw-bay, and Naw-te-naish-cum. NAM T494.

two tribes—the Ottawas and Chippewas of Michigan—attended the treaty negotiations in 1855: the Grand River Bands, Little Traverse Bands, Grand Traverse Bands, Mackinac Bands, and Sault Ste. Marie Bands. The southern Ottawas chose Paybahmesay, an ogema from Grand River, as ogemagigido, and the northern Ottawas chose Assagon, the delegate of the Cheboygan Ottawas. During the negotiations, Waubojeeg, an ogema from Sault Ste. Marie, spoke for all Chippewas, and Assagon of the Cheboygan Band spoke for all Ottawas. Individual ogemuk also spoke during the negotiations to represent the views of their bands and give assent to the speeches given by the ogemagigido. The Ottawas negotiated as their ancestors had before them: as autonomous bands representing the consensus decisions of their kin, which had united for the well-being of the Ottawa Tribe.

Even as a whole tribe, the Ottawas had no military power or material wealth that could compare with that of the United States. However, the two Ottawa ogemagigido—Assagon and Wasson—refused to stand in awe of the Americans, or to be bullied or browbeaten. Assagon in particular was an able and tenacious negotiator who knew the provisions of past treaties far more thoroughly than did the United States commissioners. When, toward the end of the negotiations, an exasperated commissioner of Indian Affairs denounced Assagon's demands as "extravagant," Assagon coolly replied: "Now I live only on corn soup at home & you have every luxury of life. It is strange that I should try to get as good as you!"[4]

What the Ottawas wanted more than anything were "strong titles" to their lands, not the uncertain tenure they received to the reservations created in 1836. These "strong titles" would "prevent any white man, or anybody else, from touching these lands," and preserve their lands for their descendants. Federal treaty commissioners also wanted to provide the Ottawas with certain, permanent tenure over their lands by creating bounded and protected reservations. The Ottawas, however, were afraid to accept federal assurances about permanent reservations, given the failure of the 1836 reserves. One Ottawa leader, Macaadupenase, expressed this fear in his response to the treaty commissioners, saying, "It seems as if you hold the land by a big string ready to pull it from us." A few young Ottawas proposed that they be given cash settlements so they could buy their lands, as many bands had already done, but the federal treaty commissioners refused to entertain this proposal. In the end, the Ottawas compromised. They agreed to make new reservations that would be divided into allotments of forty- and eighty-acre parcels owned by individual families. If, after a period of ten years, the president of the United States believed these families sufficiently competent to hold and protect their own property, he could grant them full title to their parcels of reservation land.[5]

Under the provisions of past treaties, the United States owed the Ottawas substantial debts. Federal treaty commissioners wanted to make a single, lump-sum payment of all debts to the Ottawas, but the Ottawas objected. By paying off all its debts in a single transaction, the federal government would move one step closer to severing its trusteeship over the Ottawas—a relationship it regarded as cumbersome, but which remained important to the Ottawas. While the treaty commissioners wanted the Ottawas to end their reliance on the federal government as quickly as possible, the Ottawas wanted to sustain the relationship indefinitely. Wasson explained the Ottawas' desires in a parable:

> We want this money; but wish to lock it up in your bread box. I told you then that I did not wish to do with our money, as I heard a man once did with a little swan. The little swan when he went out used to pick up shillings in his bill & bring them to his master. At last his master got to think that the swan was all money & cut him open & found no money. So he lost his little swan. Now, we don't want to cut our little swan open. We wish to let him live, that our father may feed him & he may grow & continue to bring us shillings in his bill.[6]

Waubojeeg of Sault Ste. Marie put the matter more directly: "My father with regards to the money we would like to know how much is coming to us. It is our design not to spend it all but leave it in your hands." As Wasson and Waubojeeg's words clearly show, the Ottawas and the Chippewas wanted the federal government to act as their trustee.[7]

Federal treaty commissioners objected to the establishment of a permanent trust fund, believing that it contradicted the objective of the Ottawas' eventual assimilation. If the idea was to make the "distinct" Ottawa people "one people" with Americans, the commissioners reasoned, the Ottawas could not rely on government funds indefinitely. This philosophical objection, however, was probably not as strong as the agents' desire to end government spending on the Ottawas. After much discussion, the Ottawas agreed to a ten-year trust fund, on the condition that its terms would be renegotiated at the end of its term.

At the end of the negotiations, the federal treaty commissioners achieved three of their major objectives: elimination of a permanent trust fund, continuation of government services to the Ottawas and Chippewas, and selection of reservations that would be divided into allotments for individual families. Any attempts the Ottawas made to modify these basic provisions during the negotiations were unsuccessful. However, Ottawa ogemuk were able to increase the amount of money the Ottawas would be paid. Further, because the Ottawas and Chippewas had disagreed about several treaty provisions in 1836 and in 1855, the two tribes requested and received assurance in the treaty provisions that any future treaties would be negotiated separately with the Ottawas and Chippewas. Both the Ottawas and the United States treaty commissioners assumed that when the allotment process was complete and annuities were paid, new treaties would be negotiated to settle any outstanding business. However, the Ottawas would never again make a treaty with the United States.

Ottawa leaders believed that the 1855 Treaty of Detroit would renew their cash income, guarantee their land holdings, and quiet rumors of their removal from Michigan. Grand River Ottawa ogema Paybahmesay offered the most glowing summary of the treaty:

> Our father is not aware how grateful we are today. We are glad because of his kindness. When we started here, we were like travellers on a log. We knew not when we might fall off, or where the end of it was; but we find we have not fallen off, or reached the end of it. Instead of darkness we find the bright light.[8]

The federal treaty commissioners were also hopeful, believing they had developed a workable plan to "civilize" and assimilate the Ottawas. However, the treaty's ambiguous language and unrealistic time restrictions set the stage for more than three decades of dispossession following the treaty's ratification. Despite its good intentions, the 1855 treaty would prove disastrous for the Ottawa Tribe.

The most damaging treaty provisions were those that divided the reservation into family farms or allotments. The United States intended that the Ottawas would live in reservation communities isolated from American settlers. In fact, the Grand River Ottawas who negotiated the 1855 treaty selected reservation lands that are now within the city of Muskegon. In order to prevent contact with Americans, the federal government amended the original reservation selection. The reservation described in the amended treaty moved the reserve away from the widely traveled Lake Michigan shore to a location in five inland counties: Custer and Eden townships in Mason County, Crystal and Elbridge townships in Oceana County, and Holton Township in Muskegon County. Here, the Ottawas should have been able to choose their lands without interference from others.

However, in a very short time, Ottawas who moved to the reservation would find American squatters laying claim to the land. Lumbermen claimed and cut timber from large plots of reservation land, and settlers claimed the most fertile ground for themselves. The Ottawas would also learn that the State of Michigan claimed many more acres under the authority of federal laws that granted states "swamp and overflow" land. Additionally, many sections were claimed by the Sault Ste. Marie Ship Canal Company under another federal law designed to sell public land to raise funds to construct the canal. Altogether, these claims on the reservation land reduced the land from which Ottawas could make farms and complicated the allotment process. Furthermore, the allotment process was not implemented according to the timetable outlined in the treaty provisions. Each delay allowed a larger of number of conflicting claims to ownership of reservation lands. By 1875, most of the 1855 reservation lands had been claimed by Americans. The 1855 reservation lands, which were meant to be a safe haven for Michigan Ottawas, provided the Grand River Bands with little sanctuary.

Aside from losing nearly all of their reservation lands, the Ottawas also did not receive all of the money due to them under the 1855 treaty provisions until a federal-court lawsuit forced the government into compliance fifty years later. Furthermore, because of the language that "dissolved" the "Ottawa and Chippewa nation"—a provision that both tribes had requested to assure that any future treaties would be made separately with the Ottawa Tribe and the Chippewa Tribe—succeeding generations of federal bureaucrats would later challenge and deny the very existence of the Ottawa bands as sovereign entities.[9] In 1855, both the Ottawa and United States delegates left the negotiations hopeful, but the 1855 Treaty of Detroit would prove a lamentable failure, an embarrassment for the federal government, and disastrous for the Ottawas.

The failure of the 1855 treaty strengthened Ottawa polity as the people and their leaders faced the challenges of the coming decades. They fought for what was rightfully theirs in distinctly Ottawa ways—as bands of kinsmen led by ogemuk who were respected heads of lineages, and by sharing what little land they were able to secure to support and sustain their communities. For thirty years after they negotiated the 1855 Treaty of Detroit, the Ottawas would work to obtain "strong titles" to their reservation land, and they would continue to hold the United States responsible for protection as a reliable trustee, despite the efforts of the treaty commissioners to strangle the government "swan."

■ The method of capturing images with photography was brand new when the Ottawas moved to their reservations. A few hundred images of Grand River Ottawas taken during the 1850s, 1860s, and 1870s survive, though the people in them are rarely identified. The Ottawa man in this image, who took the name of Joel Russet, is an ancestor to the Bailey family, one of the prominent family lines in the modern Little River Band. Russet was among the Grand River Ottawas who moved north to the reservations in the 1850s and 1860s. Joel Russet and wife. Courtesy of Loutit District Library (Grand Haven, Michigan).

CHAPTER 7

"Not a Tent, a Wigwam, nor a Camp Fire . . ."

The word for "reservation"—*shkwaanagan*—in the Ottawa language means "leftovers." Indeed, reservations were the leftovers of a once vast territory that had easily supported a large Ottawa population for centuries. The decision to leave their well-established villages for leftover lands in Mason, Muskegon, and Oceana counties was a difficult one for the Grand River Ottawas. They knew from experience that if they stayed in their historic villages, they would suffer the ills of a well-established whiskey trade, at the hands of traders who quickly relieved them of annuity cash by charging exorbitant prices for manufactured goods they relied upon, and from the animosity of settlers who objected to their continued occupation and use of lands that the bands had sold to the United States. The Grand River ogemuk knew that the very existence of their bands depended on moving away from the harassment and demoralization that had become part of their daily lives. By moving to less densely settled lands, the bands retained their social and political integrity, and the reservation's forested lands and marshes still housed game that required the cooperation of kin in its

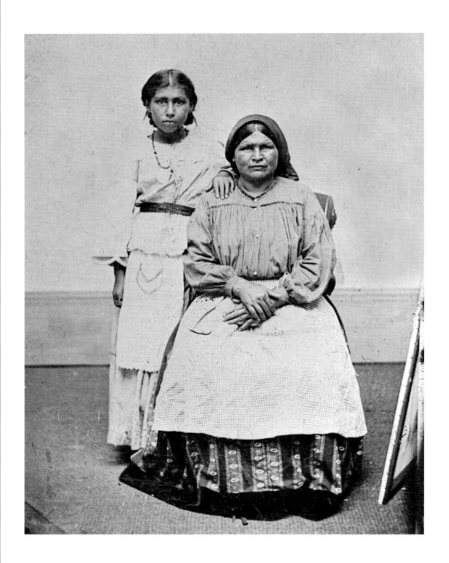

harvest and use. For the Grand River Ottawas, the reservation experience did as much to preserve their culture as it did to change it.

The move from the Grand River Valley to the 1855 reservations began in 1857, when the Grand River Bands' ogemuk and headmen traveled north to inspect the Mason, Muskegon, and Oceana county lands. They returned to the Grand River disappointed: they had found squatters already laying claim to the best agricultural lands, and much of the remaining territory was sandy and densely forested with pine, where the soil would not support farms. If the United States wished the Ottawas to become "civilized" farmers, the reserved land would contribute little toward that end. Some ogemuk told their Indian agent that they found the land "not as was represented to them nor such as they want," and

■ In their reports and other accounts, federal agents, missionaries, newspaper writers, and even casual observers noted that the Ottawas dressed like "white" people. Observers equated the Ottawas' change in dress style with a transformation of their culture—from that of the "uncivilized" or "savage" to that of the common American. Americans used this erroneous assumption to argue that the Ottawas had become "civilized," and therefore, the United States should no longer protect the properties preserved for the Ottawas in their treaties. Two Grand River Ottawa men; and Two Grand River Ottawa women. Private collection of George Pego.

some refused to move there.[1] The Grand River Ottawas who disapproved of the reservation locations had also visited the Saginaw Chippewas' reservation in Isabella County, and upon the invitation of their friends and relatives, opted to move to the Isabella Reservation instead. The majority of the Grand River Bands, however, began moving north to the Grand River Ottawa reservations the following year. In the spring of 1858, entire bands—the old and infirm, the able-bodied, and the young and vulnerable members alike—packed their belongings and carried them nearly one hundred miles north, where they built new settlements or joined their relatives' villages.

The Grand River Ottawas began their journey by traveling in their canoes to Grand Rapids, where they boarded the *Forest Queen*, a steamer bound for Lake Michigan. Hundreds of Ottawas crowded onto the small vessel on May 28, 1858. The atmosphere on the boat was strained. As the *Grand Rapids Daily Enquirer and Herald* reported: "The Indians were some afraid. They said the boat was too much loaded. . . . [They] were singing on the boat hymns in their native language, to pass away the time." At Grand Haven, the Ottawas disembarked and "lodged in the warehouses" for the night, where "Some two were sick; one very dangerously." The next morning, the Ottawas boarded the *Huron*, which took them to their reservations. On June 4, 1858, the first Ottawa immigrants finished their sixty-mile trip up the Lake Michigan shoreline and arrived at the village of Pentwater.[2]

At Pentwater, the migrating Ottawas divided into two groups, the members of which would form two distinct settlements on the reservations. A majority camped at the mouth of the Pentwater River before taking flatboats upriver to Oceana County and settling near the modern-day town of Elbridge. Elbridge, which was made up of primarily Catholic and traditionalist Ottawas, would become the center of the southern community on the 1855 reservations. A second group of Ottawas loaded up three flatboats and continued north to the Pere Marquette River, paddling inland to the northern portion of the reservations in Mason County. At modern-day Custer, they met Ogema Nawgawnequong's people, who were indigenous to the area and had already cleared about one hundred acres and planted crops. The immigrant Ottawas built a settlement alongside that of Nawgawnequong's band, and together these Ottawas formed the community that came to be known by Ottawas and Americans alike as "Indian Town." Indian Town, composed mostly of Protestant converts, became the core of the Ottawas' northern reservation community.

Not all Grand River Ottawas moved north by steamship. Some bands loaded their belongings into their canoes and traveled north by their own power and at their own speed, camping along the way. In October 1858, the *Grand Rapids Eagle* reported that one hundred Ottawas were camped in "quite a village . . . [which] sprung up . . . within a few days." The reporter continued: "They are *en route* for Pentwater, Oceana county, and are awaiting the arrival of as many more of their red brethren, when they altogether will leave for their future home."[3] About a week later, another hundred Ottawas arrived and joined this temporary village at Grand Rapids. The last Ottawas on the Grand

River, Paquodush's Fort Village Band, sold their Ottawa County land and joined the northern reservation settlement on the Pere Marquette River in November 1859.

Although the Ottawas who were indigenous to the area—the small bands of Kewaycushcum at Manistee, and Nawgawnequong on the Pere Marquette River—maintained horticultural villages in the region, most Ottawas had to build homes and clear gardens from scratch. A reporter who accompanied the traveling Ottawas noted, as did the Ottawa ogemuk and headmen who had visited the reservations in 1857, that "the land is not very good" and was "filled with pine and hemlock."[4] When emigrant Ottawas arrived at their new villages, most had insufficient food and too few tools to build homes and open fields quickly enough to meet their most essential needs. In this difficult transition period, the Ottawas depended on each other—and the values of reciprocal sharing and promoting the well-being of all bands—to survive.

However, once they had built their new villages on their northern reservations, many external features of Grand River Ottawa life changed from they way they had lived before they had treated with the United States. Still, their lives in many ways remained rooted in historic Ottawa culture. Rather than build the bark- and mat-covered structures of earlier years, they constructed one- and two-room log cabins and covered them with split cedar shakes; they erected these cabins in clusters that resembled their old villages. Families lived in the villages during the summer months, but continued to travel to fishing grounds and maple-sugar camps during the spring. They continued to keep communal gardens and to share the produce of their plots with their kinsmen and fellow villagers. Once gardens had been planted, families were free to travel during the summer to pick berries and wild plants, to work for a few days in the towns that were springing up throughout their former estate, and to visit family and friends at other Ottawa towns. Men traveled from the villages during the fall and winter to hunt and trap for meat and for furs. When hunts were successful, hunters divided the meat equally among the families in the village.

After their move from their historic villages, the Grand River Ottawas would never again hold tribal councils at the historic Grand Rapids meeting ground where they had debated issues of importance for more than a century. Sacred sites where the *Midewiwin* and *Wabano* lodges—Ottawa ritual healing societies—held annual rituals at Muskegon and burial grounds along the Grand River were left to immigrant settlers, who first converted them to fields and then to city blocks. In an article titled "Lo the Poor Indian," the *Grand Rapids Eagle* reported in May 1859:

> This is probably the first Spring . . . when the Indians have not pitched their tents . . . along the banks of our beautiful river, for hunting and fishing purposes. Not a tent, a wigwam, nor a camp fire, has anywhere this season been reared or seen upon the old tramping grounds of the red man to remind us of early days.[5]

Though the Ottawas no longer lived permanently along the Grand River, they had not stopped pitching their tents, hunting, fishing, or building campfires. Instead, they built new homes and villages, and formed new bands and confederations in their reduced territories. They would continue to rely on their cultural values, historic practices, and the leadership of the ogemuk to protect their very existence during the twenty years of dispossession that followed their northward exodus.

CHAPTER 8

New Communities, Established Leaders

I n their new villages, the Ottawas adapted to reservation life by
making decisions rooted in old cultural patterns as often as they
borrowed new materials and ideas from Americans. Americans
sought to confine the Ottawas on small parcels of land, to educate
them in schools, and to assimilate them, but the Ottawas retained their
political and cultural integrity in their new homes. Throughout the
mid-nineteenth century, the flexibility and solidarity of Ottawa bands
allowed them to resist assimilation and face the aftermath of the 1855
Treaty of Detroit. On their reservations, the Grand River Bands remade
their politics and society through the processes of band fission and
fusion, and it was through these processes that the modern-day Little
River Band would evolve from the historic Grand River Bands and the
Ottawas indigenous to the region with whom they merged.

Although the Ottawas lived in new villages, the rules of political
leadership remained unchanged. As in the days before reservation life,
village members looked to persons with exceptional skills to lead their
group. Leaders were not people who could command; instead, leaders
earned their positions and the respect of their people because they

provided for their families and led by example. The responsibilities and ethics of band membership and leadership that had supported Ottawa society for centuries sustained the new Grand River Ottawa communities even in the difficult decades that followed the 1855 Treaty of Detroit, as Americans took title to even the few acres of reservation land that the Ottawas had managed to retain during the 1860s and 1870s.

After they moved to their reservations, the Grand River Ottawas lived by rule of ancient cultural prescriptions of kinship responsibilities. Survival of the entire band remained more important than the enrichment of any individual. Members were raised and cared for by a web of extended kin, and life was guided by culturally established responsibilities of each person to the members of these large families. But the Grand River Bands did not remain static. The number of family bands changed as the southern Ottawas adapted to living in diminished territory, closer together, and for longer periods of time than they ever had before. On the Grand River, they had lived in many villages roughly ten to twenty miles from each other across an area spanning more than one hundred miles. On the reservations, bands lived side by side, with single communities sometimes housing several bands. This was common among the Grand River Ottawas' relatives and tribesmen at Grand Traverse and Little Traverse bays, who historically lived in large communities of multiple bands. However, on the reservations, hundreds of Grand River Ottawas who had once only occasionally interacted now came into daily contact with one another, and these changes initiated band divisions and mergers, as well as changes in leadership.[1]

The continuity of band leadership and systematic selection of new ogemuk was a matter of utmost importance to the Ottawas. Their livelihood depended on choosing leaders who were skilled in mobilizing band members for production purposes (such as food-gathering expeditions) and in dealing with government officials. Ogemuk also had to hold the proper kin ties linking their bands to other cooperating bands. As gradually as bands split and merged, headmen replaced aging ogemuk; ogemuk deferred to other leaders in new composite communities; and distinct communities took on identities that superseded those of the previous bands.

The first Grand River Ottawas who moved north were led by mostly the same ogemuk and headmen who signed the 1855 treaty on their behalf: Nebawnaygezhick, Shawgwawbawno, Wawbegaykake,

■ James Walker Cobmoosa was the son of Chief Cobmoosa, a prominent leader among the historic Grand River Bands. Before James Walker Cobmoosa moved to the Grand River Reservation, he owned and operated a store in downtown Lowell, Michigan. A house he built there still stands today. James Walker Cobmoosa, ca. 1850–1860. Private collection of George Pego.

Maishkeawshe, Paybawme, Opego, Chingwashe, Shawbequoung, Cobmoosa, Maishcaw, Kawgaygawbowe, Negawbe, Shayquaynaw, Metayomeig, and Maymeshegawday. Between 1855 and 1857, three headmen had become ogemuk—Negawbe, Shayquaynaw, and Maymeshegawday. Metayomeig became the leader of Meshemenocon's band. In 1858 and 1859, three new ogemuk—Aishquayosay, Kawbayomaw, and Kechekebemosay—appeared on the northern reservations. Starting as early as 1859, older ogemuk who led the Grand River Ottawas to their reservations were being succeeded by younger men. Aishquayosay took over for Shayquaynaw and led this band into the 1870s. Ogema Kawbayomaw led the Custer community, and upon his death was succeeded by Nawgawnequong. Between 1859 and 1865, Paquodush succeeded Negawbe, and Joseph Medawis succeeded Nebeneseh. Ogema Cobmoosa, who was already elderly when he and his band left the Grand River, was succeeded by his son Mawbeece, who became a leader in his own right.

Most ogemuk who led their bands north to the reservations passed authority to their successors by 1880. Joseph Medawis, who succeeded Nebeneseh in 1865, continued to lead his band into the late nineteenth century. Chingwashe (aka George Chingwash), who led one of the Ottawa bands from Bowting Village at Grand Rapids, represented his band until David Chingwash succeeded the elder leader around 1882. William Pacotush (aka William Sam) succeeded Pacquodush (aka Sam Pacquotush). Succession patterns that the Ottawas had followed for hundreds of years were still alive and well almost thirty years after the Grand River Bands moved north, and remained so well into the future.

Bands living in the close proximity that reservation life demanded sometimes lost their distinct identity, which effected change in the succession of band leadership. Less than a decade after the Grand River Bands' move north, Ogema Kechekebemosay deferred to Maymeshegawday when their two bands merged. In 1864, Penase became an ogema; by 1868 members of Kawgaygawbowe's, Payshawsegay's, and Maishcaw's bands joined with his, and Penase led this band, which had more than doubled in size, until the late 1880s. Ogema Simon Kenewegezhick's band split up between 1865 and 1870; some moved to a community at Little Traverse Bay, and others joined the Ottawas at Elbridge. Aishkebawgosh, a member of Cobmoosa's band, became a headman, and by the 1860s became an ogema. Aken Bell, a Métis whose Ottawa name was Kawequod, lived with Maymeshegawday's band until 1868. By 1870, he succeeded Maymeshegawday and led a small band of "pagans" who moved to the Saginaw Chippewa Reservation in Isabella County; Aken Bell remained an influential leader into the 1890s.[2] Nawgawnequong—a member of Kawbayomaw's band, which was indigenous to the northern portion of the Grand River reservations—succeeded the ogema in 1870. As the Grand River Ottawas' needs and common interests changed, so did the alliances and leadership that best served them.

By 1865, there were twenty identifiable Grand River bands on the reservations—thirteen of which were still led by the ogemuk who had signed the 1855 treaty and led their people north.[3] Five years later, there

■ Rodney Negake is a grandson of Chief Cobmoosa. Negake himself became a political leader among the Grand River Reservation residents. He wrote many letters on behalf of his band during the 1880s and 1890s, and also traveled to Washington, D.C., at the turn of the twentieth century to pursue redress of treaty issues. Rodney Negake and unknown man, ca. 1850–1860. Private collection of Jim Koon.

were still twenty bands, and twelve of the ogemuk who signed the 1855 treaty were still leading their bands.[4]

When the Grand River Ottawas formed new communities on their reservations, they called upon traditional rules for band membership and leadership to navigate this difficult transition. Over time, individual Ottawas moved between the southern (Elbridge) and northern (Indian Town) communities. People from the two settlements intermarried, and family members regularly traveled to visit each other or to help relatives with their work. Within a few short years, defining band membership within the reservation settlements became a matter of memory rather than a geographic fact, as it had been on the Grand

River.[5] On the Grand River, each village had been home to a separate band; but on the reservations, several bands lived together in larger settlements. Even in their new, expanded communities, individual Ottawas still knew who their band members were and which leaders represented their interests.

Elder leaders deferred to, or were succeeded by men more able to lead the bands during the dispossession and disappointment that characterized the decades following their emigration from the Grand River Valley. It is not unusual to find changing alliances and shifting spheres of influence in Ottawa society over their long history; however, the Grand River Ottawas did maintain a remarkable level of band stability during the latter half of the nineteenth century, given the radical change in their geographic and social environment. Ogemuk and headmen wielded little power in comparison to that of the United States, but by using structures of council and consensus, the Grand River Ottawas adapted by consolidating their numbers, choosing new leaders, and developing new strategies to cope with the schemes devised by Americans to dispossess them of their land and resources during the allotment years (1855–1871) and the homestead years (1872–1880s).

During the early 1900s, the reservation Ottawas could still identify their individual ogemuk, and they remembered the men who had served as leaders at the time of the 1855 treaty negotiations. It was through the historic processes of forging relationships by intermarriage and customs of band organization that the Ottawa bands at Indian Town, and the associated communities between there and the Manistee River eventually came together as the Little River Band of Ottawa Indians.

A "Great Excitement among the Indians"

When the Grand River Ottawas arrived on their reserve lands in Mason, Muskegon, and Oceana counties, they immediately began cutting farms from the dense forest and building new homes. Situated away from American settlement, they hoped to build communities on lands to which they believed they had "strong titles." Believing that the agreement they had made with the United States was binding, the Ottawas attempted to fulfill their obligations as outlined in the 1855 Treaty of Detroit. However, as their reservation lands disappeared from underfoot and the federal government failed to keep its promises, the Ottawas' hopes also failed. Living conditions on the reservations during the allotment and homestead years left the Ottawas little choice but to rely on historic ways of life to cope and survive during the 1860s, 1870s, and 1880s.

Even before the Grand River Ottawas arrived, Americans had staked claim to land within the 1855 reservation boundaries. Some Ottawas who moved to the reservations wanted to adopt American farming practices, but quickly discovered that much of the land was covered with pine timber, and the sandy soil produced limited crops. While the

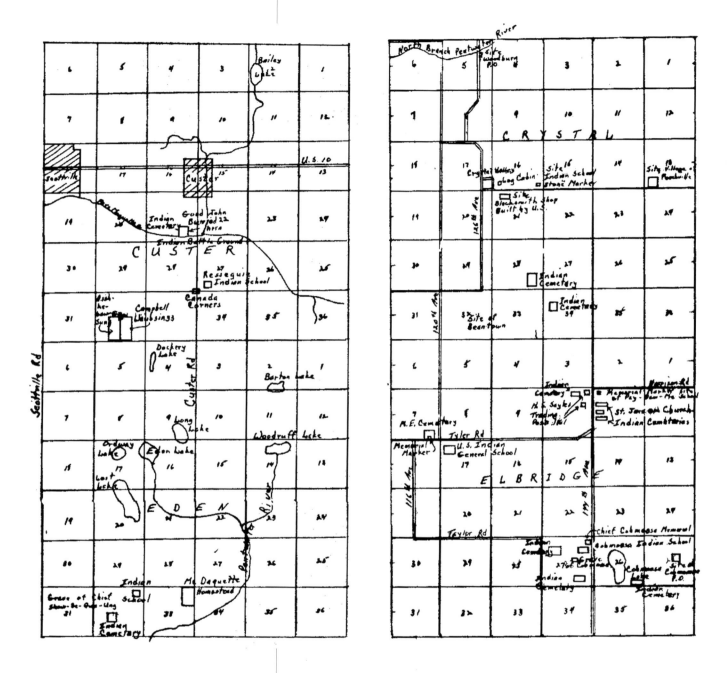

■ The Grand River Ottawas who moved to the reservations in Mason and Oceana counties cleared farms, built roads, and erected schools, churches, and houses. This map, drawn from memory by a reservation resident in the 1970s, shows how the Ottawas distributed themselves on the reservation, and the locations of their settlements. This map was reproduced in Dawn Dornbos, "Indiantown," *Mason Memories* 3, no. 2 (Summer 1975).

land was suitable for small gardens, it could not sustain the intensive cultivation required to earn a living from agricultural produce. The "agricultural implements and carpenters' tools, household furniture and building materials, cattle, labor, and all such articles as may be necessary and useful for them in . . . getting permanently settled"—all of which had been promised to the Ottawas in the 1855 treaty—were delivered sporadically, and not at all after 1875.[1] In addition, the four blacksmith shops promised to the Ottawas in the 1855 treaty simply never materialized.

Word that Ottawa reserve lands were valuable for pine timber spread quickly throughout western Michigan, and by mid-1857—before the Grand River Ottawas had even moved north—lumbermen entered private claims on Mason County lands and large pine stands were claimed in Oceana County. In October 1858, also before many Ottawas had arrived on the reservations, the local land office advertised land within the Mason and Oceana county portions of the reservation for public sale. The disregard government officials and Michigan residents showed for treaty-reserved property generated such discontent among the Ottawas that the local Indian agent wrote to his superiors about the "great excitement among the Indians," asking what he should do about it.[2]

The 1855 treaty promised that Ottawas who were twenty-one years old or who were orphan children when the treaty was ratified and became law would have five years to select land from the reservations for farms. The treaty also said that the United States would protect the titles to the Ottawas' farms—holding the properties in trust—so that they could not be sold or taken by non-Indian people for at least another ten years. At the end of the ten years, if the president of the United States believed that an Ottawa landholder was capable of managing his own affairs, he could grant the Indian landholder full possession of his property. While these treaty provisions were clear to both the Ottawa and federal officers at the treaty negotiations, they would not be carried out with any degree of precision.

Confusion quickly arose about who could select farmland from the reserves. The Ottawas had wanted all of their children to be able to select landholdings when they reached the age of twenty-one. The treaty, however, did not make provisions for people to select farms as they became adults. The treaty stated that after five years, the Ottawas had another five years to buy as much of the reservation land as they wanted for themselves. This was an exclusive right that was meant to prohibit Americans from purchasing reservation land. At the end of this five years, the treaty read, the unselected reservation lands could be sold to anyone, Indian or non-Indian.[3] Michigan Indian agents bumbled through the allotment selection process, making so many mistakes that the federal government eventually had to pass new legislation to grant Ottawas the reservation farms that the treaty intended.

■ John Baptiste Parisien was the son of a French *voyageur* (fur trader) and an Ojibwa woman. As a young boy, he traveled from his home at Flambeau, Wisconsin, to Michigan. In Michigan, he began gathering furs and doing odd jobs for the Campeaus and the Godfroys, two established Indian trading families on the Grand River. Parisien acquired a land allotment on the Grand River Reservation, and he continued his enterprise by purchasing reservation land and selling the properties to settlers and lumbermen. John B. Parrisian. Courtesy of Loutit District Library (Grand Haven, Michigan).

Between 1855 and 1870, the Ottawas tried to comply with the treaty's allotment process for selecting parcels of land for family farms. Some entered land claims only to find that their selections were already taken up by non-Ottawa people. Those who made selections on unclaimed land found that the bureaucratic process for obtaining title to the land was plagued with errors made by overworked, and sometimes incompetent and corrupt, federal agents. With each year that passed, Americans found new ways to claim reservation land, and state and local governments pressed the United States to legalize and validate these illegal claims. The state of Michigan asserted that public land grants made by the authority of federal legislation superseded the Ottawas' claim to their reservation lands, and denied the Ottawas allotments on these lands. Land speculators, lumber barons, and on occasion Ottawas themselves used ambiguous treaty language and any other opportunity to take possession of reserve land for personal gain.

There was certainly excitement among the Ottawas as they struggled to locate land and complete the claim process while, parcel by parcel, their reserve land continued to pass into the hands of non-Indian people. In September 1855, "under great anxiety," Ottawa ogemuk requested that lands on the Lake Michigan shore in Muskegon County be reserved so that they could continue to rely on these lands for horticulture, fishing, hunting, and harvesting maple sugar, while enjoying easy access to their historical travel routes.[4] The 1855 treaty commissioners had intended to isolate the Ottawas from corrupting frontier influences while they became "civilized," sedentary farmers. Federal officials objected to Ottawas continuing to live on the Lake Michigan shore, arguing that if the Grand River Ottawas received a reservation there, unscrupulous traders would ply them with whiskey and thwart the American goals. After nearly a year, the government found enough unclaimed land in five inland townships to make the reservations in Mason, Muskegon, and Oceana counties. By the time the reservation boundaries were approved by officials at the Bureau of Indian Affairs (BIA) and the General Land Office, non-Indians who, according to the treaty, had no right to be there were already squatting on reserved land.

The main culprits behind the loss of Ottawa reserve lands were inept federal agents. The first agent charged with helping the Ottawas make allotment selections made so many errors that the BIA sent the allotment list he constructed back to him. None of the Ottawas who had chosen land parcels through this agent secured farms for their families. A second agent prepared a new list of allotment selections, which the commissioner of Indian Affairs likewise deemed "ineffectual."[5] By June 1861—the year the Ottawa allotment selections were supposed to be completed—no Ottawa allotments had been selected or protected. At the end of the five-year selection period, all of the lists created by federal agents were declared irreparable, and the commissioner of Indian Affairs ordered that the allotment process start anew. Six years had passed since the Ottawas signed the 1855 treaty, and they had yet to choose and secure their allotments.

From the very start of their lives on their reserves, the Grand River Ottawas lodged complaints against American settlers who illegally entered the reservations. Ogemuk, who were disappointed and believed

■ John R. Robinson is the son of Rix Robinson and Rix's first Ottawa wife. John converted to Christianity and became a member of the Methodist Church. He served as a government interpreter and school teacher on the Isabella Reservation, and for a short time on the Little Traverse Reservation. Although John Robinson never lived on the Grand River Reservation, he purchased large quantities of reservation land and sold it to settlers and lumbermen.

■ This cabin, which stood near Remus, Michigan, is similar to those built by Ottawa allottees and homesteaders on the Grand River reservations. It was the home of Henry Pego, who would lead the Ottawas during the 1920s and 1930s. His children George, Irene, and Dorothy were all born in this house. Pego cabin. Private collection of George Pego.

that they had been deceived, marshaled all their strength and skill to protect the interests of their people. Starting in 1864, they wrote letters to federal officers demanding that the government make new treaties to assure that all Ottawas be granted "strong title" to reservation lands. They insisted that the United States address problems created by the theft, fraud, and incompetence that marked federal administration of their affairs.

When the Civil War ended in 1865, Americans flooded into Michigan. They pushed onto Ottawa reserves, squatted on the most valuable lands, and assumed that the government would validate their claims. Squatters cleared gardens and fields, built sawmills, and made lumber to construct their houses and outbuildings. At Indian Town in Mason County, squatters even claimed the Ottawas' river-boat landing. The influx of Americans onto the 1855 reservations further endangered Ottawa tenure of their reservation lands, making a mockery of the intentions of the Ottawa and federal treaty makers in 1855.

In some cases, Ottawas themselves—relying on the five-year exclusive purchase provision of the 1855 treaty—helped land speculators claim title to reserve lands. As one Michigan Indian agent reported, some self-serving Ottawas on the nearby Grand Traverse Reservation "signed a good many papers for plenty of lands" in exchange for cash payments.[6] Land speculators also acquired title to reserve lands through Ottawa buyers on the Grand River Ottawa reservations in Mason, Muskegon, and Oceana counties. To prevent the unlawful conveyance of land, the United States took action to stop the land sales by suspending the issuance of title to the newly sold land—grinding the allotment process, once again, to a halt. Still, on the recommendations of influential politicians, Ottawas John B. Parisien, Joseph Pabame, and John R. Robinson purchased land on behalf of American clients in 1868. The Ottawas could do nothing but wait while would-be settlers wrote letters to their congressmen demanding that they be allowed to stake claims on the reservation lands. These letters and the political clout of land speculators would provide willing politicians with ammunition to pass legislation giving non-Indians thousands of acres on the Ottawa reservations.

By the mid-1860s, the government's "civilization" program had col-lapsed. Few Ottawas were farmers, although many worked for American farmers in between the seasons of hunting, fishing, and harvesting wild foods. Ottawas were well aware that unspent treaty funds remained in their federal accounts, as the money had not been used to provide them with the farming equipment, seeds, furniture, or other goods promised to them in 1855. In their "great excitement" over land and financial matters, the Ottawas again mobilized their tribal governments to protect their interests. As early as 1864, they petitioned the government to sanction the visit of an Ottawa delegation in Washington to settle their tangled affairs. For the next three years, the Ottawas wrote letters to the commissioner of Indian Affairs asking that a new treaty be made to assure that all Ottawas received allotments on their reservations, not just those who were twenty-one years old when the 1855 Treaty of Detroit was ratified. They wanted the land protected from Americans. Ogemuk worked together through discussion and consensus to establish a united front, as their people continued to survive by hunting, fishing, gathering, and growing what food they could on the lands so quickly being claimed by settlers and profiteers.

CHAPTER 10

Accidents of History

The newly appointed superintendent of the Michigan Indian Agency promised the Ottawas that they would have their new treaty in 1864. He asked the commissioner of Indian Affairs to send an experienced negotiator to Michigan in June of that year, wrote proposals, made plans for his own role in the negotiations, and even began drafting a new treaty. He believed, as the Ottawas did, that the federal government had promised in 1855 that the Ottawas and the United States would make a new agreement in the not-too-distant future. The time for that new agreement had come, and between 1864 and 1870 the Ottawas, their Indian agent, and federal officials in Washington worked towards making treaty negotiations happen. Accidents of history, however, would prevent the new treaty from becoming reality.

Encouraged by their superintendent, the Ottawas prepared for treaty deliberations in 1864 and 1865. They engaged their band leaders and worked to build the consensus of their confederated bands. The Grand Traverse and Little Traverse Ottawas, in January 1866, asked for permission to visit Washington, and in May 1866 showed up there ready to negotiate on the spot. The Grand River Bands, "anxious to have these

■ Only one photograph exists of Michigan Indians in the field during the Civil War. This photograph of Indian soldiers at Fredericksburg, Virginia, may well be the famed Company K, First Michigan Sharpshooters—Michigan's only all-Indian unit.

Grand River Ottawa men who served in this unit include Amos Ash-ne-buy-nec-kay, John Battice, John E-tar-we-gezhick, Louis Genereau Jr., Samuel Going, Jacob Greensky, Cornelius Hall, Louis La-ba-o-sa, Joseph Kadah, Joseph Ka-ka-kee, D. M. Kewenaw, John Kiniewahasoipi, Thaddeus Lamourandere, Josiah Light, Joseph Mar-qua-quot, James Mash-kaw, John Mash-Kaw, Joseph Mar-qua-quot, William Newton, Adam Saw-be-com, Antoine Scott, Charles Shaw, George Stoneman, Joseph Ta-ohe-de-niw, John Wa-be-sis, James V. Watson, Charles Waubesis, Noah We-ash-kid-ba, John Wesley, and Charles Whiteface.

Civil War soldiers who returned to the reservation after 1865 were instrumental in pressuring the United States to fulfill treaty provisions. They, among other leaders on the reservation, pressed the United States to make a new treaty with their tribe. Company K, Civil War. Library of Congress, Prints and Photographs Division, Civil War Photographs, LC-B811-2342 [P&P].

matters adjusted immediately," met in council in August 1866, and asked the commissioner of Indian Affairs to treat with them at Grand Rapids.[1] In council at Indian Town, the Grand River Ottawas selected the ogemuk, ogemagigido, and delegates they wanted to represent their communities at the upcoming negotiations, installing Moses Shawbequoung as "head speaker" for the Grand River Ottawas at the expected treaty negotiations, and in all other dealings with the United States.[2]

Despite the best-laid plans of the Michigan Indian agent and the Ottawas, the crossed messages and confused arrangements of federal agents prevented negotiations from happening in 1864. The commissioner of Indian Affairs granted the Michigan Indian agent the authority to hold treaty negotiations, and appointed a special agent to travel to Michigan to participate in the proceedings. The two treaty commissioners planned to meet in the fall, at the time the Ottawas gathered to receive payment of their yearly annuities. However, the special agent from Washington did not arrive in Michigan during the late summer as planned. The Michigan Indian agent, eager to travel to the Ottawa communities by steamboat before fall, when dangerous storms swept the Great Lakes and capsized many ships, left before the special federal agent arrived. While the Michigan Indian agent traveled among the Ottawas, the special agent finally arrived in Michigan and awaited the local agent's return. When the two officers finally met, they were too late to travel to Ottawa reservations before the special agent had to return to Washington, and neither commissioner had been granted the authority to negotiate treaties with the Ottawas on his own. This delay in negotiations, caused by simple complications in travel schedules, was sufficient to end the Ottawas' chances for making a new treaty with the United States that year.

The Ottawas still hoped for a new treaty by 1867. On March 29, 1867, the House of Representatives passed a bill withholding funds for making any new treaties with Indian tribes within the United States. The Ottawas were not easily put off, however. Later that year, ogemuk from all of the Michigan Ottawa bands party to the 1836 and 1855 treaties united to petition the government to hold a treaty council; sixteen Grand River ogemuk signed the document. When the Michigan Indian agent visited the Ottawas in the fall of 1867, he barely prevented them from dispatching delegations to Washington immediately by promising to arrange a council himself.

As spring approached in 1868, the Ottawas were unwilling to wait any longer. The Grand Traverse and Little Traverse ogemuk repeated their intention to provide reservation land for their children who had come of age. Grand River ogema Moses Shawbequoung, who often spoke for the Indian Town community, prepared to send delegates to Washington, complaining that "We have laid this matter before our Agent year after year, but no answer yet; while other tribe of Indians are making treaties with the Government every year."[3] When federal officials again denied the Ottawa delegation permission to visit Washington, bands from the Elbridge and the Indian Town communities dispatched delegations to the nation's capital anyway. Although they failed in their efforts to make a treaty, the Ottawa delegation returned to Michigan believing that the commissioner of Indian Affairs had promised that federal negotiators would soon visit Michigan.

In 1868, Ottawa insistence finally led to the appointment of the Michigan Indian agent and a congressman as treaty commissioners. The congressman was to accompany the agent on his annuity rounds, and beginning on the Grand River reservations, the pair would negotiate treaties with the various Ottawa bands. However, delayed communications would once again prevent the promised treaty from materializing. The agent left for his annuity rounds before receiving instructions to wait for the congressman to arrive in Michigan, and the two men never met. This mishap, seeming minor enough at the time, would cost the Ottawas dearly.

Despite this failure to treat with the Ottawas in 1868, the United States was still willing to proceed with the Ottawas' treaties—for a while longer. In October 1868, the Mason and Oceana county Ottawas were asked to put their demands in writing and send a delegation to Washington, although they would have to pay their own traveling expenses. In response to this invitation, Ottawa bands held councils to appoint delegates; the Indian agent personally met with the Grand River Ottawas, and delegates were chosen. However, in January 1869, the commissioner of Indian Affairs refused to treat with the Ottawas, suggesting instead that their problems be solved through legislation. Even after the commissioner's refusal to treat with them, the Ottawas persisted. The Ottawas at Little Traverse Bay continued to ask for funds to visit Washington, but none were forthcoming. Two years passed before the Ottawas of Mason and Oceana counties made their final request for a new treaty. Then, on March 3, 1871, Congress formally declared an end to treaty making with Indian tribes within the United States.

By the time Congress passed this legislation, the Ottawas had lost thousands of acres of the land that was meant to become their farms. Because of the United States' failure to carry out the provisions of the 1855 treaty as they were intended, Michigan Ottawas suffered greatly. In 1855, federal treaty negotiators had viewed land allotments as part of a larger plan to assimilate and acculturate the Ottawas. With each family living on its own farm, the federal treaty commissioners believed that the Ottawas' bands and villages would break up, and that Ottawa farmers would become indistinguishable from their American neighbors. Eventually, the commissioners had hoped, the Ottawas might have no need for a reservation and would blend into the larger Michigan population. The Ottawas believed that the federal government had in 1855 promised them a new treaty in the near future, and they were persistent in their demand that the federal government make a new agreement with them to remedy the failures of the 1855 treaty. However, because the paths of federally authorized treaty commissioners twice did not cross at the intended times—purely accidents of history—the Ottawas would never again negotiate a treaty with the United States.

CHAPTER 11

The Opposite of Intentions

Congress officially ended the Ottawas' bid to make a new treaty in 1871 by passing legislation prohibiting any further negotiations between the federal government and Indian tribes in the United States. When the commissioner of Indian Affairs had refused to treat with the Ottawas in 1869, he suggested that their problems might instead be solved through legislation. Federal lawmakers recognized that the 1855 treaty makers, who meant to create protected, bounded reservations where the Ottawas could live in peace and unmolested by Americans, had failed. The ogemuk's continuing demand that their young people be allowed to select farms within the reservations received a hearing in Washington, but federal officers believed that the only way this could be accomplished was to make a new treaty. Since Congress would not make any more treaties with Indians, the ogemuk's only choice was to press for the passage of legislation that would address their most immediate desires.

In 1872, Congress passed the *Act for the Restoration to Market of Certain Lands in Michigan*, which was intended to be "remedial" legislation. The 1872 act, also referred to as the Michigan Indian Homestead

■ Many Michigan residents wanted to enter the Ottawa reservations to cut virgin timber from the land. The land on which valuable pine trees grew was sandy and not valuable for farming. Once the timber was cut, the reservation lands were often abandoned. This photograph shows the banks of the Manistee River at the turn of the twentieth century, after all of the timber had been cut. These abandoned lands along the Manistee River became a retreat for Ottawas who had lost their Mason County lands. Views of the Manistee River. Manistee County Historical Society.

Act, and the subsequent acts of 1875 and 1876, which extended time provisions of the 1872 act, did little to remedy the Ottawas' situation. Rather than protecting the reservations, these acts became legal vehicles for the Ottawas to be further dispossessed of their lands and left them nearly landless on their own reservations. All that the acts of 1872, 1875, and 1876 ensured was the complete failure of the government's "civilization program." In the end, the Ottawas, for the most part, continued to make their living from hunting, fishing, and gardening. They supplemented these economic activities with income earned by lumbering. Their kin-based society and ethics of reciprocity continued to play an important role in the evolving Ottawa society.

Under the 1872 act, Ottawas who had not yet selected allotments, and those who had come of age since 1855 had six months to choose homesteads in lieu of allotments. The Ottawas who had already selected allotments but had not received title to their chosen land were to be given patents, as well as the chance to buy additional land for a small filing fee.[1] At the end of six months—whether or not the Ottawas had chosen land—all reservation land "remaining undisposed of" would be opened to non-Indian settlers.[2] Worse yet for the Ottawas, the 1872 act validated

■ Young men often left the reservations to work in lumber camps throughout Michigan and northern Wisconsin. These two boys pose before a tree they were about to fell. Two young men with axes. Private collection of Margaret (née Bailey) Chandler.

land claims made by any "actual, permanent, bona fide settlers" prior to 1872—terms that were broadly interpreted to mean that any squatter who had moved to the reservations would receive title to Ottawa land.[3] The 1872 act—intended to remedy the Ottawas problems and protect their reservation lands—actually did the opposite.

Ottawas did not gain title to much additional reservation land under the 1872 act. Any Ottawa who wanted to choose a homestead had to first travel to federal land offices in Ionia or Traverse City to examine tract

■ Each winter, men from around Michigan would leave their farms in the south and travel north to work in lumber camps. Ottawas differed from their non-Indian neighbors in that whole families traveled to winter lumber camps together. The furs hanging outside the door of this log cabin indicate that Ottawa families continued to supplement their income by trapping. Snowshoes, an important Ottawa technology, were also still essential to their economy. Family at a lumber camp. Manistee County Historical Society.

books and find out which lands were even available. Those who did so reported that the land offices would not accept their applications, telling Ottawa homesteaders that others already had claims to the land. Ottawas often returned home without having chosen a homestead. Further, six months was not nearly enough time for all Ottawas to complete the selection process, and they had to compete with Americans who were determined to take as much unclaimed reservation land as possible, as quickly as possible.

When Ottawa ogemuk realized that the 1872 act did not allow them enough time to select land, they were quick to respond. At Indian Town, Ogema Shawbequoung immediately drafted a letter to President Grant. He wrote:

We understand that all the Reservations in the Counties of Mason Oceana and Muskegon are to come into Market this present month. We humbly pray that you will be pleased in much mercy to order not to have the Reservations to come into Market. We have many valid reasons for this petitioning. We read your communication stating that you will do just and further prosperity of the Indians in your Protection. This made us happy & much pleased & believe that you will do as you say. We have claims against the U.S. Government. We therefore pray that you will be pleased to order a Delegation to visit you at Washington City to make final settlement with this Great Government.[4]

This was one of many petitions the southern Ottawa bands sent to Washington, asking that their affairs be administered justly, preserving Ottawa reservation lands for the Ottawas. Congress, however, did little to remedy the Ottawas' problems, and continued to favor and protect American claims to reservation lands.

Nonetheless, Ottawas continued to send petitions to Bureau of Indian Affairs officers in Washington. The Indian Town community

■ By the early twentieth century, all of the lumber on the Grand River Ottawa reservations had been cut, leaving the land covered with thousands of acres of stumps. This picture was taken on the Manistee River near the site of Indian Village. Stumps in the Manistee River bottom. Manistee County Historical Society.

■ Berries soon grew among the stumps of the cutover forest on the reservation. Whole families would travel to sites where berries grew in abundance, pick them, and send them by railroad to downstate cities to be sold. Children, such as those pictured here, accompanied and helped their families on berry-picking excursions. The children in this photograph are (*left to right*): Front row: Alex Sam, Helen Sam, unidentified little boy. Back row: unidentified girl, Minnie Sam, Eunice Sam, unidentified boy, Maude Cogswell, John Sam*, and two unidentified boys. Children in a wagon, summer travel. Private collection of Rose and Alex Sams.

*Note: John Sam died when he was young and his parents named another son after him, but changed the name to Jonnie to distinguish the two boys from each other.

sent the United States a list of seventy-eight persons who had not yet been allowed to make their rightful selections. The bands in Oceana County sent another petition in February 1874 asking that their claims "be investigated and if found valid, We pray you to pass an Act which will give the right and privilege to the said Indians to claim and possess the above lands that are still vacant and unoccupied so that all who are still without any land can be provided for."[5] BIA officers who received these petitions sent instructions to field officers authorizing them to investigate the Ottawas' charges. As a result of these investigations, the BIA extended the time within which Ottawas could select their homesteads, and prevented Americans from making further claims on the Ottawa reservations until the Indian homestead selection process was finished.

However, the process by which Grand River Ottawas selected additional homesteads on their reservations after 1872 was not documented in BIA records. In 1875, the head of the Michigan Indian Agency reported to the commissioner of Indian Affairs about the homestead selection process in glowing but improbable terms:

> The last promise of the Government has just been fulfilled in the delivery of patents to those Indians that were twenty-one years of age at the formation of the treaty of July 31, 1855. The balance of the land of their reservations was opened by act of Congress in 1874 [*sic*] for homestead-entry. There were about 100,000 acres of excellent farming land. It has nearly all been taken for homesteads. Many of the younger Indians thus received lands to which they were not entitled under the treaty. This will practically determine the capability of the Indians to join with the whites in the business of civilized life, for the whites have surrounded and intersected them. I anticipate that the general result will be beneficial to the Indians. The example of that class of men that have entered upon their homesteads will show the Indian what can be done and how to do it in making the "wilderness blossom as the rose."[6]

■ Tannic acid, which is found in hemlock bark, is an essential ingredient in the process of tanning leather. Beginning in the mid-nineteenth century, families traveled into the lowlands where hemlock grew and collected bark, which they sold for cash. This photograph was taken at a family's hemlock camp near Mesick, Michigan. Peeling hemlock bark. Courtesy of Ann McClellan.

■ Ottawa families set up camps near berry patches, just as they did at lumber camps. The tent pictured here would provide shelter for the whole family during their stay at this camp. Inside the tent, a berry bucket hangs from the top rail. Berry camp. Private collection of Rose and Alex Sams.

In reality, only eighteen Grand River Ottawas selected homesteads under the 1872 and 1875 remedial legislation—selections totaling 1,509 acres of Grand River Reservation land.

Also in 1875, *An Act to Amend the Act Entitled "An Act for the Restoration to Homestead Entry and to Market of Certain Lands in Michigan"* was enacted by Congress to amend the 1872 act. Under this bill, additional patents were to be issued to Little Traverse Bay Bands Ottawas who had not yet received title to their allotments, and to allow Americans ninety days to file homestead claims on reservation lands not yet selected by Ottawas. All other Ottawa reservation lands that were not valuable for pine timber were opened to homestead claims for one year—this time to both Indians and Americans. After one year, any unclaimed Ottawa reservation land would be offered for sale. In 1876, Congress passed yet more legislation to regulate homesteading on the Ottawa reservations, this time extending the time in which settlers could stake homesteads indefinitely.

Rather than help to remedy the failed reservation allotment system, the 1872, 1875, and 1876 homestead acts further compromised the Ottawas' hold on their reservations. The injustice of these acts was twofold. First, the land the Ottawas were to homestead already belonged to them. It had been reserved for them in the 1855 Treaty of Detroit, and under this treaty, they were to have received farms on the reservations as allotments. Second, the federal government's "remedy" to its own failures only made it easier for non-Indians who wanted title to reservation land to acquire it. The acts did so by recognizing squatter claims on the reservations, and by demanding that Ottawas follow an impossible process for obtaining homesteads. If an Ottawa person successfully registered a claim at the local land office, he or she was then expected to live on the land for five years, "improving" it by clearing fields and erecting buildings. At the end of the five years, an Ottawa homesteader could apply for a patent to the land. The Ottawas had already waited twenty years for their allotment patents, and now they would have to wait another five to eight years to receive patents to their homesteads. In the meantime, enterprising Americans found new ways to dispossess the Ottawas of their homestead claims.

Further, the 1875 and 1876 legislation implemented a homestead selection process that was at odds with Ottawa culture and economy. Ottawas who selected homesteads were particularly vulnerable because of the length of time they had to live on the land before receiving title to it. To fulfill the requirements of the acts, the Ottawas had to discard their historic practices and conform to the ways of the American farmer—and do so immediately. The Ottawa idea of an allotment or homestead was not the same as that of American farmers in southern Michigan, who operated family farms year round. Ottawa life was grounded in band structures and the practices of traveling to hunt, fish, and gather while raising seasonal crops at home sites. Therefore, most Ottawa families maintained dwellings within villages very much like their historic homes on the Grand River, as well as seasonal villages at their hunting, trapping, fishing, and gathering sites. For Ottawas who lived far away from towns where they could sell crops, on land that was so sandy that farmers were not interested in crop production there, Ottawa farms were "a place on which to make sugar in the spring, raise a few potatoes and sufficient corn to supply their bread during the year, and to have a home upon, to which they may at any time return."[7] Whenever Ottawas left their homes to hunt, fish, work, or spend part of the winter at one of their other villages or traditional trapping sites, Americans declared that Ottawa homesteads had been abandoned and claimed the land for themselves.

The problem of Americans claiming Ottawa homesteads had grown to such a proportion on all of the 1855 reservations that the federal government sent a special agent to investigate what could only be described as massive land fraud. The special agent found extensive evidence of settlers and land speculators falsely claiming homesteads as "abandoned" by Ottawas, and then taking the land.[8] In February 1877, the agent reported at least forty such cases of "robbery & cruelty in the extreme," including that of William Paquodush, an ogema in the Indian Town community.[9]

The agent's report listed a number of tactics used to swindle the Ottawas. He reported that settlers saw the Ottawas as an "obstacle in the way of permanent and desirable development of the country, and for this and other reasons, every possible means is resorted to dispossess them of their lands." The simplest way for these people—this "class of sharks," as the agent called them—to obtain land from an Ottawa was to get him drunk and convince him to sign over his land for a few dollars. A more sophisticated method was to loan an Ottawa a small amount of money and then threaten to sue him, frightening him into handing over his deed, or, what the agent called the equivalent, coercing him into agreeing to a mortgage for the land. Store owners in particular specialized in obtaining Ottawa mortgages and then foreclosing. Other schemes involved providing Ottawas with "the conveniences of life," such as sewing machines and parlor organs; when Ottawas failed to make payment, they would have to forfeit their land. Even if an Ottawa refused goods or cash in exchange for a mortgage, there were other ways to deceive him. A speculator might purchase a small quantity of growing timber for a fair price, and trick the Ottawa into signing a warranty deed for the land instead of a contract for the timber. A final method was to bribe an Ottawa to impersonate the real Ottawa landowner and sign over the title in exchange for cash. Some land speculators apparently allowed this practice knowingly.[10]

The special agent himself noted that Ottawas could rarely contest the frauds successfully. Ottawas were most often too poor to travel the

seventy-five to one hundred miles to the local land office with their witnesses, and then pay the fees and an interpreter. Some Ottawas who had been educated in federally funded Indian schools wrote to their local Indian agent asking for investigations and settlements in these claims. Few of the investigations resulted in favorable rulings for the Ottawas. Despite the blunt language of the special agent's report, land fraud continued on Ottawa reservations throughout the 1870s and 1880s, as Americans used the faulty homestead legislation to gain Ottawa lands for themselves. The result was the steady erosion of the Ottawa land base, which the Ottawas remained largely powerless to stop.

County officials showed a similar lack of regard for Ottawa lands when they entered Ottawa allotment selections—supposedly protected by federal trust status—on the county tax rolls. In 1855, the Ottawas had been assured that the treaty language would exempt their landholdings from taxes. The Ottawas' reaction to taxes levied by local authorities was to ignore tax bills and notices of impending sale, either because they did not understand the taxation system or because they believed that exemption from taxes was part of their agreement with the United States. As early as 1863—seven years before the United States conveyed the first patents—Ottawa lands in Oceana County were being sold

■ Henry Bailey was among the Grand River Ottawas who became a successful farmer. He raised the money to pay taxes on his allotted land and built a log cabin on the reservation. Bailey replaced this cabin with a frame house at the turn of the twentieth century. Pictured here are Henry Bailey, Martha Smith, Sarah Sikorski, Edna Rinard, and Martha Rinard (child), a five-generation family photo. Family photo, ca. 1942. Private collection of Elaine (née Beaton) Porter.

■ Teresa Donegay was the second wife of Henry Bailey. The Donegays were one of the Mason County Ottawa families who cleared and farmed land on the reservation. Teresa Donegay. Private collection of Dorothy (née Wabsis) Bailey.

for back taxes. The local Indian agent protested loudly about Ottawa allotments being placed on tax rolls, and demanded that the practice stop. By 1877, the special agent who investigated Ottawa land frauds warned that if the United States did not place Ottawa allotments and homesteads in trust—a move that would end taxation of allotments and homesteads—Americans would soon hold title to the largest portion of the Ottawas' reservation lands. Despite his call for federal protection, tax sales continued throughout the 1870s.

As a result of fraud and tax sales, the Ottawas of Mason and Manistee counties built small settlements on the few remaining parcels held by band members. Living in such close proximity strengthened Ottawa bands, but increased the Ottawas' poverty. Peter Meshkaw, for example, managed to pay taxes on his parcel and was able to provide a home for twelve families who had lost their land. These included the families of Moses Kewagewan, Joe Donagon, Naywayquam, William Medacco, Joseph Peters (or Peete), and Henry Bailey. Many remaining allotments and homesteads became communal home sites for Ottawa families; however, with several families crowded onto these small parcels of land, there was little, if any, land left to farm. The Ottawas had no choice but to continue to hunt, trap, fish, and gather—seasonal rounds that required them to leave their allotments or homesteads for part of the year.

In 1877, the special agent reported on the Ottawas' economy as he saw it. He noted in particular the continuance of the seasonal calendar that governed Ottawa life. He wrote:

> They lead a nomadic life, subsisting largely by hunting and fishing. When they leave their homes on an expedition of this kind or for the purpose of doing a few days work to supply immediate necessities, the whole family goes together, a temporary wigwam is erected in which they all live, and while the husband is at work the wife and children subsist the family by picking and selling berries, fishing, or making baskets. . . .
>
> Most of them have small houses in the old Indian villages to which they repair during the fishing season for the double purpose of convenience, and in order that the women and children may be on hand to clean and cure the fish. . . . About the first of March such of them as have been in the villages return to their land to prepare for sugar making. Generally I think they remain on the land until about the

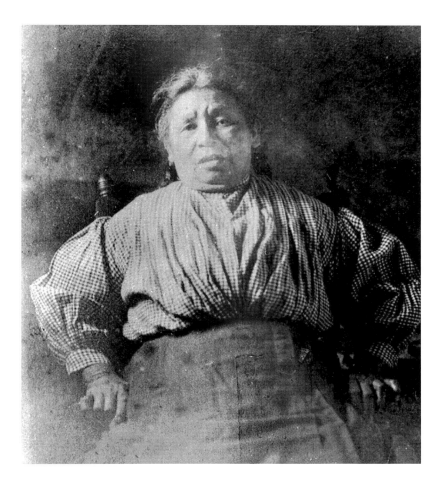

■ Helen Bailey's Indian name was Wen-da-go-qua, meaning White Giant Woman of the North. She was the first wife of Henry Bailey. She and Henry worked together to build their reservation farm and a log house in Mason County. Helen Bailey. Private collection of George Pego.

first of June when the summer fishing commences. During the summer they alternate between the fishing grounds and their farms.[11]

Early settlers confirmed the agent's observations. One local history romantically recounted that during the first years of Ottawa residence at Indian Town, they made extensive use of the natural resources at their disposal:

> Besides wolf and bear and deer and beaver, were countless numbers of marten, coons, mink, muskrat, otter and fisher and other trapped game. The lynx and wild-cat also prowled in these woods, and in short, nature presented here a model hunting-ground. The waters were full of choice fish; the air was full of edible birds, and wild duck and pigeon, in their season, darkened the air "from morn till noon and dewy-eve;" the forest glades were full of the animals of the chase, and wild berries

■ Henry Bailey was also among the few Ottawa farmers who cleared land and made a successful farm on the Grand River Reservation. Henry Bailey. Private collection of Dorothy (née Wabsis) Bailey.

grew, as they do to-day, in countless profusion; the soil was easily tilled, and produced in abundance, to the simple cultivation of the squaws and the men enfeebled by age, plentiful harvests of potatoes and Indian corn. In fact, Nature seems here to have emptied her cornucopia upon those red sons of the soil.

Such was the land chosen by the Aborigines, and the whites who have nearly supplanted them in their birthright, have reason to feel happy in their selection of a settlement.[12]

The Ottawas were, however, unhappy about the loss of their reservation lands. More of their lands were taken up by Americans every day, and they rarely received other treaty-stipulated goods, such as furniture and farming tools, that could improve their lives.

In 1855, federal treaty negotiators had looked toward the eventual assimilation of the Ottawas into American society through education, agriculture, and technical assistance; but by the end of the nineteenth century this "civilization" program had failed. The 1855 treaty achieved the opposite of its intentions: it left Ottawa bands and communities intact, created circumstances that perpetuated the Ottawas' economic practices, and maintained the Ottawas' need to sustain and engage their band and tribal governments to advocate on their behalf. The "remedial" acts of 1872, 1875, and 1876 worsened the Ottawas' poverty, made them more resistant to American "civilization," and increased their dependence on their mobile, kin-based hunting-and-gathering bands for survival.

During the latter half of the nineteenth century, the Ottawas' economic situation descended into unprecedented poverty. Annuity payments ended in 1870, leaving most families with little or no cash, except what they earned by working in lumber camps during the winter, picking berries in the summer, and selling their handmade black-ash baskets. As annuities alone could not support families, the Ottawas continued to rely on traditional economic practices and the reciprocity of their kinsmen. While Americans felled forests and undercut the basis of the Ottawas' hunting, fishing, gathering, and trapping economy, starvation became a real threat. Instead of becoming the permanent homes as they were intended, Ottawa reservation communities became launching points for off-reservation hunting, fishing, and gathering expeditions conducted by bands and led by headmen and ogemuk. The Ottawas also continued to divide natural resources, including berries and maple sugar, between community members to assure that no family went without the necessities of life. All of these cultural practices and values would continue to sustain the Ottawas well into the twentieth century.

The Ottawas' economic survival during the 1870s, 1880s, and 1890s strengthened the connections between the Indian Town community and Kewaycushcum's Band on the Manistee River—the forerunners of the Little River Band. Because Americans did not want the inland marshes along the Manistee and Pere Marquette rivers for agriculture, the sheltered wetlands along all of these river systems continued to provide rich winter hunting and trapping. Ottawas who had moved to Mason, Muskegon, and Oceana counties in 1857 and 1858 regularly left their allotments and homesteads to travel to the Manistee River tributaries and estuaries, where they fished, shot game birds, and trapped fur-bearing animals. Eventually, the two communities intermarried, shared resources, and formed a new community.

CHAPTER 12

The Council of Ogemuk

The Grand River Ottawas continued to rely on the skills of their ogemuk to lead their reservation communities, particularly as they were dispossessed of their lands by Americans. Ottawa ogemuk regularly met in council and addressed representatives of the United States, in person or in writing, to voice grievances and press for solutions to their problems; the historical record is filled with letters addressed by the ogemuk to Michigan Indian agents, the commissioner of Indian Affairs, and the president of the United States. When major issues affected all the historic Grand River Bands, the northern and southern reservation communities wrote joint petitions. On regional matters, communities or bands acted independently. By 1865, the northern and southern communities had developed separate identities, similar to band identities, and were concerned with issues distinct to their communities. However, the ogemuk and their constituents from all of the reservation communities united to fight for the "strong titles" and the allocation of land to young Ottawas that they believed they had been promised in 1855.

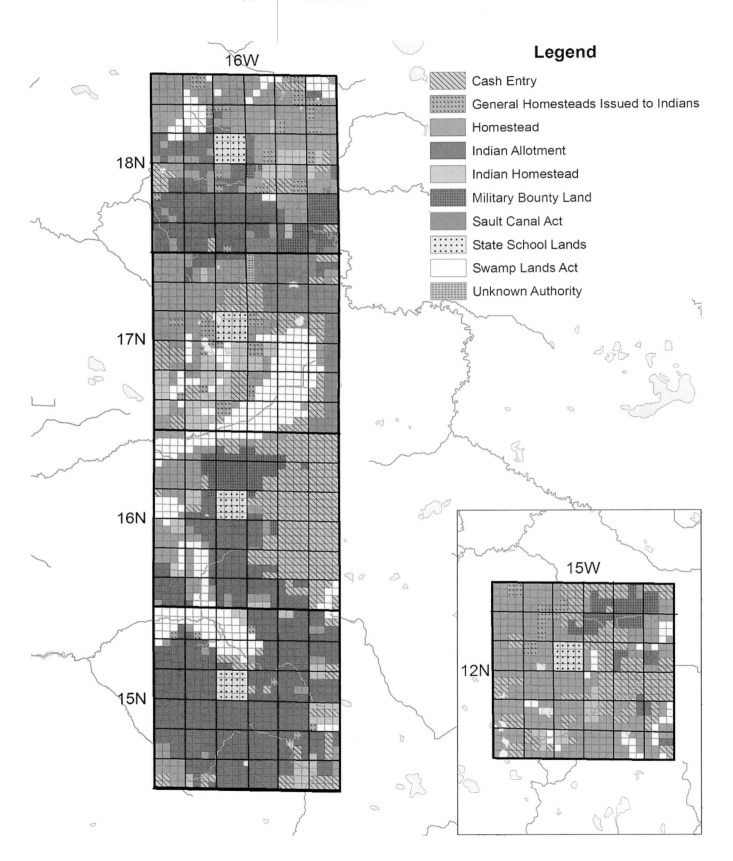

Legend

- Cash Entry
- General Homesteads Issued to Indians
- Homestead
- Indian Allotment
- Indian Homestead
- Military Bounty Land
- Sault Canal Act
- State School Lands
- Swamp Lands Act
- Unknown Authority

During the late 1860s, pressure mounted from settlers who wanted the United States to complete the allotment selection process on the Grand River reservations, to issue the Indians patents for Indian lands, and to open the remaining reservation land for sale to Americans. The words of frustrated ogemuk who saw their lands slipping away from them actually mirrored those of would-be settlers: both wanted control and ownership of land and for the federal government to issue titles to Indian landholders. The ogemuk, however, believed that their land should be saved for themselves and their children; they demanded that the United States issue "strong title" in the form of patents, and redoubled efforts to obtain these proofs. Americans who wanted titles issued to Indians spoke of fee-simple patents—documents that conveyed all right, title, and interest in the parcel to the Indian landholder, but reserved no federal trust over the land so it could be sold to any purchaser.

Leaders from the Elbridge community in Oceana County and the Indian Town community in Mason County came together in June 1865 to determine how they could correspond more productively with the federal government in their efforts to protect their reservations. At a well-attended council at Indian Town, the northern and southern communities drafted a resolution to the "United States of America [and the] State of Michigan."[1] The purpose of the meeting was to "form and establish some foundation by which, *We* may be better enabled to conduct all our public Conventions and councils in a more *legal* and systematic form; and to carry into full effect all of our public *Acts*, Treaties, Resolutions and agreements."[2] Ottawa leaders were in no humor to capitulate to settlers who wanted their land, and they would not allow the federal Office of Indian Affairs to order them about. The ogemuk, for example, upheld the right of their people to select their own leaders. Their insistence on continuing this tradition prevented attempts by federal Indian agents to manipulate the political process in a way that would undermine their tribal authority.

The BIA tested the determination of the ogemuk to select their own leaders when it attempted to install Joseph Medawis as ogemagigido of the Indian Town community. The Michigan Indian agent, upon the death of Ogema Nebeneseh in 1864, took it upon himself to select a successor to represent the Indian Town community. The Ottawas immediately objected to this infringement on their political prerogative. Ogema Shawbequoung spoke out against the agent's violation of Ottawa band sovereignty:

■ The Grand River Ottawas reserved, by treaty, land in Mason and Oceana counties as their permanent homes. Their treaty included language that would both protect the reservations and allow the Ottawas to divide the reservation into family farms. However, shortly after the Ottawas moved to their reservations, they learned of a number of legal loopholes that allowed other parties to claim land within the reservation boundaries. The state of Michigan claimed many acres within the reservation. Settlers made illegal land purchases with the aid of corrupt federal agents at the Ionia and Traverse City land offices, and were allowed to obtain title to their claims. Non-Indian homesteaders were allowed to claim additional reservation lands after the Civil War. In the end, the Ottawas were only allowed to make farms on a small portion of the reservation. Map of Ottawa land dispossession. Courtesy of Little River Band of Ottawa Indians Historic Preservation Department.

> I beg leave to address these few lines informing you that it has created much grief and sorrow in the minds of those Indians of Band which belonged the late Chief Nebinnesa in appointing Joseph Metaywis to be the successor of the late Chief (Nebinnesa) contrary to the wishes of the late Chief and his Band. It has produced much dissatisfaction, [and] ill feeling. . . . The new Chief (Jos. Metaywis) appointed and elected is altogether ignorant and utterly incompetent to discharge or transact the public affairs between the Government and the Indians. They have no confidence in him.[3]

Shawbequoung made it clear that this usurpation of power had caused discord in the Indian Town community. He explained the Ottawas' position on the issue of selecting their own leaders:

> The Commissioner G. W. Manypenny [the United States negotiator of the 1855 treaty] gave the Indians distinctly to understand that should any of the head Chiefs die who were parties and signed the Treaty of 1855 at Detroit, the headman under the Chief that dies, should then be immediately appointed and elected to be his successor in office, and no other should or could not usurp that office. And whenever the Government should see fit and proper at any time to renew and extend the Treaty with the Indians, the Commissioner is instructed properly to recognise only those Chiefs who signed the Treaty, and those headmen who may be appointed to fill vacancies occasioned by death. Those, and only those persons I have alluded to are the only persons that can be properly recognised as Chiefs, and no others.[4]

According to Shawbequoung, it was the "unanimous wish and request of all the other Chiefs both at Pentwater [Elbridge] and Pere Marquette [Indian Town]" that Nebeneseh be succeeded by his son Noteenokay.[5] Replacing a respected ogema with a man who was trusted by the ogemuk, they believed, would bring peace to the community.

Also at the June 1865 council at Indian Town, the Ottawas informed the Indian agent that they would choose their own "Head Speaker" by traditional criteria, resolving that

> by the powers of this convention that we the Chiefs and people do hereby nominate and appoint Moses Shawbekoung (Chief) to the

Office of head Speaker who shall preside in all our public Councils and Conventions; when and wherever held; and in all Treaty; or Treaties which may hereafter be held and negotiated, between the United States Government and the Grand River Ottawa and Chippewa Indians.

He shall hold his office during good behaviour, and be compensated so much for his services as the Indians may see fit and proper to allow and direct. His knowledge and influence, His honesty, and integrity, the public confidence of our people; and his philanthropic regard for the welfare of our people, all this preeminently qualifies him for that important Office.[6]

These Ottawas insisted that their decision be respected, asserting that "The Indian Department and all Officers connected with the Indian Agency is hereby informed and acquainted to recognize Moses Shawbekoung as the *Head Speaker* for the Ottawa and Chippeway Indians."[7] Nebawnaygezhick, Kawgaygawbowe, Paquodush, Chingwashe, Payshawsegay, Kawbayomaw, Shawgwawbawno, Penase, Maishcaw, Cobmoosa, and even Joseph Medawis all signed this document.[8] Many of these leaders also signed the 1855 treaty and continued to represent their bands throughout their lifetimes.

The council at Indian Town shows the Ottawas' adaptability. While maintaining their band and leadership structures and traditional "offices," such as that of the ogemagigido, they also created a new community-wide council made up of the formerly distinct and autonomous Grand River Bands. Several bands originally made up the northern and southern reservation communities, and their members slowly came to identify with their new communities more than with their Grand River villages of origin as historically distinct bands intermarried and intermingled for common purposes. For example, Ottawas at Indian Town no longer identified themselves exclusively as members of Shawbequoung's, Chingwashe's, Paquodush's, Kawgaygawbowe's, or Nebeneseh's band (among others), and instead identified themselves as members of the Indian Town community. The same can be said for the southern reservation community at Elbridge.[9] Still, these communities chose leaders and spokesmen by the same criteria the Ottawas had used for centuries. The adjustments the Grand River Ottawas made did not represent a loss of culture; rather, they were a sign of vitality and their ability to adapt to changing conditions.

A number of Grand River ogemuk rose to ascendancy in their respective communities during the 1860s as they led their people into a new era of political action. Cobmoosa, Mawbeece (Cobmoosa's son), Aishkebawgosh, Paybawme, Maishkeawshe, Payshawsegay, Aishquayosay, Wawbegaykake, Nebawnaygezhick, and Opego regularly sent letters and petitions to state and federal governments from the southern settlement at Elbridge between 1859 and 1870. The ogemuk who wrote from the northern Indian Town settlement in Mason County were Shawbequoung, Chingwashe, Paquodush, Kawgaygawbowe, Nebeneseh and his successor Joseph Medawis, and Penase. The immigrant Ottawas at Indian Town joined two indigenous communities whose settlements predated the creation of the 1855 reservations. Those villages were headed by the ogemuk Kewaycushcum at Manistee, and Nawgawnequong (Kawbayomaw's successor) at Indian Town (later called Custer). Many headmen, the leading males of families of lesser prominence, joined the ogemuk by adding their names to letters and petitions.

In 1869, Ottawa ogemuk who were fed up with unkept promises made by powerless Indian agents incorporated another new element into their political process when they hired an attorney to help them bring a lawsuit against the United States. Ogemuk had been "doing all in their power to procure a recognition and present their rights and secure the pittance allotted to them," but had not been heard. On behalf of the Ottawas, attorney W. T. Howell charged the federal government with allowing "several thousand acres of the choicest and most valuable lands reserved under the provision of the [1855] Treaty . . . [to be] sold and patented under circumstances of fraud and criminality, which in ordinary transactions would amount to felony." In short, Howell pointed out the federal government's neglect, and its mismanagement and illegal handling of Ottawa affairs.[10]

The agent then in charge of Michigan Indian affairs was furious with the Ottawa ogemuk for taking action without his supervision. In a private council with the ogemuk, the agent made it clear that he would "brook no outside interference."[11] He threatened to discredit Howell and demanded that the Ottawas cease legal action at once. Each ogema who responded to the Indian agent spoke for his band. Nebawnaygezhick, an ogema of the Indian Town community in Mason County, responded sharply:

I am one of those who employed the attorney. What was we to do. The promises had been made but never fulfilled. For instance one agent Mr. Leach promised us that each of us should have a yoke of oxen. Did we get the oxen? Yes we got them, four yokes each, but in promises. The Agent would come up here all smiles and promise anything, and then would show us his backside for one year. Then he came again with smiles and promises, then his backside for another year. Then for the third time his promises, then for the third time, his backsides. At last he would come the fourth and last time, and bring the oxen with him, but they were in his mouth, smile go home and be put out of office and the last that we would see of him would be his backsides.[12]

Nebawnaygezhick used oxen as an example of broken promises; however, Ottawa ogemuk were most concerned about gaining "strong title" to their lands and keeping non-Ottawa people from claiming more of their reservations.

After the end of the Civil War in 1865, the Ottawas faced intense pressure to sell their reservation lands to settlers and leave southern Michigan. The rapid growth of midwestern cities led to a demand for light and easy-to-work-with pine timber. Lumbermen took timber outright from reservations—doing so illegally, as reservation lands and the resources thereon were supposedly protected by the federal government, held in trust for the Ottawas, and therefore ineligible for sale.[13] Whether or not an Ottawa owner gave his permission to cut timber from an allotment, according to the Indian agent, was irrelevant, because all allotments were held in trust for individual Ottawas. Some Ottawas sold lumbermen the right to cut timber from their allotments despite the objection of their agent.

The desire of lumbermen to cut pine timber on the Grand River reservations proved powerful, and the threat to Ottawa reservation land increased in 1870. When the Michigan Indian agent charged with protecting the Ottawa reservations attempted to use federal courts to stop the deforestation of reservation lands, the court-issued ruling itself became a tool for further stripping the land. A federal-court judge in Grand Rapids was called upon to decide if an Ottawa who had selected an allotment on the reservations but had not received title to it could sell timber from the land. The agent who had brought the suit argued that since the United States held the reservation land in trust, individual

Ottawas were not allowed to sell lumber. The judge, however, ruled that a person who claimed an allotment actually owned the land, and resources on the land. Therefore, the United States only had a right to protect title to the land, but could not deny the Ottawa person who owned an allotment the right to sell timber from his own property.

With this ruling, lumbermen descended on the Ottawa reservations, cutting timber both legally and illegally. In the winter of 1870–1871, an estimated twenty to thirty million board-feet were cut from Ottawa reservations. Ottawas who opposed the entry of non-Indians could not rely upon the federal courts or the BIA to stop the lumbermen. A number of lumbermen who came to the reservations stayed there, increasing the number of squatters who waited for the United States to grant them title to Ottawa lands.

The Ottawas knew that unless they received patents for their allotments, neither the federal nor the state governments would honor the protected status of their reservation lands. In another council, Ogema Paybawme spoke up on this issue. He said:

> We have thought that perhaps it would be best to visit Washington and have a talk with the Commissioner. We have felt that when we should tell him of our trials, of our poverty, that his ears would be open to us and his heart feel for us, and we wanted you to go on there with us. . . . We do not mean any disrespect by our words, but we have had so many disappointments, we have suffered so much that our hearts have turned sick and we have looked in vain for aid. To add to this white men have come and settled on the land we could not buy and are still there. Then they tell us we are not to have our deeds at all, but are to be moved, and when year after year passes and we do not get our deeds it appears like proof of what they have said. Cannot we have a chance to purchase some land, and will not our Great Father let our children who are grown & are now heads of families have an equal share with us.[14]

Ottawas wanted their right to reservation lands protected, they wanted their children who had come of age since 1855 to have land, and they wanted the sale of their lands to settlers to stop. The ogemuk agreed to wait before making a trip to Washington, but they would do so only if the Indian agent kept his promise to stop settlers from moving onto the reservations and to get the Ottawas patents for their allotment selections.

The Michigan Indian agent's promises to procure for the Ottawas patents that supposedly conveyed "strong title" to allotments ended in disaster and loss of Ottawa lands, not protection of the reservation property. Although he corrected many errors made by agents who compiled earlier allotment lists, the agent requested that the Ottawas be issued fee-simple patents—a landownership status that would end federal trust over the land—instead of patents that would sustain federal protection of the land. Removing the trust status from Ottawa land was contrary to the wishes of the ogemuk, who wanted the United States to protect reservation lands for their young people, and to protect the property from fraud and theft. Federal officials' haste to settle the Ottawas' affairs, driven mainly by a desire to gain support for political candidates in an upcoming national election, ended in yet another shortsighted solution that had devastating effects for the Ottawas.

Members of Michigan's delegation to the United States Congress and members of the Michigan legislature used their offices and influence to expedite delivery of fee-simple patents to Ottawas. Most patents were delivered to the Grand River Ottawas in 1870, though there remained eligible allottees who had not yet confirmed their land selections in 1871. Under pressure to act, the BIA resumed allotment selection in 1871, while Congress investigated the flawed allotment process as it had transpired on the Grand River reservations. In the end, the BIA appointed special agents to provide allotments to persons who were twenty-one years old at the time the 1855 treaty was negotiated. Having allowed every person they could find who met that criteria to select allotments, the special agents declared the process complete in December 1871. However, the Ottawa children who had come of age were not given an opportunity to select land on the reservations—a request the ogemuk had made consistently for nearly fifteen years.

Within one year, 90 percent of the allotments for which the Ottawas received patents passed into the hands of others by way of fraud, trickery, unlawful tax foreclosures, and outright theft, leaving the Ottawas in an even more precarious position. Meanwhile, government agents continued to ignore Americans who squatted on the reservations, and defend those who entered the reserves to cut timber from the land. By early 1871, the Ottawas lived on Indian reservations where non-Indians owned title to most of the land.

In mid-1871, the Indian agent who had issued fee-simple patents to Ottawa allottees was replaced by another Indian agent who immediately recognized the detrimental effects that his predecessor's issuance of fee-simple patents had created on the Grand River reservations. This agent immediately took steps to reverse the damage done to the Ottawas by asking his superiors in Washington to withdraw the fee-simple patents and issue trust patents to the allotments. He insisted that doing so was the intention of the men who had negotiated the 1855 Treaty of Detroit, who had wanted protected reservations for the Ottawas. This agent, who worked to protect title to Ottawa land within their reservations, died in a shipwreck on Lake Huron while traveling to Ottawa communities to make annuity payments, before he achieved his goal of restoring federal trust over allotment lands.

More than fifteen years after their last treaty, the Ottawas were no more secure in their land tenure than they had been in 1855. They had been denied a new treaty and had not received titles to their allotments, and the records of their allotment selections were an incomplete mess. Many Ottawa children had come of age, but none were allowed to choose allotment land for farming as their elders had intended. The federal government failed to honor provisions of the 1855 treaty that called for the protection of allotments, restriction of squatters from reservation lands, and issuance of trust patents. Those who had selected allotments did not receive patents for them, leaving the land vulnerable to the claims of any lumberman or squatter who wished to settle on an Ottawa's chosen parcel. With treaty making at an end, the Ottawa ogemuk took new initiatives to press the United States to safeguard their reservation properties.

Ogemuk asserted claim to all remaining reservation lands. They petitioned the president, asking that the not-yet-delivered patents be conveyed to the Ottawa landowners. They also requested, once again, that their adult children be allowed to select land. This time the ogemuk sent a delegation to carry their demands to Washington. Afraid that angry Ottawas would vote against Republican candidates in the upcoming elections, the incumbent congressman from the western Michigan district expedited the delivery of patents. Had the congressman also pressed the United States to allow young Ottawas to choose allotments on the reservations, the Ottawas might have secured title to about 80,000 acres of prime Michigan real estate for themselves. Congress did not so act. Instead, it enacted the 1872 *Act for the Restoration to Market of Certain Lands in Michigan*, and its subsequent remedial acts of 1875 and 1876—legislation that further reduced the Ottawas' chances of protecting their remaining reservation lands for themselves (as discussed in chapter 11).

The Ottawas' dispossession of their lands encouraged the continuity of their distinct communities as the council of ogemuk worked to protect the interests of their families. The Ottawas continued to rely on their ogemuk—now representatives of larger communities—who used new methods to act in the changed political environment. The Ottawas still met in formal council for discussion and to arrive at consensus decisions, but during these years they increasingly presented their demands in letters and petitions, and even through attorneys. The Ottawas were, however, unsuccessful in saving their lands from settlers, speculators, and lumber barons. Ironically, it was the resulting lack of a stable land base—their lost "trust" lands—that promoted the continuation of Ottawa cultural, political, and economic patterns. The Ottawas had no choice but to rely on their kin-based bands and the authority of their ogemuk—their trusted structures—as the basis of their survival.

■ The Pete and Sam children traveled with their parents to this blueberry camp. By the early twentieth century, temporary shelters like *tipis* and *wagenogans* had been replaced with canvas tents, but life in the woods remained much as it had always been. Notice the black-ash basket in the lower right corner. Families spent their spare time making baskets to trade or sell for food and cash. The children in the picture are, from left to right: Dennis Pete, Mary Pete, John Sam, Helen Sam, Minnie Sam, and Alex Sam. Children in a berry camp, ca. 1912. Private collection of Katherine (née Sam) Glocheski.

CHAPTER 13

On the Outskirts

T he Ottawas remained a distinct people from treaty times into the twentieth century because of the unique geographical and social space they occupied at the edge of American society. When Americans were not exploiting the Ottawas, they largely ignored them. Over time, the Ottawas changed their practices to enhance their survival in ways that did not undermine their unique cultural identity. For example, some Ottawas adopted Christianity, yet did not abandon traditionalist beliefs, ceremonies, and rituals. As Ottawas engaged in wage labor and commercial production, they did not abandon their historic economic practices of hunting, trapping, fishing, gathering, and gardening. During the final decades of the nineteenth century, Ottawas were more closely integrated into the regional economies of Mason, Muskegon, Manistee, and Oceana counties, yet they remained on the outskirts of American society as a distinct and separate people.

The Ottawas remained religiously distinct from their American neighbors into the twentieth century. For decades, Catholic and Protestant missionaries had vied for Ottawa converts. At Elbridge, Catholics built

■ Nawgawnequong was the ogema at the Mason County Reservation community that came to be known as Indian Town. He became a Methodist preacher and served his people honestly and with integrity all of his life. Nawgawnequong was known as Good John by settlers who came to the reservation in the 1870s. Good John, Department of the Interior, Census Office, Report on Population of the United States at the Eleventh Census: 1890, pt. 1. Washington, D.C.: Government Printing Office, 1895.

■ Ottawas continued to rely on relatives for support. The eldest family members contributed to the family by working near to home—tending gardens, cutting wood, and caring for children. Adult men and women cared for the home and met their family's economic needs by hunting, fishing, and gathering. Extended families often shared houses and traveled together to lumber camps and farms where they were employed. This photograph dates to the 1890s. Family photo. Private collection of Margaret (née Bailey) Chandler.

a mission church that became a center of reservation community life. Catholic church members made up the congregation and filled all of the roles of lay leadership in the institution. Even Ottawa converts to Christianity remained part of a unique Christian group that preserved the integrity of the Ottawa community. Catholics, however, had little spiritual influence on the Indian Town community. Ottawas of Mason and Manistee counties were more reticent and had only sporadic contact with Christian denominations—most often Methodist. Henry Jackson, Joseph Elliott, and Peter Greensky were Ottawas who occasionally preached at Indian Town. Throughout their careers, even these Ottawa ministers demonstrated varying degrees of dedication to the Christian sect. Nawgawnequong (Good John), who led the village originally located at Indian Town, "converted to Christianity, and joined the Methodist Church, and has since that time preached more or less among

the Indians."[1] Shawbequoung, an ogema at Indian Town, affiliated with the Methodist church.

Many Ottawas held to their own beliefs, traditions, and culture more resolutely than they accepted Christian lifestyles and ideologies. Although many of these Ottawas still maintained loose attachments to Christian churches, attending services conducted by itinerant Indian circuit riders and traveling to camp meetings held at various Michigan Indian settlements, they were primarily traditionalists who carried on an indigenous way of worship. There was tension between the Methodists and Catholics because each wanted to convert members of the traditionalist community. These divisions are evident in the four Ottawa cemeteries on the reservations—one for Catholics, one for Methodists, and two for traditionalists.

Even those Ottawas who affiliated with Christian denominations often did so with nominal conviction. Few Ottawas in either the northern or southern reservation communities were strongly committed to attending church regularly. At the height of the Methodist influence at

■ Ottawa families traveled through the Great Lakes region between 1870 and the early 1900s to earn money as laborers in the lumber industry. Unlike other lumber-camp laborers who worked in camps only during the summer, Ottawas camped there year-round. Ottawa workers brought their entire families with them and set up temporary villages on the outskirts of the lumber camps. These Ottawas, who are dressed for church, stand outside a typical lumber-camp cabin made of boards and tar paper. Lumber camp. Private collection of Marcella (née Moore) Luesby.

■ At the end of the nineteenth and the beginning of the twentieth centuries, Ottawa families provided the manual day labor that Michigan's agricultural economy required for planting, crop care, and harvests. They traveled throughout the state working in orchards and fields, picking fruit and vegetables for wages. Here, women and children rest at the edge of a field. Families at a farming camp. Courtesy of Little River Band of Ottawa Indians Historic Preservation Department.

Indian Town during the 1860s, fewer than 160 Little River Ottawa people were Methodist Church members. After 1871, the reservation-based mission ended. New off-reservation churches formed at Crystal Lake (1874–1880) and Riverton (1873–1894), but there is little evidence that they attracted any significant number of Ottawa members. The Methodist church did not sustain appropriations to support the churches in Ottawa communities, making its commitment to the Ottawas short-lived. The Ottawas, too, showed a marginal interest, preserving instead their traditional beliefs and practices.

In 1890, a United States census taker found an Ottawa settlement on a single homestead at the northern edge of the reservation in

■ Emma Keoquom Battice, Joseph Battice, and their children Maggie and Jim pose here for a family portrait. Emma's family lived near the reservation town of Lattin. Joseph supported his family by working in lumber camps. When work in the camps slowed, he resorted to hunting and trapping for food and furs. He died young, having fallen through ice while hunting.
Joseph Battice family. Private collection of Maud Battice.

Sherman Township, near modern-day Fountain. These Ottawas, living in isolation from Americans, had not forgotten their beliefs, rituals, and traditions. Enduring Ottawa spiritual and ritual practices resonate in the enumerator's words:

> In the deep woods of Sherman township is a band of pagan Indians. . . . They believe in witchcraft and worship imaginary gods, each having his own deity, though all recognize the existence of a Great Spirit. There are no farmers among them and no stock whatever. They use their own medicines and employ no physicians, and prefer to live by themselves, as far from civilization as possible.[2]

■ Ottawas began to acquire automobiles during the early twentieth century. A whole family would climb into their car and drive along roads cut from the footpaths their ancestors had made. Cars made visiting other Ottawa communities easier and increased the frequency of all-Ottawa baseball games, Protestant camp meetings, and travel between work sites. This photograph, taken ca. 1910–1920, shows Billy Gilbert (*sitting on the fender*), Sam Tapakeya (*tall man in light-colored shirt*), and the Methodist pastor Isaiah Wasaquam (*man in the hat standing on the far right*). Men in a car. Private collection of the Wasaquam family.

The settlement that the census taker described was located on a homestead that was the summer residence for Paquodush's band. Throughout the early twentieth century, this settlement was home for many prominent families who formed the Little River Ottawas, including the Medaccos, Mickos, Shagonabys, Johns, Baileys, Kelseys, Wabindatos, Saugies, and Sands. As this Ottawa band of "pagan Indians" demonstrates, many Ottawas lived on the fringes of society, continuing to live in historic ways and preserve traditional beliefs.

Many Ottawas, however, were not as secluded from American settlement as Paquodush's band. As Americans moved onto reservation lands, cleared farms, and built industries, the fences they constructed and property lines they drew increasingly diminished the area in which Ottawas could hunt, trap, fish, and gather. The Ottawas still relied

■ Women who followed lumber camps cooked and cared for their families. Many women also did laundry and cooked for the lumberjacks. Here, Katie (née Pete) Medacco holds baby Steve Medacco. Rose Medacco stands on the right and Jesse Medacco on the left. Ca. 1913.

Medacco family. Private collection of Steve and Dorothy Medacco.

primarily upon these historic economic practices to survive, but by the late 1870s, these activities alone could not sustain their communities. To provide for their families' basic needs, Ottawas began participating in the growing wage-labor economy, and they integrated these activities into their yearly cycle. Ottawas became farm laborers, lumbermen, and commercial fishermen. They harvested wild berries and produced crafts for sale.

One observer described the beginnings of new economic practices— "how the Indians supported themselves in this land." He wrote:

■ Like other Ottawa families, the Campeaus followed lumber operations from Michigan into Wisconsin at the end of the nineteenth century. This photograph, taken at Phelps, Wisconsin, shows the family standing in front of a log barracks. Campeau family at Wisconsin lumber camp. Private collection of Percy Campeau.

■ The grandchildren of traders and Ottawa women continued to live in the reservation communities. James Campeau, shown here with his son Benny, lived in the log cabin that his parents built on Hamlin Lake. James's son, Percy Campeau, continued to live in this same home until his death in 2004. James and Benny Campeau. Private collection of Percy Campeau.

There were but seventeen small bands, not exceeding 1,300 in all, it will be easily understood that there was no surplus population to feed. In Summer they peeled hemlock bark,—mainly for Charles Mears, of Pentwater—picked berries and fished, and in the Fall they secured their potatoes and corn, then went to the hunt and to trapping.[3]

A few families, like that of George Paquodush, owned their allotment or homestead land and made a living from farming, but many worked as migratory day laborers to supplement the food and materials they gained from hunting, fishing, gathering, and gardening.

The Ottawas first began working as seasonal wage laborers on fruit farms in the Manistee region. Mason and Manistee counties are bounded

■ Many Ottawas found work in Michigan's fruit orchards. These four Ottawa women are thinning peaches at the Nine Snede Farm, ca. 1915. The women in photograph are (*left to right*) Nancy Fitch, Eliza Crampton, Matilda Smith, and Lydia Crampton. Women in a peach orchard. Private collection of Margaret (née Bailey) Chandler.

■ George Sam lived at Indian Village on the Manistee River much of his life. He was the first Ottawa to graduate from Manistee High School. Here, George is standing in the center of the photograph, immediately behind the horses. He and his crew are hauling logs from the forest to transport to the sawmill. George Sam. Private collection of Jay Sam.

■ Ottawa men were famed for their log-driving skills. They used cant hooks and poles to break logjams and move logs downstream to sawmills. This photograph of the Medacco brothers was taken on the Pere Marquette River. The men are (*left to right*) Gus Pete, Isaac Medacco, unidentified, unidentified, Moses Medacco, unidentified, and Joe Medacco. The Medacco brothers. Private collection of Steve and Dorothy Medacco.

■ The Ottawas who farmed during the late nineteenth and twentieth centuries used horse teams to plow, cultivate, and harvest their crops. Horses were often the property of a community, or of extended families who shared the teams and cooperated in their labor. Here, Pete Saugie and Charlie Pete stand with a team that their families used. Pete Saugie and Charlie Pete. Courtesy of the Pete family.

■ The Pete family followed lumber operations from Mason County northward to the Upper Peninsula and into Wisconsin at the turn of the twentieth century. Here, the Petes are pictured in front of a barracks at a Wisconsin lumber camp. The Pete family. Courtesy of the Pete family.

■ Ottawas who earned money in the woods or working as day laborers sometimes used their discretionary income to have their portraits taken. These two young men are dressed in the clothes of working men. The man on the left is Jake Aikens. Portraits from the end of the nineteenth century. Courtesy of Little River Band of Ottawa Indians Historic Preservation Department.

on the west by Lake Michigan, whose warm waters extend the growing season long enough to shelter the apple, peach, pear, and cherry orchards that settlers planted in the 1860s. Within twenty years, fruit growing was the region's predominant agricultural activity. Ottawa families moved from orchard to orchard, trimming trees and picking fruit and vegetables. They packed fruit for shipping and hauled it to the ports of Manistee and Ludington, where it was loaded onto ships that made regular runs to the rapidly growing cities of Chicago and Milwaukee. Ottawas harvested enough berries to can and ship them to downstate cities. By 1882, a railroad ran through Manistee and expanded the market for local commercial fruit production as well as for Indian-harvested berries, and the fruit and berry industry continued to grow into the early twentieth century. During the late nineteenth and early twentieth

■ Catherine "Kate" (née Skimhorn) Antoine is seated and holding Sylvester Antoine. Mary Hinmon, half sister of Kate's husband Moses, stands beside her. Courtesy of Ann McClellan.

centuries, demand for labor in the fruit farming industry, as well as continuing hunting, fishing, trapping, and gathering, drew Ottawa families northward to Manistee, Benzie, and even Leelanau counties for an increasing number of months each year.

Like the work of hunting, trapping, and gathering, farm labor was organized by extended families, a modern manifestation of the historic band. During the late summer, entire extended families of three or four generations would travel in wagons from orchard to orchard. These families would leave their home villages to travel during the summer and fall, staying temporarily in orchard camps until the end of the season. In their orchard camps, the Ottawas conducted all the work of maintaining their families: obtaining food, fixing tools, cleaning and mending clothing, and educating their children, as well as making

■ Agnes Bailey. Courtesy of Ann McClellan.

■ Sylvester (*left*) and Moses (*right*) Antoine.
Courtesy of Ann McClellan.

traditional arts and crafts for cash. They traveled, worked, and lived as self-sufficient, kin-based bands. They camped on the outskirts of the orchards and farms, gleaned what they could, and moved on, eventually returning to their villages to start the cycle once more.

The Ottawas were also employed in lumbering, which by 1870 was a major industry in Mason and Manistee counties. Ottawas were hired to cut cordwood for steamboats, and later to collect hemlock bark for tanning. In 1876, a Michigan Indian agent reported that a large number of the Ottawas who lived at Mackinac and southward "do considerable in the way of supporting themselves by cutting wood in winter, which they sell at the ports on Lake Michigan."[4] The Ottawas' adjustment to lumbering seems to have been an easy and natural one. Like trapping, lumbering was seasonal work and centered in the forests. They quickly

became known as expert woodsmen, sought out by lumber companies for their skills as choppers, sawyers, and boat loaders, but especially for the dangerous work of running logs down the rivers—a skill in which the local Indian agent claimed "they cannot be excelled."[5] The Medaccos, among other families, were known for their excellence in this profession.

By the end of the 1880s, a few Ottawas, like Peter Espiew (aka Asaboon or "Raccoon") of Hamlin Lake, worked independently in the woods, using their own teams and equipment and employing their kinsmen. However, American lumber companies employed most of the Ottawas working in the lumber industry. An agent writing in 1879 noticed this shift in Ottawa economic practices, writing that "The habit of subsisting solely by hunting and fishing is being abandoned,

■ The generation of men and women who moved to the Oceana and Mason county reservations during the 1850s brought with them knowledge of the technology, seasonal cycles of plant and animal life, and spiritual beliefs of Ottawa culture. Amos Wakefield (Pay quay nay skung) stands here, holding an Ottawa-made canoe paddle. Amos Wakefield. Private collection of Elaine (née Beaton) Porter.

and very many of the young and able-bodied men find employment as sailors, as lumbermen, and wood choppers, and in the various mills."[6] Lumbering became one of the mainstays of the Ottawa economy in Mason, Muskegon, Manistee, and Oceana counties.

In fact, Ottawas became so closely connected with the lumber industry that when companies erected sawmills, Indian villages often sprang up nearby. Sawmills operated at Ludington, Hamlin Lake, Freesoil, Fountain, and Manistee, and in the 1880s and 1890s, there were seasonal Ottawa villages near all of these mills. Although lumbering was new to the equation, Ottawas still moved seasonally, camping on the outskirts of American settlements until it was time to go back to their home villages.

Despite their skills in the woods and on fruit farms, the Ottawas' work in the lumber and agricultural industries did little to relieve their poverty in the final decades of the nineteenth century. Even with the income they earned from working and selling their crafts, the net result was only basic survival. In 1885, an Indian agent described the Ottawas as "very poor," remarking that if "they held the lands given to them by the Government," they might be comfortable. He also claimed that "it is too late to remedy the evil, and as a result the race will disappear in Michigan within fifty years."[7] The agent correctly appraised the depth of Indian poverty, but, like most Americans, he underestimated the Ottawas' endurance.

Many Indian agents emphasized in their reports to Washington that the Ottawas were at least nominal Christians and dressed much like their American neighbors. Agents claimed that the wigwam had all but disappeared, except as a temporary shelter, and that Indians lived in cabins or board houses. However, these were merely external observations. When pressed, most agents harbored few illusions about how acculturated the Ottawas had become. Band members stubbornly held to their own communities, and they refused to adopt the kind of agriculture that Americans believed was synonymous with civilization. The Ottawas were, for instance, astonished at suggestions that they clear and plant the land where their maple groves stood; they wanted to save these groves so that their children could make sugar. The special agent sent from Washington to investigate homestead frauds in 1877 found the Ottawas "possessing all the habits and customs which have ever been characteristic of their race."[8] Living on the outskirts allowed the Ottawas to continue their distinct cultural practices, with some adjustments, largely free of interference from Americans.

The Ottawas continued to travel for hunting, fishing, trapping, and gathering in the 1880s and 1890s. An 1890 census report documents the Ottawas' continued reliance on their historic economic practices, describing the integration of new elements into traditional Ottawa life. In Mason County, there were 335 Ottawa people living at and around Indian Town, where

■ Jesse and Steve Medacco are dressed for their First Communion. Steve Medacco both practiced Catholic Christianity and taught traditional Ottawa beliefs throughout his life. Private collection of Steve and Dorothy Medacco.

ninety families own houses, 10 frame and 80 log, for the most part neat and comfortable, with a patch of ground upon which vegetables are cultivated. The greater number of Indians follow a variety of callings, sometimes logging and laboring, then fishing, hunting, trapping, picking berries, gathering roots, according to the season. Three-fourths of the tribe are at this time (last of September) in the woods gathering ginseng root, which commands a good price. They raise no produce for market.⁹

In many ways, Ottawa life had changed from their days on the Grand River. By the 1890s, many lived in frame or log houses and traveled for wage labor. However, these adaptations allowed the Ottawas to survive without undermining or replacing the foundations of their historic practices and culture.

The Ottawas' involvement in wage labor did, however, erode some of the ogemuk's influence over Ottawa bands. During the 1880s and 1890s, Ottawas built seasonal villages on small tracts of land owned by relatives. Ottawas left these villages regularly and lived on the outskirts of lumber-mill towns and railroad centers at Fountain, Freesoil, Hamlin Lake, Custer, Eden, Ludington, Manistee, and Brethren. This separation from the home community diminished the ogemuk's role in the day-to-day life of Ottawa bands. The ogemuk did not disappear—much to the surprise of federal agents who visited the bands during the early twentieth century—but their function diminished. While migrating as bands and living on the outskirts of American settlements did much to allow the Ottawas to preserve their culture, the Ottawas' adaptations for survival also made some practices difficult to maintain.

In the final two decades of the nineteenth century, the Ottawas underwent significant change due to the loss of their lands and their need to survive—but Ottawa culture, beliefs, and practices were not lost. Even those who accepted Christianity did not abandon the beliefs of their ancestors. The Ottawas lived in villages much like their historic settlements on the outskirts of American settlement. They traveled seasonally to hunt, fish, trap, and gather, and also to engage in wage labor. When they traveled for work, Ottawas stayed in orchard camps or temporary villages on the outskirts of lumber towns. Although the 1880s and 1890s saw the addition of wage labor and commercial production of crafts, and a subtraction in the influence of ogemuk over more mobile bands, Ottawa life was regulated by the same basic principles that had sustained it throughout time. By remaining on the outskirts, the Ottawas preserved the practices, beliefs, and culture that made them distinct and separate from their American neighbors.

Teaching the Children

F ederal agents from the 1820s forward believed that offering Indian children a formal education in American-style schools offered the best hope for instilling in them the values of "civilized" living. The Ottawas on the Grand River reservations were not exempted from federal education efforts, and the education Ottawa children received from the mid-nineteenth century through the 1930s did eventually direct change in Ottawa culture. Provisions for teachers' salaries and the operation of schools were written into each treaty that the Ottawas negotiated with the United States during the nineteenth century, and the 1855 Treaty of Detroit continued this federal plan. During the 1860s, the United States built one-room schoolhouses at Ottawa band settlements, including both the Elbridge and Indian Town communities. By 1863, six day schools were operating on the Grand River reservations. Among these were the Paybame, Genereau, and Cobmoosa schools in Oceana County, and three others near Indian Town that are not well documented.

The reports of Michigan Indian agents suggest that the Grand River reservations' schools were well attended during months when Ottawas

■ Percy and Hazel Campeau posed for this photograph at a studio in Ludington. Private collection of Percy Campeau.

■ As Ottawa children reached school age, their parents had to decide where their children would be educated. Ottawas who lived at the edges of small towns and in rural communities were poor, and children were often not dressed as well as their non-Indian classmates. Ottawa children who attended public schools were often ridiculed. Some Ottawa parents opted to send their children to federally operated boarding schools or schools run by the Catholic Church. Here, Jesse Medacco (age six) poses with his dogs. Jesse Medacco. Private collection of Steve and Dorothy Medacco.

■ Baby James Campeau is photographed with his older brother Benny. Private collection of Percy Campeau.

■ The children of Henry Pego—Irene, Dorothy, baby Betsy, and George Pego—stand in the yard on their farm. George Pego, who stands at the right of this photograph, recalled that his father put his education to work in his effort to restore federal recognition to his tribe under the Indian Reorganization Act during the 1930s. Private collection of George Pego.

■ Elizabeth (née Jett) Pauneshing and her son Albert, ca. 1915. Private collection of George Pego.

occupied the villages at their garden sites. However, during the rest of the year, Ottawa children traveled with their parents, doing their part to support their extended families. Teachers often reported that Ottawa children progressed well in their studies during the weeks that they attended school, but teachers also complained that the children were too often away from the classroom. As an Indian Town ogema said in 1865, "There is no such a thing as regularity in the School."[1] The time Ottawa children spent away from the reservation schools increased greatly as the Ottawas lost title to their reservation lands, and families more frequently traveled away from their reservation homes to search for work in the fields of settlers or in the lumber camps being established

■ Teachers at rural schools often complained that Ottawa children missed too many classes to learn effectively. Each year, many Ottawa children accompanied their parents into the woods to make maple sugar, gather plants, and hunt, as well as to work in lumber camps or on farms. Here, Marie Cogswell, Helen Sam, Minnie San, and Alex Sam stand in front of their tent at one of the places they camped during the summer. Marie Cogswell, Helen Sam, Minnie Sam, and Alex Sam. Private collection of Rose and Alex Sams.

■ Katie (née Pete) Medacco holds baby Steve Medacco. The boy standing on the left is Jesse Medacco, and the girl on the right is Rose Medacco, ca. 1913. Private collection of Steve and Dorothy Medacco.

■ Elizabeth Bailey spent her early childhood at Indian Village on the Manistee River, where she suffered her mother's death at a young age. Elizabeth's father sent her to boarding school, first at Holy Childhood of Jesus Indian School at Harbor Springs and then at the Mount Pleasant Indian Industrial School. She graduated and returned to Indian Village, where she raised her family. Elizabeth lived at Indian Village for over sixty years. Elizabeth (née Theodore) Bailey. Courtesy of Elizabeth (née Theodore) Bailey.

■ Henry Pego was among the first generation of Ottawas who attended government-run boarding schools. He received his education at Carlisle Institute, an Indian boarding school in Pennsylvania. When Pego and other Ottawa students of his generation returned to their Michigan communities, they were often unable to find employment. Like many others, Henry farmed and worked as a day laborer. He also wrote many letters to federal officials on behalf of his people. Henry Pego. Private collection of George Pego.

on and around the reservations. Federal funds for operating the schools ran out by 1872, and that year all but one of the schools on the Grand River reservations were closed down.

After the federal government closed the reservation day schools, Michigan Indian agents tried to integrate Ottawa children into American public schools. The Resseguie School at Custer, meant to serve both Ottawa and American students, opened in 1872. In areas where American settlements surrounded Ottawa communities—in Mason, Manistee, and Oceana counties—the local Indian agent attempted to send Ottawa

■ A school picture taken at Orchard Beach Park on the last day of school. All of these girls, Indian and non-Indian, were friends. Back row (*left to right*): Leelah Arquilla (*crouching*), Grace Schmidt, Betty Hillsamer, Margaret Bailey, Marke Saugee, Katie Sam, Caroline Somsel, Lucile Johnson (*partial face*). Front row (*left to right*): Lavern Wahr, Anna Mae Sam, and Pauline Saugee. Girls at Orchard Beach. Private collection of Katherine (née Sam) Glocheski.

■ School picture taken at Dickson High School at Brethren in April 1936. Ottawa children from Indian Village walked or rode in wagons over the three-mile distance between their settlement and the town of Brethren to obtain an education.

Front row, left to right: fifth child is Margaret Bailey, eighth is Anna Jean Sams, ninth is Anna Mae Sams. *Back row:* twelfth child is John Sam, whose Ottawa name was Shabit (a dialectical variation of Zhaabdiis [or shabitese] which is the Ottawa pronunciation for the French Jean Baptist, John or Johnny [Jonnie] for short). The single African American (*eighth boy from the left in the back row*) is actor James Earl Jones. Brethren School classes. Private collection of Rose and Alex Sams.

■ Thomas and Alvina Bailey, children of Moses and Delia Bailey. Many of Alvina's children, the Lones family, are tribe members. Courtesy of Elizabeth (née Theodore) Bailey.

■ Stella and Elizabeth Theodore Courtesy of Elizabeth (née Theodore) Bailey.

■ Arthur and Henry Pete. Courtesy of the Pete family.

children to public schools. However, these schools did not meet the special needs of Ottawa children who spoke only the Ottawa language, whose families traveled on a seasonal basis, and who did not have the same quality of food and clothing as American children. Ottawa children were often ridiculed by American students, and they received very little education.

As early as 1878, the Michigan Indian agent advised his superiors that the only way to help the Ottawas cope with the loss of their lands was to establish boarding schools to educate Ottawa children. He argued that Ottawa families had lost their land, after all, because the heads of families did not understand mathematics and the workings of governments. Without property, children would be more dependent upon education if they were to support themselves in the new Michigan economy. The federal government responded, and by the late 1880s, it established boarding schools for the Ottawas that operated for many years and served many Ottawa families.

In 1888, the United States contracted with the Franciscan Order to operate a boarding school on the Little Traverse Reservation at Harbor Springs, called the Holy Childhood of Jesus Indian School. That year the school accepted fifty resident students, in addition to day students who lived in the area and returned home after school each day. The school received so many requests to board students in 1887 and 1888 that the Catholic Church collected donations to enlarge the school buildings to accommodate an additional twenty to thirty students. By the early 1900s, the school housed hundreds of children from all over Michigan and Wisconsin, including children from the Little River Ottawa community. The Holy Childhood School was the first successful effort to educate Ottawa children. Little River tribal elder Elizabeth (née Theodore) Bailey went to Holy Childhood School when she was nine, and tribal member Joe Lawrence also attended the school. Unlike its predecessors, the school was prepared to teach English as a second language to children like Bailey and Lawrence who only spoke the Ottawa language. The Holy Childhood of Jesus Indian School served the Ottawas for nearly a century, from 1886 until 1981.

The federal government also opened several large boarding schools in the final years of the nineteenth century. Ottawa children were enrolled at federally operated boarding schools at Carlisle, Pennsylvania; Haskell, Kansas; and Genoa, Nebraska. Closer to home, the United States

■ Alice Theodore. Courtesy of Elizabeth (née Theodore) Bailey.

■ (*Left to right*) Brothers Ron, Ken, Bob, Tom, and Larry Pete. Pete brothers (5). Courtesy of Ron Pete.

opened a boarding school at Mount Pleasant, Michigan, where Indian children from all over the state were taught basic reading, math, and manual-labor skills. Ottawa students from Mason and Manistee counties attended the Mount Pleasant Indian School from its opening until its closing in 1934.

Many Little River Ottawas remember attending the Mount Pleasant Indian School during the twentieth century. Elizabeth (née Theodore) Bailey moved to the Mount Pleasant Indian School from the Holy Childhood School in Harbor Springs in 1919. There, she met her future husband, Peter Bailey. George and Joe Lawrence, whose father was a log driver on the Muskegon and Manistee rivers, both attended school at Mount Pleasant, as did Delia Cadotte and Viola Wilson of Freesoil. Isaac Peters, whose family lived at Highbridge on the Manistee River, two miles east of Indian Village, also attended Mount Pleasant during the early 1930s. All of these students would later become active in the Ottawas' political affairs.

At the Mount Pleasant Indian School, Ottawa students led regimented and disciplined lives. The control that school officials had over children was so complete that they could even deny parents' requests that their children be sent home for family emergencies. Elizabeth (née Theodore) Bailey, for example, was only allowed to return home once during her six years at the Mount Pleasant School. This was difficult for homesick Ottawa children to endure, but Ottawa parents continued to enroll their children because federal boarding schools could provide for their children's most important needs. At the schools, their children would be fed, clothed, and given medical and dental care. Although sometimes children were poorly fed and received substandard medical care, for many desperately poor Ottawas, the enticements of boarding schools simply could not be ignored.

Michigan Indians complained loudly when the Mount Pleasant Indian School closed in 1934. Despite the rocky beginnings and faults of federally sponsored schools, these schools eventually succeeded in providing Ottawa children with quality education, and in meeting their most basic needs. These schools also educated the Ottawas who would become leaders of their communities and transform Ottawa concepts of governance during the twentieth century.

■ Anthony Bailey, ca. 1915. Private collection of Dorothy (née Wabsis) Bailey.

■ Elizabeth (née Theodore) Bailey (*far right*) and two of her companions at the Mount Pleasant Indian Industrial School. Courtesy of Elizabeth (née Theodore) Bailey.

■ Jacob Walker Cobmoosa, the grandson of Ogema Cobmoosa, was educated at the Carlisle Institute in Pennsylvania. When Cobmoosa returned to Michigan, he began the work of creating a constitutionally run government for his tribe. He drafted and introduced language in the U.S. House of Representatives. He prepared lawsuits to be brought before the U.S. Court of Claims, and he filed claims before the Indian Claims Commission after World War II. James Walker Cobmoosa spent nearly forty years of his life serving his tribe before his death in 1952. Jacob Walker Cobmoosa. Courtesy of Marcella (née Moore) Luesby.

CHAPTER 15

A Small Victory

A	t the turn of the twentieth century, the Ottawas entered a
	new era of change. In the nineteenth century, Ottawas had
	adapted to new geographic situations as bands moved to
	the reservations and settled into new communities. They
adapted their hunting, fishing, and gathering lifestyle in order to survive
in Michigan's growing economy and among the Americans who moved
into their territories. Ogemuk and headmen acquired new skills to allow
them to effectively deal with the United States government and with the
settlers who claimed so much of the Ottawa estate for themselves. In
the twentieth century, Ottawas formed new political organizations that
united all of their communities in order to seek redress of grievances
against the United States. They pooled their leadership talents, wealth,
and labor to identify claims for money that had not been delivered to
them, and for land that had been illegally or unconscionably taken
from them. Ottawa peoples—as a whole tribe—sought restitution for
the injustices they had endured for nearly a half a century, educating
new leaders and building political organizations that would evolve into

■ Sampson Robinson was an educated man who, after the turn of the twentieth century, attempted to build a constitutionally governed form of republican government for the Michigan Ottawas. In his profession as a Methodist preacher, Robinson visited Indian communities throughout western Michigan, preaching and attempting to win support for his vision of a united Ottawa government. Sampson Robinson. Private collection of Percy Campeau.

modern, constitutionally governed tribal councils during the latter half of the twentieth century.

In May 1900, the ogemuk of Indian Town and Elbridge joined with the Little Traverse Ottawas to file a lawsuit against the United States in the Court of Claims. Little Traverse ogemuk Simon Kijigobenese, John Miscogeon, and John Kewaygeshik instigated the lawsuit and traveled south to win support for their efforts. Following Ottawa tradition, communities throughout western Michigan selected trusted leaders who formed a council, and this council was charged with exploring potential Ottawa claims against the federal government, hiring attorneys, and bringing suits to trial. The joint action of the Ottawas as a consolidated tribe inspired a new generation of leaders to invest their energies in strengthening pan-Ottawa cooperation.

The new organizations that came together at each community in 1900 were headed by a chief, chairman, and secretary—new titles used to describe traditionally defined positions the ogemuk had always filled in Ottawa society. Leaders from Elbridge headed the Grand River Ottawa organization, with Ashkebyneka (Amos Green) as chief, William Genereaux as chairman, and James Cogsequom as secretary. These three men worked with an executive committee of five persons representing the other reservation communities: Charles Genereaux, Rodney Negake (grandson of Cobmoosa), and Charles McDaguett (Medacco) represented the Elbridge community, and William Sam (William Paquotush) and Isaac Shogwabno represented the Indian Town community. The organization worked with other Michigan Ottawas who were parties to the 1855 Treaty of Detroit to file a suit alleging that the United States had not paid the Ottawas a substantial amount of money due under the provisions of both the 1836 and 1855 treaties.[1]

The formation of this organization was an important and widely debated issue within and among the Ottawas' reservation communities. Not all Ottawas agreed with or supported the organization's leadership. Leaders of the Battice, Bailey, Pete, McClellan, Wakefield, and Hinmon families, who claimed to represent "Hundreds of Others," wrote a letter rejecting the Elbridge ogemuk's right to provide leadership for their band. They wanted the Little Traverse leaders Simon Kijigobenese and John Kewaygeshik to represent their band's interests instead. Sampson Robinson worked to bring the Indian Town and Manistee River communities together—an amalgamation that would eventually form the Little

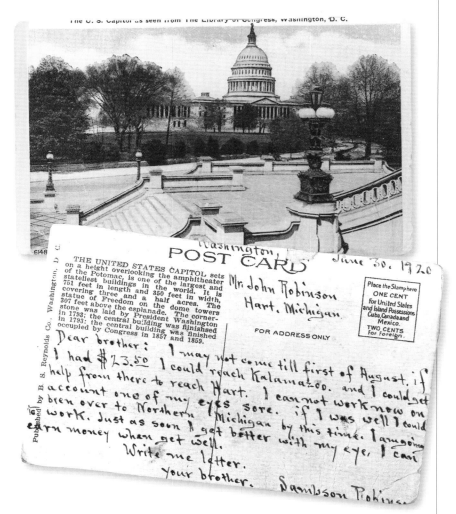

The U. S. Capitol as seen from The Library of Congress, Washington, D. C.

POST CARD

Washington, June 30, 1920

THE UNITED STATES CAPITOL sets on a height overlooking the amphitheater of the Potomac, is one of the largest and stateliest buildings in the world. It is 751 feet in length and 350 feet in width, covering three and a half acres. The statue of Freedom on the dome towers 307 feet above the esplanade. The corner-stone was laid by President Washington in 1793; the central building was finished and occupied by Congress in 1857 and 1859.

Mr. John Robinson
Hart, Michigan

FOR ADDRESS ONLY

Place the Stamp here
ONE CENT
for United States
and Island Possessions
Cuba, Canada and
Mexico.
TWO CENTS
for foreign.

Dear brother:
I had $23.50 I may not come till first of August, if I could reach Kalamazoo. and I could get help from there to reach Hart. I cannot work now on account one of my eyes sore. if I was well I could been over to Northern Michigan by this time. I am going to work. Just as soon I get better with my eye, I can earn money when get well.
Write me letter.
Your brother.
Sampson Robinson

■ Sampson Robinson was convinced that the United States owed the Michigan Ottawas money under provisions of the 1836 Treaty of Washington and the 1855 Treaty of Detroit. Robinson traveled to Washington, D.C., where he met with Michigan's representatives in the Senate and the House of Representatives. Robinson urged the Michigan delegation to introduce two pieces of legislation that would allow the Ottawas to bring their claims against the United States in the U.S. Court of Claims. Both pieces of legislation died in committee. Robinson returned to Michigan and continued to work on Ottawas' issues until his death in the mid-1920s.

Sampson sent this postcard to his family while on one of his visits to Washington, D.C.

Postcard sent from Washington, D.C., by Sampson Robinson. Private collection of Percy Campeau.

River Band—and helped them organize their first elections to select representatives. Robinson continued to work for these communities for another forty-five years.

Despite some disagreement and internal struggling, the Ottawas filed their lawsuit with the U.S. Court of Claims in 1905. The plaintiffs were primarily from the Little Traverse and Grand Traverse areas, as well as the Mashkaws from Elbridge, the Akins from Newaygo, and the Robinsons who lived near Indian Town. The Ottawas won this lawsuit when the court ruled that the federal government had inappropriately placed the Ottawas' trust-fund money into the United States' general treasury. The court ordered that the Ottawas should receive payment in full, including the accrued interest on the amount that had been taken from them. The suit was a small victory, because the monetary

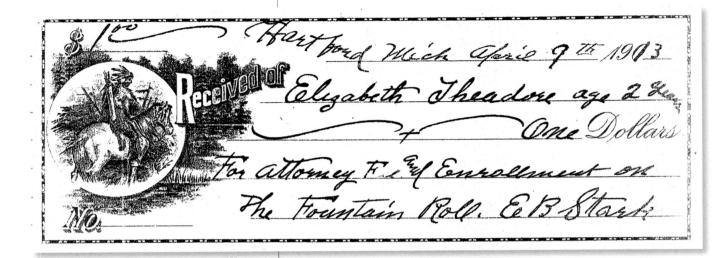

$1⁰⁰

Received of

Hartford Mich April 9ᵗʰ 1903

Elizabeth Theadore age 2 years

One Dollars

For attorney Fee & Enrollment on

The Fountain Roll. E B Stark;

No.

■ Ottawas who received payment as a result of the Ottawas' lawsuit against the United States received a receipt to show that they received cash. This receipt was written to child Elizabeth Theodore (Bailey). Fountain payment receipt. Courtesy of Valerie Chandler.

compensation due to the Ottawas amounted to little when divided on a per capita basis; however, it was immeasurably successful in motivating the Ottawas to continue their efforts to unite and press further claims against the United States.

The successful completion of the Court of Claims lawsuit also compelled the United States to take an accurate and detailed census of the Ottawas—the first one compiled since 1870.

In 1905, the Bureau of Indian Affairs was charged with distributing cash payments to every Ottawa person whose ancestors had participated in the 1870 annuity payment. Special agents came to Michigan expecting to find a handful of individuals who might be paid: but, much to their surprise, the agents found whole Ottawa communities intact and functioning, with populations far more numerous than expected. The first agent sent to Michigan estimated that there were three thousand to six thousand Ottawas living throughout western Michigan in more communities than he could visit in a reasonable time. Rather than attempt to do so, the agent took hotel rooms near major Ottawa settlements and asked the Ottawas to come to him. Entire Ottawa bands traveled to the agent's hotels to be enrolled on the payment list. As leaders and protectors of their communities—and according to Ottawa custom— ogemuk insisted that only a band's appointed ogema could certify its membership. The BIA agreed with the Ottawa leaders and accepted the word of the ogemuk as sufficient evidence of individual Ottawas' ancestries and band memberships.

Payment of the settlement funds for the Ottawas of Mason and Manistee counties, where the majority of Little River Ottawa ancestors lived during the early twentieth century, took place at Fountain in 1910. The amount of money that individual Ottawas received in settlement was small, about $21 per person. However, the political benefits the Ottawas gained—from working to build support for the suit and being recognized as cohesive communities of culturally distinct people—were incalculable. The payroll—named the Durant Roll for special agent Horace Durant, who completed it—is still widely used as a genealogical base roll for determining membership in modern Michigan tribes. By pursuing this lawsuit, which was led by ogemuk who emulated the organizational plan of the American governments around them, and by the enrollment process that followed, the Ottawas of Mason and Manistee counties won a victory that launched them into the new century.

■ Baseball became a favorite pastime of the Ottawas in the early twentieth century. Members of Ottawa baseball teams traveled to other settlements to play against their relatives and rivals. This game at Peacock, Michigan, was photographed between 1910 and 1920. Women and children often attended games, pictured here on the sidelines, using umbrellas to shield themselves from the sun. Baseball game at Peacock. Courtesy of Marcella (née Moore) Luesby.

CHAPTER 16

Community Councils
to Business Committees

Ottawas who made up the Grand River reservation settlements increasingly circulated in the American communities on and around their reservations. By 1905, Ottawa families from the Grand River reservations and the Pere Marquette and Manistee river settlements lived on the outskirts of Custer, Fountain, Freesoil, Millerton, Brethren, Hamlin Lake, and Manistee—American towns built within the Ottawas' traditional homeland. The Ottawas increasingly worked in these towns as migrant laborers for American farmers, traveled to provide labor in lumber camps in the winter, and worked at sawmills in the summer. The organization of the band—so important for regulating hunting, fishing, and gathering—slowly became less necessary to family survival as Ottawas worked for wages, and the band political structures that had served the Ottawas from prehistoric times and through the reservation years gradually became less meaningful. Ogemuk who were once responsible for the tasks of feeding and clothing all of the family members who made up the village were increasingly unable to exercise the same influence over the day-to-day lives of people now spread over a wide territory. Nevertheless, the Ottawas continued to be held together

143

■ Activities that brought together Ottawas from several communities were in effect reunions of the historic bands. It was not uncommon for whole communities to attend baseball games. After the games, adults socialized and discussed topics of social and political importance. Tribal elders living today recall that their parents and grandparents often sent them to play while the adults conversed at social events. This photograph was taken after a baseball game at a community near Manistee in the early twentieth century. Community after baseball game. Courtesy of Lavern (née Wahr) Oren.

■ Brothers Jesse (*left*) and Steve (*right*) Medacco don their baseball uniforms, ca. 1920s. Medacco brothers. Courtesy of Marcella (née Moore) Luesby.

■ Because Ottawa settlements were made up of a small number of families, community baseball teams were usually made up of players who were relatives of one another. Most of the players on this team are brothers (members of the Medacco family). They appear to be getting ready to travel to a game at another Ottawa community, ca. 1929.

Back row, left to right: Joe Medacco, Moses Medacco, Jim Medacco, Jerry Medacco, Isaac Medacco, Gus Pete, Jim Theodore. *Front row, left to right*: Mitchell Pete, George Kelsey, Johnny Pete. Private collection of Steve and Dorothy Medacco.

■ This baseball team is made up in part of Medacco men (brothers), all of whom are standing in the second row. They are (*left to right*) Joe Medacco, Moses Medacco, Jerry Medacco, and Isaac Medacco. The other players' identities are unknown. Private collection of Steve and Dorothy Medacco.

■ Ottawa men left their communities to serve in all branches of the U.S. Armed Forces during World War I. Before enlisting, many of these men had never left their reservation communities. Returning soldiers were highly respected by their families and fellow Ottawas because they had earned the status of warriors. Frank LeHay was one such soldier. He was an honored soldier during the war, whose fame spread by way of local papers that printed stories about his wartime experiences. Frank's fame was propelled to a national level when the *Saturday Evening Post* published a story about him. Here, Frank poses in his army uniform with his niece, Hazel Campeau. Frank LeHay. Private collection of Percy Campeau.

■ Isaac Medacco warms up for the pitch while the women in the background, seated in front of a Model A Ford, look on. The women, dressed in long, heavy skirts, take refuge in the shade of their umbrellas. Private collection of Steve and Dorothy Medacco.

by their shared history and cultural understandings. They continued to count relationships by blood and marriage, hold common beliefs, produce traditional crafts, and engage in seasonal ceremonies. The next generation of leaders, however, shared a new political awareness and learned new ways to meet the twentieth-century needs of their relatives and communities.

The community councils that had served individual villages gave way to the establishment of business committees, which were

■ When Frank LeHay returned from his tour of duty during World War I, he traveled around the United States performing in "Wild West" shows that were popular at the time. Here, Frank and his sister Eliza enjoy the beach at Ludington, garbed in head-dresses and costumes from one of the shows in which Frank performed. Frank LeHay and Eliza LeHay Campeau. Private collection of Percy Campeau.

■ Nelson Theodore also served in the U.S. Army during World War I. Nelson, on the left, poses for a portrait with an unidentified friend. Private collection of Margaret (née Bailey) Chandler.

■ Nelson Theodore poses for a portrait, dressed as a cowboy in chaps and a holster. Private collection of Margaret (née Bailey) Chandler.

comprised of elected officials drawn from the Ottawas' on-reservation and off-reservation communities. The Ottawas of Mason and Manistee counties—the ancestors of the Little River Ottawas—elected their first government in 1911. Sampson Robinson was chosen to serve as chief, William Sam as secretary and treasurer, and William Mickcoo as the overseer of the committee. The committee consisted of a number of other related individuals from Ottawa communities throughout southwestern Michigan.

The newly formed and unnamed committee organized by Robinson, Sam, and Mickcoo was headquartered at Fountain, only a few miles north of Indian Town. Its organizers were mostly Grand River Ottawas of the Mason County area, as all the elected officials were from well-established Ottawa families who resided in that community. Their goal was to pursue a second claim against the United States in the federal courts—a case through which they hoped to recover additional money in return for wrongs they had suffered during the reservation years. Under federal law, however, a party may only sue the federal government if it is granted permission to do so. If the Ottawas wished to bring a lawsuit against the

■ Anthony Bailey in his military uniform, World
War I. Dorothy (née Wabsis) Bailey Collection.

■ Land on and around the Ottawa reservations was, by the early twentieth century,
transformed from the thick, canopied forest for which the Ottawas had named the
land, to a vast terrain dotted with tree stumps. The Ottawas who remained on the
land at the beginning of the twentieth century relied on a combination of hunting,
fishing, trapping, gathering, and farming to provide for their families' most basic
needs. This photograph, taken at the beginning of the twentieth century, shows the
railroad bridge, known locally as High Bridge, in the background. Several Ottawa
families lived at the foot of this bridge, on the northern shore of the Manistee River.
Stumps in the Manistee River. Manistee County Historical Society.

■ Enos Pego was one of the few Ottawa farmers who successfully earned a living for
himself and his family. Enos was educated at the Carlisle Institute in Pennsylvania
and went on to serve as an important political leader among the Ottawas in the
1930s and 1940s. Pictured here (left to right) are Dorothy Pego, Enos Pego, Irene
Pego, and Myrtle Pego. This photograph was taken in 1917. Enos Pego family. Private collection of George Pego.

■ Here, Christine Theodore sits at the door of her plank house in 1911. Many Ottawas lived in houses like this at the turn of the twentieth century. Private collection of Margaret (née Bailey) Chandler.

■ A young Julia Theodore, who lived at Indian Village on the Manistee River, poses for her portrait, wearing a fashionable turban hat and a coat made of raccoon fur. Julia lived her entire life on the river and was the last Ottawa resident to leave Indian Village, in 1980. Courtesy of Marcella (née Moore) Luesby.

■ Pete Espiew was one of the better-known Ottawa farmers of Mason County. He and his family raised livestock and vegetables, which they traded locally. His cabin, on "Indian Pete" Bayou in Hamlin Lake, still stands at that place today. In this photograph, taken around 1910, Pete sits with his daughter Nora (née Espiew) Theodore. The boy to Pete's left is Charles Theodore, and the baby Nora holds is Earl Theodore. The man and woman in the second row are unidentified. Private collection of Dorothy (née Wabsis) Bailey.

CLOCKWISE FROM TOP LEFT:

■ Jenny (née Espiew) Koon, daughter of Indian Pete, married into a prominent Manistee Ottawa family. Jenny's son, Jim Koon Sr., served as a community leader between 1950 and 1970. Her grandson, Jim Koon Jr., was a code talker during World War II. Jenny Espiew Koon. Private collection of Jim Koon.

■ Rix Robinson moved to Michigan early in the nineteenth century, and several of his brothers followed soon after. Like Rix, some of the Robinson brothers also married Ottawa women. The Robinson family name was still carried by their descendants who lived in the Ottawa reservation communities in the 1920s. This portrait of Mary (née Robinson) Medacco was taken early in the twentieth century. Mary Robinson Medacco. Private collection of Rose and Alex Sams.

■ The lives of Ottawa women who resided on and around the reservations were difficult. They lived in homes that would be condemned by local authorities in this century. Most worked from sunup until sundown, gathering and preparing food, clothing their families, and working to earn money from their crafts, the foods they raised, and the medicinal plants they gathered. This picture of Rosie Pete, taken at Indian Village during the late 1920s or early 1930s, reflects the poverty in which the Ottawas of Manistee County lived. Rosie Pete. Private collection of Steve and Dorothy Medacco.

■ Pete and Elizabeth Bailey lived on the last homestead taken into federal trust for an Ottawa family by the United States. This homestead at Indian Village remains the home of the Bailey family today. Here, Pete Bailey's mother Margaret (*left*) poses with Martha Cogswell. Ca. 1920. Margaret Bailey and Martha Cogswell. Private collection of Margaret (née Bailey) Chandler.

United States, they had to obtain permission from the Bureau of Indian Affairs to hire an attorney, and from Congress to file the suit.

From 1911 through 1916, Sampson Robinson's organization sought BIA support for its efforts to bring additional claims in the U.S. Court of Claims for lands wrongfully taken from the Ottawas of Mason, Muskegon, Manistee, and Oceana counties. The Ottawa business committee was twice denied BIA funding that would allow them to hire an attorney. Undeterred, Sampson Robinson applied directly to Congress for support of his organization's lawsuit. When Robinson and his group approached their congressman for help, the congressman responded, "I doubt if there is anything I can do for the Indians of my district," and claimed that the Ottawas had been granted their due restitution in 1905. Despite all their efforts, the Ottawas' first attempt at creating a political organization operated by elected officials was unsuccessful, and their

■ Owning a horse was a luxury beyond the reach of many Ottawas during the early twentieth century, and people who owned horses were considered wealthy. Jim and Rose Medacco sent this photograph to Jim's mother, with a note on the back that reads: "From your daughter Law and son. Mr. and Mrs. James Medacco. To Mrs. Wm. Medacco." Jim and Rose Medacco. Private collection of Steve and Dorothy Medacco.

CLOCKWISE FROM TOP LEFT:

■ Some Ottawas, during the early twentieth century, continued to make their homes at the edges of towns and cities within the lands their ancestors had ceded to the United States in nineteenth-century treaties. Moses Medacco and his family lived on the outskirts of Man-istee. Moses was considered to be the leader of the Manistee Ottawas during the 1920s and 1930s. Here, he poses (*right*) with Jerry Medacco (*left*). Ca. 1910. Jerry and Moses Medacco. Private collection of Steve and Dorothy Medacco.

■ Those Ottawas who lived in and around towns and cities often had their portraits taken in professional studios. This portrait of Isaac Medacco and Joseph Medacco was taken in the 1920s. Private collection of Steve and Dorothy Medacco.

■ Amy Foster, Mary Robinson, and Mary Walker. Ca. 1910. Private collection of Steven and Dorothy Medacco.

■ Here, an unidentified Ottawa poses for a studio portrait wearing an ornate dress, which she likely sewed and embroidered herself. Ca. 1920s. Stylish girl. Courtesy of Little River Band of Ottawa Indians Historic Preservation Department.

pursuit of claims against the United States soon disappeared from the historical record.

The failure of this first business committee did not diminish the Ottawas' belief that the United States owed them, at minimum, retribution for property taken from them. Individual Ottawas continued to write letters to federal officers about their claims. They also asked the United States to help them to overcome the increasingly difficult economic conditions they were experiencing. For example, the Hinmon family, some members of which had also signed the 1900 document forming

CLOCKWISE FROM TOP LEFT:

■ Jim and Benny Campeau on the day of their First Communion at the Church of the Sacred Heart, east of Hamlin Lake, Michigan. Private collection of Percy Campeau.

■ Annie Pete, the sister of Gus Pete. Annie Pete. Private collection of Steve and Dorothy Medacco.

■ Earl Theodore and Ed Espiew. Private collection of Dorothy (née Wabsis) Bailey.

■ Phil Wabindado and George Bailey. Courtesy of Little River Band of Ottawa Indians Historic Preservation Department.

the elected council at Fountain, sought compensation in 1915 for the illegal sale of their allotment on the 1855 reservations. Although the Hinmons did not receive the federal aid they requested, they and other band members nonetheless continued to perceive themselves as the legitimate heirs to treaty-reserved properties and rights. They also believed—as they had for almost a century—that it was the BIA's duty to protect those obligations and rights.

■ Francis, Dee, and Anna Antoine. Courtesy of Ann McClellan.

By 1915, the idea of elected committees formed to achieve benefits for Ottawa communities had become a fundamental and permanent part of the Ottawas' thinking. The formation of these organizations was often marked by political difficulties and conflict as several individuals vied for authority to represent their fellow Ottawas. By 1918, Sampson Robinson of Mason County, who had been working on behalf of the Ottawas for several years already, and Jacob Walker Cobmoosa of Elbridge competed for authority to file another lawsuit in the U.S. Court of Claims in an effort to recover Ottawa lands.

Jacob Walker Cobmoosa began his work toward a court case in 1918 by petitioning the BIA to recognize him as the attorney for the Michigan Ottawas and asking for the cash the Ottawas needed to pursue the claim. To support his request, Cobmoosa circulated a petition in Ottawa communities, asking his fellow tribesmen to grant him power of attorney. In return for his work, Cobmoosa would claim a percentage of the money the tribe recovered. Cobmoosa's bid for community support yielded few signatories outside his home community at Elbridge, and his request was met with indifference by BIA officers, who refused to recognize his authority as a leader, grant him funds, or otherwise further his work.

Sampson Robinson of Mason County redoubled his organizing efforts in 1919 with a different vision for his organization than that of Jacob Walker Cobmoosa. Robinson wrote letters to the leaders of Ottawa communities throughout western Michigan explaining that the organization he envisioned should be incorporated under state law, would have "permanent officers" and an "Executive Committee" made up of representatives from each community, and would conduct meetings at places where most members "could most conveniently gather."[1] He intended to hire a lawyer who understood tribal issues, was familiar with Indian-claims cases, and had successfully tried similar cases in U.S. courts. Robinson traveled to all of the Michigan Ottawa communities to gather support for this organization and to create a roll of members. He made a concerted effort to raise cash donations from his supporters to finance the hiring of an attorney to argue the Ottawas' case in federal offices. The poverty of his supporters, however, prevented Robinson from raising much money for the cause. Even without compensation from the community, Robinson and Cobmoosa traveled to Washington, seeking the federal validation of their organizations and the BIA support they needed to move Ottawa claims to the U.S. Court of Claims.

Neither Cobmoosa nor Robinson were able to win federal support for their organizations or the claims they wished to bring against the United States. The BIA responded to the Ottawas' elected leaders by insisting that their "alleged" claims against the government were unfounded, and that everything the United States owed to the Ottawas had already been paid.[2] Robinson and Cobmoosa, after making many trips to Washington and persistently visiting the Michigan delegation to Congress, convinced congressmen and senators to write and introduce bills whereby Congress granted the Ottawas permission to sue the United States without the BIA's support. Although the legislation gained important sponsors, it stalled in Congress and eventually died, as would each of the Ottawas' later attempts to receive federal permission to press claims in U.S. courts.

Sampson Robinson's efforts to form a constitutionally governed organization to serve all of the Ottawas were no doubt hindered by his competition with Jacob Walker Cobmoosa, as well as with Paul Kijigobenesse and Albert Shananquet of the Ottawa communities at Little

■ Ottawas traveled throughout their historic territories, working as migrant farm workers. Here, Adams Gables cherry pickers sit on the porch of Two Gables in Acadia in 1939. *Front row, left to right*: Mable Sam, Adam Gable holding his daughter, Helen Sam, Jimmy James, Inez Gable. *Middle row:* Jesse Medacco, Joe Medacco, John Sam, Gus Pete, George Sam, Stanley Sam, Lavern (née Wahr) Oren, Marie Sam, Sophie Pete, Agnes Pete, Minnie Sam Danks, and Amos James. The two old men in the back are the brothers of Adam Gables. Group shot of Little River Ottawas who picked cherries at Adams Gables. Private collection of Katherine (née Sam) Glocheski.

■ Emma (née Lewis) Austin carries a black-ash picnic basket like those that so many Ottawas made and sold or exchanged for groceries, clothing, and provisions. Courtesy of Larry Romanelli.

Traverse Bay. All of these men traveled throughout Michigan, enrolling support and asking individual Ottawas to grant them power of attorney. In return for their efforts, each man expected to take up to one-quarter of any successful settlement as payment. The independent actions of these men raised skepticism among the Ottawas and demeaned the authority of their community leaders who had for so long dealt with federal officials on their behalf.

Although Cobmoosa, Kijigobenesse, and Shananquet had good intentions, Sampson Robinson's concept of community government won him the Ottawas' favor—except at Elbridge, where Cobmoosa enjoyed the strong support of his family and friends. Robinson's approach reflected his vision of drawing all Ottawas together under a single elected body of leaders who continued to value a concept of tribal leadership for the sake of all Ottawa people. When Robert Aiken, an Ottawa man from Newaygo, challenged Sampson Robinson's credibility, Robinson responded:

> What I am trying to do is for the benefit of the whole Ottawa and Chippewa Indian people. I have given up several years to the work of laying the foundation for recovering our tribal claims. . . .
>
> I know that there are some others who have followers and who want to be the leaders in the work of pressing these claims. I am not opposing them; I am only doing what I can to organize the members of the band that are following the leadership of me and the headmen who are associated with me.
>
> In the end the results of all our work will have to be combined because none of us is trying to collect individual claims, but the common claims of the whole tribe, and no one can make any progress towards this end without first getting the assistance of Congress and then going to the courts.[3]

Robinson had already worked to organize the Ottawas for at least three years without pay. Before he was finished, he would invest another three years in the pursuit of claims in federal courts, an effort that ended only upon his death.

By 1923, after the Ottawas' attempts to achieve legislative permission to file claims had been repeatedly defeated in Congress, Robinson tried one last time to unite the historic Ottawa bands under a single administrative committee. Based on his five years of work among the

Ottawas, Robinson founded the Michigan Indian Organization. The Michigan Indian Organization's constitution read:

> Section 1. Each band may have and to hold Chart of this Michigan Indian Organization. They shall have the right to transact any and all business that may come before the band, and they shall have the right to make laws for themselves, but never to construe or contradict and must obey all orders of the organization.

> Section 2. Each and every chart shall have officers elected by the people members of the chart, above said namely, Chairman, Secretary and Treasurer.[4]

The Michigan Indian Organization's constitution and bylaws were intended to be a governing document to help consolidate the political

■ Ottawas continued to rely upon their extended-kin network at the turn of the twentieth century. Here, Nim-kee-qua, or Helen Pego (*center*), stands in front of her home on the Mason County Reservation. The child in her arms is her newborn son, Douglas Pego (Pierson). The man in the white shirt, standing to her right, is the child's father, Bert Pego, and the rest of the people in the image are members of the Pego family. That same day, Emma and Bert "adopted out" their newborn to Frank and Emma Pierson, a childless couple, to raise. Family on the Mason County Reservation. Courtesy of Larry Romanelli.

■ The Pego family on the steps of their reservation home. Courtesy of Larry Romanelli.

divisions of the Ottawa Tribe, yet respect the integrity of individuals and communities. The constitution reflected the distinctly Ottawa ideas of equality and autonomy among bands: each community would elect officers to represent them on the tribe-wide business council, which would make decisions by consensus vote. In many ways, the Michigan Indian Organization was a reincarnation of Ottawas' historic regional and tribal confederacies, described in writing in its constitution for a newly literate Ottawa community.

The creation of the Michigan Indian Organization was more a triumph for the Ottawas in organizing themselves, establishing new and revised self-government practices, and uniting Ottawa peoples than it was in achieving their legal aims. The BIA did not take the organization seriously and repeatedly denied its legitimacy; the acting commissioner of Indian Affairs even declared that the pamphlet in which the bylaws and constitution of the organization were printed had "the earmarks of an organization probably created by one man for some propaganda purpose."[5] The acting commissioner, in his attitude of bureaucratic arrogance, miscalculated the strength of Ottawas' political will in the face of federal intransigence.

The Michigan Indian Organization may have been the conception of one or two educated Ottawa men, but it developed to meet the twentieth-century needs of Ottawa communities throughout the state. Although it failed to achieve the political ends to which it aspired, the organization was an influential forerunner of Ottawa organizations that would follow some twenty years later. The Ottawas of Grand Traverse and Little Traverse bays formed a similar organization called the Michigan Indian Defense Association in 1934. In 1947, former Michigan Indian Defense Association members created the Northern Michigan Ottawa Association, a constitutionally governed organization that succeeded in uniting and organizing all of the independent Michigan Ottawa communities. Descendants of the Indian Town community who lived in Mason and Manistee counties—the Ottawas who would become the Little River Band—became Unit Seven of the Northern Michigan Ottawa Association. The Northern Michigan Ottawa Association and its constituent units would enroll and represent thousands of members and successfully represent Ottawa political interests for the coming forty years.

After nearly fifty years of effort—from the pan-Ottawa organization of 1900 to the Northern Michigan Ottawa Association—the Ottawas had reformed their political structures. The Ottawas' organizations of the mid-twentieth century were in many ways adaptations of older band councils and business committees, formed through distinctly Ottawa political practices of councils, consensus building, and confederacy among independent but related Ottawa communities.

■ The Grand River Ottawas were famed for their sleek, lightweight dugout canoes. Unlike their northern neighbors, the Ottawas who lived in the Lower Peninsula did not have easy access to birch bark to make canoes. Instead, they hollowed out the trunks of white cedar trees. These cedar dugout canoes were so light that a man could easily carry the vessel on his shoulders. Newspapers sometimes reported that Ottawa men carried their canoes on railroad cars en route to their winter hunting and trapping territories. In this photograph, Jim Peters paddles his canoe on the Manistee River. The people who lived at Indian Village in the 1920s and 1930s continued to rely on earlier Ottawa technology as an essential part of their economic pursuits.

Jim Peters in dugout canoe. Courtesy of the Manistee County Historical Museum.

CHAPTER 17

A Desperate Decade

During the Great Depression of the 1930s, the Ottawas of Mason and Manistee counties—those who would become the Little River Band—were destitute. They no longer owned title to any significant amount of land, and the few properties they did hold title to were the crowded home sites of entire extended families, leaving no room for farming beyond planting small garden plots. The meager income Ottawas earned in lumbering and farming ebbed away as jobs became scarce and any available wage-labor jobs went to Americans over Indians. Ottawas sometimes earned a few dollars as laborers, but their wages alone could not feed their families. During these difficult years, most Ottawas in Mason and Manistee counties continued to live as their ancestors had for generations—by keeping small gardens, gathering wild plant foods, hunting, fishing, trapping, and occasionally selling baskets made of splints they cut from black-ash logs. Even these essential pursuits became dangerous for Ottawas when the State of Michigan began enforcing game and conservation laws in territories they relied on for their food supply. Ottawa men who were arrested for hunting without state-issued licenses could not afford to pay even minimal fines, but Ottawa families

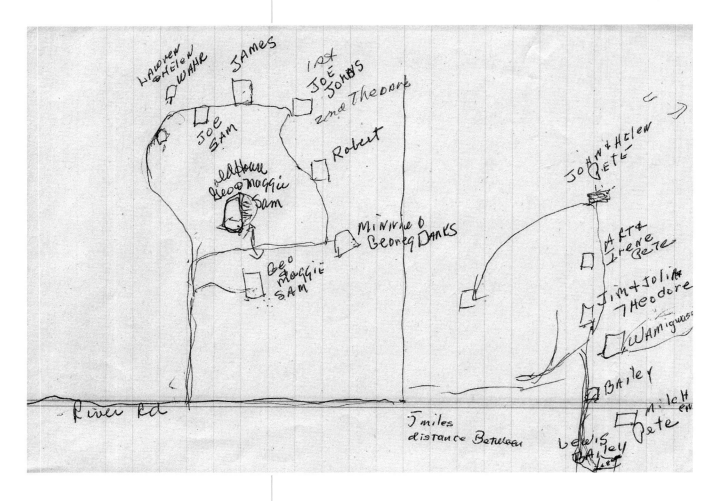

■ The Ottawa residents of Indian Village formed a distinct community. These maps, drawn by elders who once lived at Indian Village, show the families who resided there in and around the 1930s. This is the community that Louise Armstrong described in her 1938 book *We Too Are the People*. Indian Village maps, drawn by Alex Sams and James M. McClurken. Private collection of Rose and Alex Sams.

could not live without their hunters and fishermen if their men were sent to jail. As poor as they were, the Ottawas received no aid from the Bureau of Indian Affairs, and very little from local or state governments. If the Ottawas had not relied on traditions of reciprocity and sharing between kin, and on knowledge about the plants and animals in their historic territories, they would not have survived the 1930s.

In 1933, United States relief administrator Louise Armstrong arrived in Manistee County to aid the destitute people who lived there, including the Ottawas. Armstrong, unlike county or state officials, genuinely attempted to serve the "underprivileged" residents under her charge. At Indian Village, one of the Ottawa settlements on the shores of the Manistee River, Armstrong found poor and nearly starving Ottawas. Armstrong commented that for the Ottawas, "it was not just a matter of depression. Apparently they had always been kicked about, and there is no knowing how many of them had died from want and disease in the process." Armstrong was determined to provide the Ottawas the same assistance that their American neighbors received: she brought them food in equal quantities and assigned Ottawa men to work-relief projects as often as American men.[1]

During her work in Manistee County, Armstrong was so impressed by the distinctiveness of Ottawa culture that she dedicated an entire chapter—titled "The Redskins"—of her 1938 memoir to the Ottawa people she came to know. Her clients lived at Indian Village, on the outskirts of the City of Manistee, and in two smaller settlements along the Manistee River between Indian Village and Brethren. The size and location of these Ottawa settlements had changed little between 1910 and 1930, and their total population still numbered about five hundred persons. The Mason County Ottawas continued to live on the outskirts of Custer, Ludington, Hamlin Lake, Fountain, and Freesoil, though many families moved seasonally to hunting and trapping grounds along the

■ Indian Village residents participated in the 1936 Manistee National Forest Festival. The festival was conceived of as way to draw attention to the successes of federal programs intended to improve the lives of Manistee's residents during the Great Depression. Festival planners hoped to educate local people, as well as draw tourists to the area and bring additional money to Manistee's economy. One way to showcase the unique history of the Manistee area was to highlight the Ottawa community there. Festival staff recruited local Ottawa youth to make canvas *tipis* that resembled the birch-bark structures the Ottawas used during their early history. Local Ottawas consulted with festival staff and volunteers to add culturally accurate decoration to the lodges. Ottawas also made their own headdresses and decorated their clothing with beads and ribbons. The 1936 Forest Festival marked the first time during the twentieth century that non-Indian Manistee residents called public attention to the Ottawas who lived among them. Indian Village at the 1936 Forest Festival. Private collection of Margaret (née Bailey) Chandler.

■ William Sam is the son of Sam Paquotush, who led his band from the Grand River to the Mason County Reservation, and then to Indian Village on the Manistee River. William Sam was considered to be the leading elder of the Indian Village settlement during the 1930s. His grandchildren recall that he cut firewood while kneeling because his legs hurt him. William Sam helped to supervise the creation of regalia and decoration of the *tipis* for the 1936 Forest Festival at Indian Village. William Sam. Private collection of Katherine (née Sam) Glocheski.

Manistee River. Some families still owned land—if only the soil on which their houses and gardens stood—and extended Ottawa families shared these sites and supported each other during these desperate years.

The Ottawas were able to survive the 1930s only because they continued to engage in their historic economic practices. Although Ottawa families lived all over Manistee County, most Ottawas remained isolated and insulated from their American neighbors. The "majority of them lived together" at Indian Village, and another band lived near Brethren.[2] Armstrong was amazed by this feature of the Ottawas' geography, and commented:

> Relatively few white citizens in the city [Manistee] have any idea where the Indians live, and even the few who might venture on the River Road and the adjoining woodland trails would be likely to pass

■ John Peters also lived at the Indian Village. Here he is pictured wearing regalia (formal clothing denoting Indian identity) from the 1920s. The simple shirt and pants are decorated with ribbon appliqués, arranged in designs that the Ottawas have used for centuries. Peters is wearing silver brooches on each shoulder, and perhaps another on his chest. His necklace is made of bear claws. The headdress is not commonly associated with the Grand River Ottawas at that time, and was made to resemble those worn by Native people on the Great Plains. John Peters. Private collection of Steve and Dorothy Medacco.

■ William Sam takes a break from the Forest Festival events to smoke his pipe. He favored Peerless Tobacco. Private collection of Katherine (née Sam) Glocheski.

■ Ottawas from Indian Village used the opportunity the Forest Festival provided to market their crafts. Peter Bailey and his daughter Margaret Bailey (Chandler) showcase beadwork made by Pete's wife and Margaret's mother, Elizabeth (née Theodore) Bailey. Elizabeth learned beadworking from a matron while attending the Mount Pleasant Indian Industrial School during the 1920s. Pete Bailey and Margaret Bailey Chandler. Private collection of Margaret (née Bailey) Chandler.

within shouting distance of those interesting, primitive little houses without even noticing that they were there. The Indians, shoved away from the white community like unwanted stepchildren, might be cheated of their just share of some of the more civilized blessings of the county; but in their poverty and friendlessness, at least they had selected a paradise in which to live.[3]

Apart from their homes, now made of logs and boards, the Ottawa settlements Armstrong visited were much like those of a century earlier. They were composed of several cabins, made from "odd bits of material," with a common garden near the shores of lakes or streams that provided food and water. Armstrong reported that just "one of the families owned the land on which they lived." With the exception of some American-style adaptations of housing and agriculture, the Ottawas existed much as they

■ *Tipis* were painted with symbols that were significant to the families to whom they belonged. William Sam, an elder of the Indian Village community, sits in front of this tipi talking to three young guests. The design on William's tipi is of two girls—his twin granddaughters Anna Mae and Anna Jean Sams. Twins are rare in Ottawa families, and the birth of the Sams twins was celebrated at the 1936 Forest Festival. The children standing in the background in the upper left corner of the photograph are (*left to right*) Katherine Sam (Glocheski), Johnny Pete, and Anna Jean Sam (Guenthardt). The twins' tipi. Private collection of Katherine (née Sam) Glocheski.

always had, depending on wild food sources and living in concentrated, kin-based villages.[4]

The Ottawas still placed a great deal of importance on perpetuating their family lines and names—the very basis of their kin-based band structure. Although Ottawa names had been Anglicized, they were nonetheless passed down to children. Armstrong wrote that Ottawa names were often "combinations of two Christian names, as Pete John or Sam George," adding that, for example, "Pete John's son might be Bill John, and his grandson Arthur John."[5] However, within their families and communities, the Ottawas also still used their Indian names. Armstrong wrote:

We always thought that they probably also had Indian names, but knowing the Indian's dislike of curiosity, we never asked them. My

husband found out about these names just by accident. He had stopped at the Chief's house one day when nearly the whole family were at home. In the course of the conversation, he referred, jokingly, to the Chief's young daughter as Memengwa, the Ottawa word for butterfly. Her mother laughed. "Her real name is E-wan-kwe," she said. "That mean Mist Girl—'Girl in Mist.'" This was the key that unlocked another door in coming to know our Ottawas. . . . Our old Chief had the most beautiful name of all: Ke-way-ge-wan—which means "The River that Flows towards Home." His handsome grown son was Wabibinesi—"The White Eagle." The son's pretty little wife was Sibi-kwe, "The River Girl." The Chief's fourteen-year-old son, who became a great favorite

■ Twins Anna Mae and Anna Jean Sams stand in front of their *tipi* with their parents. Left to right are Alex Sams, Anna Jean Sams, Elaine Sams, Anna Mae Sams, and their mother Rose Sams. Private collection of Steve and Dorothy Medacco.

■ Pete Bailey feeds a tame black bear for
onlookers at the Forest Festival. Private collection of
Margaret (née Bailey) Chandler.

■ Elizabeth (née Theodore) Bailey, her daughter
Margaret Bailey (Chandler), and Jenny (née
Espiew) Koon stand in front of a Forest Festival
tipi. Private collection of Margaret (née Bailey) Chandler.

of my husband's, was Jawin-ikom, "South Thunder," and his married
daughter, the wife of Nen-ya-she (for whose name we were never able
to get a translation), was Bosh-ta-win, "Before Daylight." Her little son,
the baby with such immense dignity, was Ogima-binesi, "The Eagle
Chief," and he certainly lived up to his name. The eagle seemed always
to connote distinction. William [William Sam], our old wise man, was

Kije-go-ne-si, "The Great Sky Eagle." In one family the names all had to do with some phase of light. The father was Gisiss, "The Sun," his son was "Bright Day," and his daughter was "Twilight." The attractive young couple were Ne-gan-ko-wom, "The Man Who Paddles in Front in the Canoe," and his lovely wife was Wabish-esh-ikwe, "The White Marten Girl." I always loved the name of the gentle little squaw who was such a good housekeeper—Monqui-Dokwe, "The Passing Cloud."[6]

Because she was deeply interested in and involved with her Ottawa charges, Armstrong learned and understood more about Ottawa community than most of her contemporaries. She cautioned that "if any social worker or other person who comes in contact with them cannot assume right from the start that they are different, he had better not try to work with the Indians."[7]

The Ottawas were perhaps most notably different from their non-Indian neighbors because they relied so greatly upon wild plants and game for their survival. Conservation laws limiting the kinds of game they could hunt and trap, the number of animals and fish that each person could take, and the seasons in which they could be taken made little or no sense to the Ottawas. As early as 1918, the state game warden

■ Pete Bailey Jr. and Robert Bailey stand in front of their *tipi* at the Forest Festival. Tribe members recall that they enjoyed the festival, especially camping in the tipis. Private collection of Margaret (née Bailey) Chandler.

■ Pete Bailey and his family stand in front of their Forest Festival *tipi*. The children are (*front row, left to right*) Robert, Margaret, Peter Jr. In back, Elizabeth, who is holding their son Jerry, stands next to her husband Pete. Private collection of Margaret (née Bailey) Chandler.

■ Louis Medacco, Moses Medacco, and John Peters stand on the road that led Forest Festival visitors to Indian Village. Private collection of Margaret (née Bailey) Chandler.

■ One of the most popular events at the 1937 Forest Festival was the crowning of the Indian Princess. Irene Pete was one of Manistee's first Indian Princesses. Here, she stands with Art Pete. Princess Irene and Art Pete. Private collection of Rose and Alex Sams.

■ Few jobs were available to Ottawa men during the 1930s. Racial discrimination ensured that Indians were passed over for any good, available jobs. When Ottawa men did find work, they often performed manual labor, most often cutting cedar logs for fence posts, or new-growth trees for paper pulp. Pictured here (*left to right*) are Jim Theodore, Louis Theodore, John Theodore, and Nelson Theodore. These men worked cutting wood for pulp. Jim, Louis, John, and Nelson Theodore. Private collection of Margaret (née Bailey) Chandler.

■ Although Manistee recognized and celebrated its Ottawa residents at the Forest Festival, little was done to improve the Ottawas' economy, health, or education. This photograph, taken during the 1930s, shows a typical Ottawa home at Indian Village, built with scrap planks and tar paper. Standing in front of the house are Rose Sams, who is holding one of her twin daughters; Joe Thomas, who is holding the other twin; William Sam; and Mae Thomas. Rose Sams, William Sam, and guests. Private collection of Rose and Alex Sams.

■ Gus Pete and Moses Medacco stand in the second-growth forest at Manistee, where logs were cut for pulp. Private collection of Rose and Alex Sams.

closed Mason, Manistee, and other Michigan counties to deer hunting, and eventually to trapping also. The Ottawas were particularly pressed by this order, as it "was just as natural for them to hunt as it was for them to breathe, and here they were in a forest filled with game." Deer, or "government rabbit," became a crucial part of the Ottawa diet during the Great Depression. It is little wonder that Ottawas wrote letters to federal officers asking that they be allowed to hunt and fish in places where none of their American neighbors farmed. They believed that the 1836 Treaty of Washington had guaranteed them the right to do so regardless of laws passed by the State of Michigan. State conservation laws left the Ottawas two choices: starve or break the law. Most, of course, chose the latter option.[8]

In the context of unfair laws and deplorable conditions, the Ottawas had little choice but to continue to rely on their hunting and trapping economy, as well as their custom of reciprocal division of game. This practice was so important that Little River Ottawas who lived at Indian Village during the 1930s recall how it worked. Rose and Alex Sams (grandson of William Sam) explain that men "went hunting and fishing then, whoever got the fish then they'd go around and divide them or give everybody fish, see. . . . Now, somebody get a deer—maybe a couple of deer—they split that deer all up, and then . . . , divide the meat up, then go get some more. They didn't try to store it away."[9] Katherine (née Sam) Glocheski and Margaret (née Bailey) Chandler, who also lived at

Indian Village, remembered that when men returned from fishing trips, they stacked their catch in piles—one for each family in the village. To be sure the division was fair, one man would turn his back on the piles and call out names, and each named person would choose his family's lot. If hunters killed a deer, they butchered it as soon as they arrived home. The tenderloins and steaks would be roasted immediately, and the whole neighborhood would eat. Women then divided the rest among the households in need of meat. The same divisions were made of raccoon, beaver, and even turtle. Over time, every household contributed to the well-being of the community.

The ethic of reciprocal sharing and immediate consumption of food is common in band and tribal societies throughout the world. As federal agents learned throughout the nineteenth century, this ethic prevented individual Ottawas from accumulating material wealth and fully participating in America's capitalist society. Rather than taking and keeping goods for themselves, every person in an Ottawa village shared whatever food, clothes, or shelter were available. Armstrong found this cultural trait alive and well at Indian Village in the 1930s. She complained that the Ottawas, among other Michigan Indians, were "unable to grasp the white man's idea of planning for the future," and that they "quite literally took no thought of the morrow." Armstrong had trouble explaining capitalistic concepts to the Ottawas, who also did not quite grasp the idea of stretching out a paycheck. Exasperated but concerned, Armstrong wrote: "I am quite certain that most of them spent their pay checks the very first day they received them. If the food lasted through until they got the next pay check, so much the better, but if it did not, they simply went hungry."[10]

Armstrong did note that several individual Ottawas generated some cash income from selling their black-ash baskets. Basketry, though, demanded fine craftsmanship and hard work that often did not pay well. A well-made black-ash basket would earn its maker only 25¢ during the 1930s, when the actual cost of producing one was close to $5.00. Instead, Ottawas made baskets to trade for food and commodities at stores or neighboring farms, and for other essentials, like clothing. Trading was another element of Ottawa life that survived in their communities and helped them cope during the years of the Great Depression.

The Ottawas of Mason and Manistee counties also carried their spiritual beliefs into the twentieth century. In the 1930s, they still practiced Ottawa rituals and held pre-Christian beliefs, as well as carried out revised

■ When Louise Armstrong wrote her book titled *We Too Are the People*, she recognized Moses Medacco as the leader of the Manistee Indians. Moses Medacco's status is also denoted by the feathers in his headdress. While Ottawas of lesser status than Moses wore turkey feathers, community members believed that it was beneath Moses and a handful of other community leaders' rank to wear them. Community members hunted sandhill cranes on the Manistee River, from whom they plucked the feathers to make headdresses for their leading men. Moses Medacco. Courtesy of Elizabeth (née Theodore) Bailey.

■ The Ottawas continued to rely on hunting, trapping, and fishing for a large part of their daily sustenance during the early twentieth century. Ottawa men were known for being able to shoot a fur-bearing mink from a long distance, through the eye so as not to damage the pelt. In this rare image, Lawrence Wahr and a male member of the Medacco family stand beside a night's take of raccoons. Raccoons were killed both for their meat and their furs. Deer were commonly hunted for food and sale to people in the local towns and cities. Lawrence Wahr and Theodore. Courtesy of Marcella (née Moore) Luesby.

seventeenth-century Christian customs introduced to them by the first Europeans to set foot on Ottawa homelands. In Armstrong's words:

> Our Ottawas were very religious in their way, and also very superstitious. Nearly all of them were Roman Catholics, and their forefathers had been ever since the days of the Jesuit missionaries. However, though they were very serious about their belief in the Christian God, we found that the old religion of their ancestors had by no means disappeared. A few were frankly of the old belief and had not embraced Christianity, but even the true believers had mixed up a good deal of ancient superstition with their Christianity.[11]

In the early to mid-twentieth century, Ottawas had only adopted and integrated certain elements of American influence into their culture. They blended new customs with old ones, allowing them to adhere closely to their traditions and to each other.

There were many components of the Ottawa spiritual and ritual system that Armstrong never witnessed. Sweat lodges, for example, continued to be an important practice for physical and spiritual renewal. In the spring, Ottawas performed a rite to ensure the productiveness of crops, and in the fall, another to give thanks for abundance. Ottawas routinely practiced the traditional ceremonies of the *Wabano* Lodge, an alternative and sometimes rival of the more commonly known *Midewiwin* Lodge. When individuals joined a lodge, they learned why and how their group was distinct from all others. This knowledge gave adherents to the lodge special powers to contact and communicate with the spirits that resided in the world (*aki)* around them. Into the 1930s and beyond, Ottawas continued to conceive of their world as a place filled with spirits who must be cared for if people and spirits were to coexist. For example, relatives continued to place small wooden canoes in the graves of their loved ones to carry their spirits into the other world. Ottawas continued to send the spirits of the dead on their journey to the other world, accompanied by the sounds of *Jebencobmooemaen*, traditional wake songs sung continuously for three days after death, as well as by holding Christian funerals. Ottawas have celebrated *Jebiwesening*, or Ghost Supper—an annual feast held by the living to feed souls of those who have gone to the other world—from ancient times into the present day.

The federal government had attempted to impose a "civilization program" on the Ottawas in 1836 and again in 1855, but by the mid-twentieth century, the Ottawas had still not assimilated. They continued to cling to their traditional belief systems, precapitalist economic practices, and historic kin-based band communities—all of which indicate the survival of a strong, distinct Ottawa culture during the first half of the twentieth century. They remained a separate people living on the margins of American society, exercising all of their skills to survive in the face of the economic collapse, racial discrimination, and political powerlessness that characterized the 1930s. The cultural integrity of the Ottawas who lived in Mason and Manistee counties bound them together and allowed them to sustain and perpetuate Ottawa culture rather than adopt American lifestyles. If it had not been for their trusted and historic strategies of survival, the Ottawas would have perished during the desperate decade of the 1930s.

■ Ottawa life was characterized by extreme poverty during the years of the Great Depression of the 1930s. This photograph shows the typical lifestyle of the Ottawas who lived in Manistee County at that time. Jonnie Sam, Lavern Wahr, and Gus Pete stand in front of their home at Indian Village. While almost all of the people in Manistee were poor during the Depression, the Ottawas' poverty significantly exceeded that of their neighbors. Sams home at Indian Village. Private collection of Marcella (née Moore) Leusby.

CHAPTER 18

New Deal, Renewed Hope

T he Ottawas' relationship with the federal government began
to change when President Franklin D. Roosevelt introduced
New Deal policies and agencies during the mid-1930s. The
New Deal was a federal program designed to offer jobs and
services to the country's poorest residents, and to alleviate the desperate
economic and social conditions caused by the Great Depression. President
Roosevelt and Commissioner of Indian Affairs John Collier's philosophy
for reforming the federal government's dealings with American
Indians was to use federal resources to empower local communities
and reverse the policy of assimilation. These ideas were embodied in
the Wheeler-Howard Indian Reorganization Act—commonly referred
to by its acronym, the IRA—which became law in 1934. This legislation
was the federal government's first attempt in more than a century to
revitalize Indian communities instead of forcing Indians to assimilate
into American society.

The IRA was designed to relieve Native Americans' economic dilem-
mas by strengthening their communities, providing them with land,
and creating constitutionally operated tribal governments. Michigan

177

■ Mable (née Medacco) Atkins dressed in urban fashion of the late 1920s and early 1930s. Private collection of Marcella (née Moore) Leusby.

■ Agnus Pete sits in front of a Model A Ford parked in front of a board and tar-paper house at Indian Village. Private collection of Rose and Alex Sams.

■ Young Ottawa men were given the opportunity to leave the poverty of their homes and work in programs established by President Franklin D. Roosevelt's New Deal legislation. Many young Ottawa men, such as these two unidentified boys, joined the Civilian Conservation Corps (CCC) during the years of the Great Depression. They traveled to CCC work camps established throughout northern Michigan, where they worked to repair ecological damage caused by the destruction of Michigan's forests. Ottawa men planted trees throughout Michigan to stop the erosion of soil, repaired buildings and infrastructure required for monitoring and maintaining Michigan's ecology and wildlife, and created many of the parks that tourists enjoy today. In return, the young men were housed in barracks, fed, and paid wages for their work. Unidentified Indian boys with shovels. Private collection of Marcella (née Moore) Leusby.

Ottawas, like Sampson Robinson, had been trying to organize a business committee that represented their several communities at Little
Traverse Bay, Grand Traverse Bay, and on the Grand River reservations
for more than thirty years. The IRA gave the Ottawas renewed hope
and a federally sanctioned plan for creating the modern tribal government they had envisioned for decades. From 1934 to 1939, the Ottawas
attempted to organize a tribal government under IRA provisions that
would consolidate the Ottawa Tribe, represent their interests, relieve
their poverty, and restore their land—desires that had patterned the
Ottawas' interactions between bands and with the federal government
since 1855. The IRA offered Ottawas their first real opportunity to build
a constitutional government capable of repairing some of the damage
done to their culture and polity during the preceding eighty years of
devastating federal policies.

In 1934, the Ottawas who began the work of petitioning the United
States to implement the IRA in Michigan were hopeful. Federal officials

■ Moses and Catherine Antoine pause for
a family photograph with their children. The
picture was taken during the Great Depression.
Courtesy of Ann McClellan.

■ The young Ottawa men who worked together
in the CCC often made lasting friendships.
Some young Ottawas used their leisure time to
engage in sports not available to them in their
home communities. This photograph shows a
CCC boxing team at Camp Steuben, Company
669. Steve Medacco stands on the far left in
the back row. CCC boxing team. Private collection of Steve
and Dorothy Medacco.

■ Steve Medacco participated in a boxing league organized by CCC workers. Private collection of Steve and Dorothy Medacco.

■ Steve Medacco also acquired a reputation for playing guitar and singing during his enlistment in the CCC. He is shown here in a publicity photograph, which Steve hoped would help him land some air time on a Chicago radio station. Later in his life, Steve's children, who shared his musical talent, would perform throughout the United States. Steve Medacco with guitar. Private collection of Steve and Dorothy Medacco.

■ Jim Koon and David Medacco display a sign they made as part of their employment in the federally sponsored National Youth Corps in 1938. Signs like these were used to mark trails in the newly established Manistee National Forest. Private collection of Jim Koon.

in charge of IRA programs in the Great Lakes region encouraged Ottawa leaders and advocated for them in Washington. Agents who visited the Ottawas noted the desperate condition of band communities; in particular, one agent reported that "certainly there are none in more urgent need of rehabilitation."[1] Two agents who visited Michigan in the summer of 1935 observed that the Ottawas were "poorly housed and unfavorably situated from an economic point of view," and encouraged the Bureau of Indian Affairs to act favorably on the Ottawas' behalf.[2] So sure were these federal agents that the Ottawas would be granted a federally sanctioned IRA constitution that they, with the support of their superiors in Washington, initiated plans to buy land that would be a home for the Ottawas and a place where they could pursue future economic development.

However, even as plans for reorganization were forming, they began to fall apart. The agents who visited Michigan first decided to gather all the historic Ottawa bands—the Grand River Bands, the Grand Traverse Bay Bands, and the Little Traverse Bay Bands—into a single community. Aside from the fact that this plan did not account for the independent nature of Ottawa bands and communities or for the Ottawas' ties to their own historic communities, Congress refused to adequately fund

■ Ottawas were too poor to purchase professional photographic portraits during the Great Depression years. This photograph of Mose Thomas and Earl Theodore is one of the few portraits taken during the early 1930s. Private collection of Dorothy (née Wabsis) Bailey.

■ During the 1920s, the Bureau of Indian Affairs helped Alice obtain an allotment on the Manistee Reservation. She and her family lived on this small farm throughout the Great Depression. Like other Ottawas, they later moved from their rural settlements to nearby towns where they hoped to find work. Alice (née Pete) Moore is pictured here with her daughter in the yard of her house in town. Alice Pete Moore and daughter Hazel. Courtesy of Marcella (née Moore) Luesby. ca. 1940.

IRA projects. As a substitute for direct federal involvement in advancing economic programs to help lift the Ottawas from poverty, federal agents suggested instead that the American Legion purchase lands in the northern Lower Peninsula, using federal loan money, and resettle the Ottawas there.[3] The Civilian Conservation Corps could then establish camps around the new reservation where Ottawas could be employed to earn money to repay the federal loan.

The American Legion loan plan failed. It did so, in part, because the Ottawas were understandably unwilling to leave their homes and communities, but mostly because the BIA claimed that it did not have the money to implement even this downscaled plan. Still, BIA agents

■ The camera captures Jim and Jenny (Bailey) Peters in a happy moment. Courtesy of Elizabeth (née Theodore) Bailey.

who visited Michigan quietly continued to encourage Ottawa efforts toward reorganization. In February 1935, the commissioner of Indian Affairs advised an Ottawa leader from Cross Village that the BIA still favored organizing Michigan Indians, but not as a single tribe; instead, the commissioner encouraged "smaller Indian Groups or Bands" to reorganize separately.[4] From that time forward, Ottawa communities throughout Michigan petitioned the United States individually, asking for the opportunity to benefit from provisions of the IRA. All of the Ottawa communities of Emmet County, Charlevoix, Beaver Island, Garden Island, and the north shore of Lake Michigan filed petitions. Another 268 members of the Grand Traverse Bands from Omena, Peshawbestown, Elk Rapids, Northport, and Suttons Bay signed these petitions by mid-1935.

■ These Ottawas were among the few who were able to purchase a professionally photographed portrait in the midst of the Great Depression. The men in the back row (*left to right*) are Phil Memberto and Jacob Walker Cobmoosa. The women in front (*left to right*) are Josie Memberto and Anna Pete, who is holding baby Mary Walker Cobmoosa. Courtesy of Marcella (née Moore) Luesby

Grand River Ottawa communities in Mason, Manistee, and Oceana counties filed petitions as well. Enos Pego took the lead for the Ottawas of Mason and Manistee counties. Pego and other Grand River Ottawas met with the commissioner of Indian Affairs in Grand Rapids in October 1935, and by July 1936, Pego submitted a petition for IRA reorganization. Arthur Moby of Honor in Benzie County, and Bill Peters of Indian Village in Manistee County coordinated the petition efforts. This petition, on behalf of the "Grand River Ottawas," was signed by Ottawas at Indian Town (Custer) and from the Manistee River area at and around Indian Village—the Ottawas who would become the Little River Band. Ruth (Koon Smith) Dean is the only living Little River Band member who signed this petition to establish a constitutional government for her tribe.[5]

Despite their nearly unanimous positive response to the IRA, most Ottawas were confused about how exactly they would benefit from the law. While they grasped the broad intentions of the IRA, they misunderstood the specifics. The petition that Arthur Moby and Bill Peters

■ Visiting relatives was a common pastime for Ottawas during the years of the Great Depression. The Skimhorns, Saugies, and Shagonabes captured one of their get-togethers in this photograph. Pictured (*left to right*) are John Skimhorn, Alex Fred Saugie, an unidentified boy, Elly Shagonabe, Louis Snay, and Solomon Shagonaby, who holds Elizabeth Shagonaby. Courtesy of Ann McClellan.

■ The poorest of the poor Ottawas lived in a
village at the foot of High Bridge, on the cutover
land through which the Manistee River flowed.
These Ottawas were among the first to petition
the United States for extension of federal jurisdiction over their village under the 1934 Indian
Reorganization Act. High Bridge. Courtesy of Margaret
(née Bailey) Chandler.

submitted on behalf of the Manistee County Ottawas demonstrates this
misunderstanding:

> We all hope to get what we want from George Washington promise
> us. This is what we want. Please help us, anyhow. We all hope to get
> Reservation to live on, to eat some white games, and get some wood
> to burn. Some Indians han't got any home, so could have Reservation
> home to go too, and if you could helpe us any, and is enough of us to
> get Reservation so never mine about other Indians don't want give
> they names. So please helpe us.[6]

As social worker Louise Armstrong noted, the Ottawas in Mason and
Manistee counties were poor and desperate. They wanted access to
natural resources and they wanted reserve land. Their petition reveals
as great a concern with these issues as with creating an IRA tribal
government to administer their affairs.

The Ottawas pressed forward and were no doubt encouraged by
the positive results of similar petitions made by neighboring Chippewa tribes. In spring 1935, the Chippewas at L'Anse, Bay Mills, and

■ Arthur John Moby led the Little River Ottawas' effort to obtain federal recognition under the Indian Reorganization Act. In this photograph, Moby holds the petition signed by the Ottawas who lived on the Manistee River. The petition was sent to the Bureau of Indian Affairs in 1936 and is currently on file at the National Archives in Washington, D.C. Arthur John Moby with petition. Private collection of Sue Thull.

Hannahville in the Upper Peninsula, and the Saginaw Chippewas at the Isabella County Reservation held federally sanctioned referenda, voting in favor of creating new tribal governments under the IRA. Federal officers immediately undertook the work of drafting tribal constitutions, acquiring land, and issuing loans for community development for these Chippewas. All of these new tribal governments became officially "recognized" by the United States—a status under which the federal government acknowledges the right of a tribe to exercise sovereign powers to govern its people. The efforts of the Ottawas of Mason and Manistee counties to do the same would go unrewarded for nearly six more decades.

In response to the Ottawas' petitions, the BIA sent officials to hold public meetings in various Ottawa communities in March 1936. Federal

■ Josephine Hinmon. Courtesy of Elizabeth (née Theodore) Bailey.

■ Alex Keoquom Jr. Courtesy of Ann McClellan.

officials met with descendants of the Grand River Ottawas of Grand Haven, Muskegon, and Manistee; with Grand Traverse Ottawas at Suttons Bay; and with Little Traverse Odawas at Petoskey and Cross Village. Instead of unanimous community support for the IRA and its programs, a small but vocal opposition sponsored by a Catholic priest from Harbor Springs fomented dissent in the Little Traverse and Grand Traverse communities. The priest accused local Ottawa leaders of misguiding and deceiving the Ottawas into petitioning for reorganization when, as he claimed, no Indians wanted to return to reservation life. The federal agent who had worked to restore the governments of local Chippewa tribes left these meetings skeptical about the chances for Ottawa reorganization. The priest became convinced that the Ottawas did not live on defined reservations or as defined bands, and therefore believed they were ineligible for reorganization.

Local BIA agents were incorrect in their limited knowledge of Ottawa history, the continuity of the Ottawas' community, and the strength of the kin relationships that bound the Ottawa communities together. Special agents of the federal government had taken a roll of the Mason and Manistee Ottawas in 1908 and 1909—less than thirty years earlier—and found the Ottawas living in distinct communities still led by ogemuk whom the federal government relied upon to identify the members of the various Ottawa bands. Ottawas lived in communities on and around reservations created for them by the 1836 Treaty of Washington and the 1855 Treaty of Detroit. These communities grasped the hope offered to them under provisions of the IRA and quickly mobilized to benefit from the law. However, based on one agent's misunderstanding of Ottawa history, BIA officers in Washington adopted a new perspective on Ottawa reorganization. They accepted the agent's recommendation that "either arrangements must be made to purchase lands for these people or they should be definitely informed that they cannot be considered under the Act."[7] In 1937, lack of congressional appropriations for the IRA eventually halted all federal moves to acquire land or create constitutional governments for the Ottawas. The Ottawas, however, continued to recognize leaders of their communities and to function politically, participating in efforts within and among their communities to improve living conditions for themselves and their kin throughout Michigan.

CHAPTER 19

No One's Responsibility

The Ottawas' need for social and economic assistance, and their ongoing desire for redress of past grievances compelled Ottawa leaders to continue pressing for reorganization under the Indian Reorganization Act (IRA) during the late 1930s. While the Bureau of Indian Affairs' desire to extend the benefits of the IRA to Ottawas waned by 1938, Michigan officials pressed the BIA to "formulate some plan to rehabilitate these Indians."[1] State officials and county relief workers, such as Louise Armstrong (discussed in chapter 17), recognized a reality that eluded other observers: the Ottawas were a distinct, unassimilated group, and their poverty was of a nature quite different than that of their American neighbors. As the Ottawas continued to act in the interest of their communities, officials at the local, state, and federal levels denied responsibility for the impoverished conditions in which the Ottawas lived.

In 1937, BIA officials in Washington and at the Great Lakes Indian Agency declared that the Ottawas of Mason and Manistee counties were too poor for the federal government to assist adequately. Even agents who had initially supported the Ottawas' efforts to benefit from the IRA

■ Enos Pego graduated from the Carlisle
Institute, a federally operated and funded
Indian boarding school in Pennsylvania. Enos
returned to the Grand River reservations, where
he joined in the work of filing claims for unkept
treaty provisions before the United States
courts and creating a constitutional government
under provisions of the 1934 Indian Reorganization Act. He wrote articulate letters arguing
against federal officials who cited inaccurate
historical accounts to justify termination of the
federal trust relationship between the Ottawas
and the United States. Enos Pego. Private collection of
George Pego.

recommended that their communities not be allowed to reorganize,
adopting the view that it would be "unwise for the Indian Service at this
time to make any gestures that might be interpreted as evidence that it
was about to assume responsibility for the welfare of these Indians."[2]
The federal government could not, in fact, assume responsibility for
Ottawa economic development, because Congress refused to appropriate
enough money for the BIA to do so. The Ottawas, the agents argued,
had become the responsibility of state and local governments, and the
federal government should not interfere with this relationship because
it already provided adequate economic schooling and safeguards to

Ottawa communities. In reality, the Ottawas received only meager assistance from state and local governments, and then only when they faced actual starvation. Although the Ottawas met IRA criteria, the BIA refused to allow the Ottawas to reorganize, claiming that doing so would worsen their economic position and drain already insufficient government funds.

The BIA's refusal to allow the Ottawas to reorganize, and its passing of responsibility to state and local governments, motivated Ottawa leaders to act. Enos Pego and Peter Stone, who had become the spokespersons for the Ottawas of Mason and Manistee counties, initiated action by writing to Senator Burton Wheeler, the creator of the IRA legislation. Pego and Stone asked why their band had not been allowed to benefit from the IRA, and requested copies of Michigan Indian constitutions that had already been approved. Other Ottawas mobilized as well. George Antoine of the Grand Traverse Bands wrote to the BIA in May 1938 to ask whether his community had been acknowledged yet, and if not, to request an investigation to determine why not. Little Traverse Bay Ottawas demanded reorganization and a reservation under the IRA. To these inquiries, the BIA apathetically responded that the Ottawas would be contacted "in the event of a decision."[3]

The Ottawas also addressed their concerns to the Michigan congressional delegation, urging Michigan's senators to press the BIA into action. They received a response that had become standard among federal officials by 1938: the BIA suffered from a lack of funding, but might reconsider granting Ottawa petitions if funds became available in the future. When pressed by Michigan's senators to account for their slow responses to Ottawa requests, BIA officials hardened their ambiguous position regarding Michigan Ottawas. BIA officials firmly opposed extension of the IRA to Ottawas, saying, "They have for years been dealt with by the State. . . . For the Indian Service to go among these people with inadequate funds and to attempt to take over functions and services . . . [t]here is no doubt that . . . the State will withdraw. If we cannot do an equally good or better job, then we should not interfere."[4]

Ottawa leaders did not passively accept the federal government's decision to pass responsibility for providing relief to their communities to the state of Michigan. Enos Pego wrote to the commissioner of Indian Affairs directly, accusing BIA agents of poor judgment based upon little knowledge of history and a gross misunderstanding of the Ottawas' political and economic conditions. Pego refused to accept the BIA's pat answer that the Ottawas were the responsibility of the state, declaring that "Its the condition the white man left us after swindling us of our land that has more to do with our problem."[5] Pego demanded to know why other Michigan tribes had been allowed to reorganize, but his people were repeatedly denied the same privilege. Pego received noncommittal replies to his charge.

Pego, now understandably frustrated, commented directly about the BIA's insistence that the Ottawas were Michigan's responsibility. On December 12, 1938, he wrote again to the commissioner, stating: "The United States government has never the right policy in trying to solve the Indian's problems. The Indians have always been the victim of the ever changing policy of the government. Each change of administration changes the policys."[6] It was because of the federal government's habit of changing policy and contradicting its positions that the Ottawa bands were so confused about the IRA, and Pego began to doubt that they would ever be able to complete the process.

Even so, Enos Pego remained unwilling to accept the federal government's denial of responsibility for the failures of federal policy. In his letter to the commissioner of Indian Affairs, he argued that if the state of Michigan, not the federal government, was responsible for the Ottawas' deplorable living conditions, then the state should make reparation for all that Americans had taken from his people. Pego boldly wrote:

> Have the state give these Indians a place to live or a home. Not only a place to live, but give them land, good land, so they may raise something.
>
> The State owes it to these Indians as a reparation for what the State has taken away from them. . . . The State should have a plan to give these Indians some good State land and a location along some good stream or river where the Indians could hunt, fish, or trap three or four months out of a year. Why not?[7]

Pego proposed that the state should grant each Ottawa family eighty acres that would pass to heirs upon the owner's death, and that each family would pay a small tax to support a school. Pego's demand that state government become involved in reparations prompted a response from the assistant commissioner of Indian Affairs, who told Pego that the BIA remained deeply concerned and was "continuing to search for a satisfactory course of action."[8]

Enos Pego, no matter how correct and persuasive his arguments, faced the BIA's de facto policy that encouraged the intervention of state agencies, provided they not be called upon to make payments to Ottawas, and as little federal intervention as possible. To make matters worse, new BIA appointees chosen to coordinate IRA programs in the Great Lakes area announced in 1938 that the state services to the Ottawas would soon be discontinued. With this declaration, the Ottawas faced total abandonment by local, state, and federal governments. The Ottawas desperately needed assistance, but—as no one's responsibility—they received none.

■ By the end of the 1930s, Little River Ottawas still lived in rural communities throughout their historic homelands. However, the means by which they had made their living from the end of the nineteenth century forward—by lumbering, hunting, fishing, trapping, and subsistence farming—no longer provided adequate support. Families began to move from their rural communities to the cities and towns that now occupied the sites of the Ottawas' historic villages. Here, the Medacco and Bailey families stand in front of the house that Pete Bailey built on one of the last homesteads made at Indian Village. Pictured (*left to right*) are Robert Bailey; Louis Medacco Jr.; Alice (née Theodore) Medacco, who holds baby Shirley Mae Medacco; Elizabeth (née Theodore) Bailey, holding Jerry Bailey; Margaret and Pete Bailey Jr. (*the children in the foreground*); and Louis Medacco. Bailey and Medacco families. Courtesy of Elizabeth (née Theodore) Bailey.

CHAPTER 20

The Whole of the Holst Report

T he Ottawas' prospects for creating a new federally recognized, constitutionally guided government and receiving federal assistance under the Indian Reorganization Act died in 1939. That year, Enos Pego, who had worked to establish IRA programs for the Ottawas of Mason and Manistee counties, passed away. While Pego's death was a misfortune for the Ottawas, it was a small setback when compared to the effects of an investigative report ordered by the Bureau of Indian Affairs, popularly called the Holst Report after one of its authors, John Holst. The Holst Report declared that Ottawa culture, tradition, and way of life were all but lost; that the Ottawas were no different than any other citizens in rural Michigan communities; and that neither the federal government nor the state need provide the Ottawas with any additional assistance. However, the whole picture of Ottawa life and culture in 1939 was quite different than the one drawn in the Holst Report.

Three BIA employees drafted the Holst Report, which was purportedly a summary of the findings of their investigation into how the state and federal governments could best cooperate to provide assistance to the Ottawas. Of the three investigators—a field agent, an anthropologist, and a social worker—only the social worker had visited a significant number of Ottawa families, while the other two passed quickly through Ottawa settlements and spoke to few Ottawa people. The authors shared a common perspective—one that would be cited repeatedly during the next fifty years as the Ottawas worked to reverse the social and political damage created by the Holst Report.

The Holst Report, actually titled "A Survey of Indian Groups in the State of Michigan, 1939," began with a wildly distorted account of Ottawa

■ Into the 1930s, fishing continued to provide rural Ottawa families with badly needed protein. Here, Lois Brubaker proudly displays her day's catch. Courtesy of Elizabeth (née Theodore) Bailey.

■ RIGHT: Siblings Sherman and Hazel Moore stand in front of their family's home in rural Manistee County. Courtesy of Marcella (née Moore) Luesby.

■ OPPOSITE, TOP: Deer hunting remained the primary method of supplying meat in the diets of rural Ottawa families during the 1930s. Elaine Pete, Alex Sam, Jerry Medacco, and John Pete stand by a deer that they would divide among their families. Deer hunting at Indian Village. Private collection of Rose and Alex Sams.

■ OPPOSITE, BOTTOM: Ottawas who moved to cities and towns returned to the country to hunt—an activity that continued to be a vital subsistence practice, even for urban-dwelling Ottawas such as Raymond Cannon, pictured here with his kill. Urban hunter Raymond Cannon. Courtesy of Little River Band of Ottawa Indians Historic Preservation Department.

■ Some Ottawa families continued to earn part of their living by farming, though few owned farms that produced sufficient food to provide surplus cash crops. Here, Patsy and Sarah (Sally) Hewitt pose with their family's team of horses at their home in Engadine, Michigan.
Girls with horse team. Courtesy of Patsy (née Hewitt) McPherson.

■ Just as their ancestors throughout their history, whole families still traveled to the woods during the summer to harvest berries, ginseng, and other plants throughout the twentieth century. They also traveled to local orchards, where they picked fruit and vegetables for local farmers. The women in this photograph, Josephine Wakefield and Martha (née Bailey) Smith, are at a cherry-picking camp in the Traverse City area.
Summer camp. Private collection of Elaine (née Beaton) Porter.

history, followed by brief descriptions of Ottawa settlements during the 1930s. Based upon their brief visits to Ottawa towns, the authors made a central statement—that little Ottawa culture remained intact—which guided their recommendations. According to the Holst Report's authors, the Ottawas had assimilated: they spoke English, were "indistinguishable from their white neighbors in dress," and were on "equal terms with other citizens."[1] The authors continued, writing that the Ottawas

no longer maintain any tribal organizations or traditional ceremonies, except for the benefit of tourists. Their ancient arts and crafts survive only in half-forgotten imitations, or newer adaptations for tourist trade. They are in the transitional stage in that they have abandoned their old laws and customs while they have not learned to use the civic and social instruments which they have tacitly accepted.[2]

■ Ottawas from Indian Village picking cherries on the Adams Gables farm at Arcadia, Michigan. Cherry pickers. Private collection of Katherine (née Sam) Glocheski.

They specifically mentioned that the Manistee County Ottawas near Brethren had no "community interest."[3] This is a peculiar statement, as this was the same community that Louise Armstrong had written about only five years earlier. Contrarily, she had observed the continuity of Ottawa bands and ethics, and the persisting Ottawa economy of hunting, fishing, trapping, and gardening, along with some wage labor.

In many ways, the Ottawas of Manistee County maintained more traditional culture than reorganized Indian communities in other parts of Michigan. However, the authors wrote:

Brethren is another inland group widely scattered. Several of them own land but it is poor or uncleared. They do have gardens. The 15 families

■ Nancy (née Medacco) Wahr and her daughter Carol Ann Wahr (Bennett) pose for a snapshot outside of their home. Carol Ann would become a tribal leader and serve on the Little River Ottawa's first Tribal Council after federal reaffirmation of the Tribe in 1994. Courtesy of Marcella (née Moore) Luesby.

■ Francis, Lucille, and Stanley Antoine stand in the yard in front of the Antoine home, just north of Manistee. Courtesy of Ann McClellan.

are divided into four small groups a few miles apart. In general their condition is not hopeful. Native crafts have been forgotten and work for wages is scarce. At this season the bean and potato fields furnish some employment and so does berry picking.[4]

Unless the authors expected to find Ottawas in traditional dress and living in bark lodges in villages on the shores of Lake Michigan, it is hard to know what to make of these statements, except that the authors did not visit Ottawa settlements at all. If they had visited Indian Village, for example, they would have seen Ottawa men traveling in and fishing from traditional cedar dugout canoes. Had the authors arrived when a catch was brought back to the village, they could have witnessed the

reciprocal division of game among community members. In fact, many parts of traditional Ottawa technology—from *potagons* for grinding corn, to gill nets for fishing—were still used on a daily basis.[5] Further, the authors' comment that the Ottawas participated in wage labor and lived in log and frame houses was the equivalent of complaining in 1855 that because log cabins and shipbuilding were "un-Indian," the Ottawas had lost their culture by living in cabins and building plank boats. The Ottawas' kin-based band structure remained strong enough to support several hundred people by the organized exploitation of traditionally harvested natural resources, even during the darkest days of the Great Depression. The notion that the Ottawas lacked "community interest" was simply naive and superficial.

Ironically, the Holst Report suggested expanding the manufacture of traditional crafts to provide an additional source of income for the Ottawas. BIA officials, perhaps seeing a cheap and easy cover for their failure to make meaningful contributions to Ottawa communities, planned to create a Works Progress Administration (WPA) program to manufacture Indian crafts at Brethren—a program focused on the "revival of native crafts . . . to develop a means of self help for families." The authors qualified their proposal by adding that Native crafts such as "Basketry, the tanning of skins, the making of rustic furniture, snow

■ Marie (née Aikens) King stands with her daughter Roxanne. Courtesy of Little River Band of Ottawa Indians Historic Preservation Department.

■ Mrs. Anse, Stella Theodore, and their dog. Private collection of Margaret (née Bailey) Chandler.

shoes, bows and arrows, [and] work with birch and elm bark" had always received the attention and admiration of non-Indian people. Despite the Ottawas' supposed loss of culture, the report proposed marketing traditional skills that the Ottawas continued to practice, not teaching them new ones.[6]

The oversights and exaggerations of the Holst Report were relentless. The authors looked at marginally churched Ottawa communities and saw devout Christians. Admittedly, by the mid-twentieth century Ottawa religion was colored with Christian beliefs, music, and rituals. Since the relationship between the Christian churches and the Ottawas' ancestors had begun centuries before—predating, for example, the founding of the United States—it was hardly a recent innovation that proved some sort of cultural decline. Given the many contemporary accounts of continuing traditional, non-Christian belief and its expression in ceremonies, any Christianity practiced by the Ottawas of Mason and Manistee counties was clearly more syncretic than orthodox.

The Holst Report also exaggerated the Ottawas' level of interaction with their American neighbors. The authors wrote that the Ottawas participated with Americans "on a common basis of understanding," were "everywhere component parts of the communities in which they live," and "in no sense constitute a separate and distinct group"—adding that "any attempt to deal with them as such would be detrimental both to Indians and whites, and very probably disastrous to the Indians." Despite the petitions and letters written and signed by Ottawas and sent to Washington, particularly during the 1930s, the Holst Report authors asserted that the Ottawas "neither need nor ask help, special favors, or gratuity from the Federal Government." The authors argued that no lands, such as reservations or allotments, should be held in trust for the Ottawas by the federal government, as such "class privileges and prohibitions" were a "menace to Indian welfare and progress." Specifically, they recommended that the federal government diminish welfare and educational aid to the Ottawas, that it not institute any new such programs, and that "there be no further extension of organization under the Indian Reorganization Act in Michigan."[7]

The Holst Report conclusions are incredible given the existence of exclusively Ottawa communities like Indian Village in Mason and Manistee counties, the observations of federal relief agents such as Louise Armstrong, the reluctance of local officials to aid the Ottawas through programs designed for all citizens, and finally, the Ottawas' persistent attempts to organize, to secure reservation lands, and to receive federal economic assistance. The authors of the Holst Report ignored the reality of the Ottawas' condition and presented a false and facile picture of Ottawa society. Their statements are understandable only as the foreordained result of a report intended as an apology for decisions already reached by the BIA to end IRA efforts in Michigan. The resolution not to organize the Ottawas was, in reality, an administrative decision based on a lack of funding.

However, not all BIA employees accepted the Holst Report. Federal agents who actually worked in Michigan Indian communities, and who were familiar with the Ottawas' true condition, objected to many of the report's conclusions. One agent who criticized the report had visited many Ottawa homes and communities during his tenure as superintendent of the Tomah Agency, under whose jurisdiction the Ottawas were at the time, and knew that the Holst Report had seriously underplayed the extent and depth of Ottawa poverty. The agent knew that the Ottawas desperately needed federal aid. The Ottawas and their southern neighbors, the Potawatomis, were the only Indian groups in Michigan denied the right to reorganize, and these tribes could not be expected to quietly accept the BIA's decision to halt IRA efforts while other tribes received federal aid. As long as other Michigan tribal groups were under BIA supervision, "a ray of hope and a realization that there is an Indian Service" would persist among the Ottawas and Potawatomis, and they would continue to press for reorganization.[8]

The recommendations of the Holst Report helped justify a policy shift that had already taken place at the highest level of the BIA; thus, in May 1940, the commissioner of Indian Affairs announced the end of all further IRA efforts in Michigan. This proclamation barred the Ottawas of Mason and Manistee counties from receiving the federal aid they needed and, by the provisions of the IRA, for which they were once thought eligible. Although these Ottawas did not benefit directly from the IRA—an act originally intended to revitalize Indian culture and polity—their efforts to implement the act helped to sustain their community by mobilizing tribal leadership in pursuit of a common goal. The families who provided leadership in the effort to create IRA governments would continue to pursue the interests of the Ottawa community in other contexts following World War II.

■ Leona Cogswell and Jenny Bailey stand at the front door of a local store. Private collection of Margaret (née Bailey) Chandler.

■ Events of the 1940s forever changed Ottawa communities. So many Ottawa men enlisted in the U.S. Armed Forces to fight in World War II that some rural communities were left without adult men. In some Ottawa communities, women assumed complete responsibility for providing for their elders and children.

Here, George Pego and his cousin Doug Pierson pose for a photograph while attending a Methodist camp meeting at Mount Pleasant, Michigan. These men would lose the innocence of their youth during battle in Europe. George Pego and Doug Pierson. Private collection of George Pego.

CHAPTER 21

"Indian Problems"

During World War II, men and women from every Michigan Ottawa community enlisted in the United States Armed Services. Michigan Ottawas did so even while the United States refused to recognize their tribal status and to provide the Ottawa Tribe or its independent communities with services that the federal government offered to neighboring Chippewa tribes. The Bureau of Indian Affairs, however, continued to monitor the condition of Ottawa communities—conducting investigations and making proposals—during and immediately after the war. The BIA concluded that Michigan Ottawas faced unique struggles, issues that BIA officers referred to as "distinctly . . . Indian problems."[1] These problems affected the Ottawa communities in Mason and Manistee counties as much as any other Michigan Ottawa community. Throughout the 1940s, Ottawa women, children, and the few men who had not joined the war effort continued to receive poor educations, live in poverty, and go without federal aid as they waited for their men to come back to continue fighting the Ottawas' war at home.

■ This photograph is a joke for the families back on the Grand River Reservation. George Pego, dressed in the uniform, had not yet enlisted in the army, and Paul Lewis, in the business suit, had. They exchanged clothes for this photograph. Private collection of George Pego.

■ Brothers Paul T. Lewis (*left*) and Fred M. Lewis (*right*) both gave their lives in World War II. Private collection of George Pego.

■ All of the able-bodied men from the Indian Village community enlisted in the U.S. Armed Forces during World War II. Even forty-year-old Alex Sams, the father of the famous Ottawa twins Anna Mae and Anna Jean, served. This photograph was taken when the Sam family sent Spencer Sam to serve. Pictured (*left to right*) are John Sam, Stanley Sam, Spencer Sam, and Alex Sams. Soldiers at Indian Village. Private collection of Rose and Alex Sams.

■ Young Jim Koon served in France. He became famous as an Ottawa code talker. Jim, living on the French side of the English Channel, spoke to his cousin Pete Saugie, who was stationed in England, in the language *Odawa Anishinaabemowin*. Together they provided logistic information to English fighters. Jim Koon. Private collection of Jim Koon.

■ Pete Saugie, U.S. Army; Irene Medacco; and Pete Savage. Private collection of Steve and Dorothy Medacco.

■ Francis Cogswell, U.S. Navy. Courtesy of
Little River Band of Ottawa Indians Historic Preservation
Department.

■ Albert Hardenburg, U.S. Army. Private collection
of Steve and Dorothy Medacco.

■ Billy LeHay (*left*) and an unidentified
friend, U.S. Army. Private collection of Steve and
Dorothy Medacco.

■ Glenn Dale Hewitt, U.S. Navy.
Courtesy of Patsy (née Hewitt) McPherson.

■ Thaddeus Theodore, U.S.
Army. Courtesy of Marcella (née Moore)
Luesby.

■ Joe Medacco Jr., U.S. Army,
participated in the Normandy
invasion. Private collection of Steve and
Dorothy Medacco.

■ Van Moore, U.S. Army. Courtesy
of Little River Band of Ottawa Indians
Historic Preservation Department.

■ Robert Akins Wahr, U.S. Army. Private collection of
Steve and Dorothy Medacco.

■ Spencer Sam went to war in 1942. Here, Minnie and Rose Sam pose for a photograph in front of their Indian Village home. Sending Spencer Sam to war. Private collection of Rose
and Alex Sams.

■ George Pego was seriously injured by an
explosion that tore away part of his abdomen.
He was rescued from a French orchard and
survived his injury. He was one of hundreds
of Ottawa men who returned to Michigan and
began building a family. George Pego married
Lucille Lewis, and the couple began raising
children, helping to create a post–World War II
baby boom among the Ottawas. George and Lucille
Pego. Private collection of George Pego.

■ Women took responsibility for almost every part of community life at places
like Indian Village while their men were away during World War II. Here, the village
midwife, Maggie Pete Sam (right), poses with her daughter Helen Sam Wahr, Helen's
granddaughter Loretta Skocelas (Becarria), and Maggie's grandson George Sam. The
midwife. Private collection of Katherine (née Sam) Glocheski.

■ Ottawa men who returned from the war participated in the economic plenty of postwar America. Many moved their families to cities throughout the Ottawas' historic territories. Frances Cogswell and Jenny (née Bailey) Peters are pictured here during the postwar years. Francis Cogswell and Jeanne (née Bailey) Peters. Courtesy of Little River Band of Ottawa Indians Historic Preservation Department.

■ Katie Sam Glocheski (*left*) and Rose Sam (*right*) pose with John Pete. Private collection of Rose and Alex Sams.

■ Minnie Sam (*left*) and Julia Theodore (*right*) pose with Spencer Sam. Sending Spencer Sam to war. Private collection of Rose and Alex Sams.

■ Stanley and Mabel Tyler Sam. Courtesy of Elizabeth (née Theodore) Bailey.

■ Anna Mae Sams (Lempke) poses in her stylish ice-skating costume at Indian Village in 1943. Private collection of Rose and Alex Sams.

■ Ottawa women, for the first time in history, were hired by non-Indian businesses to work for wages. Here, Lena Cogswell (*left*) and Virginia Cogswell (*center*) pose with a friend, dressed in their work clothes. Working women. Courtesy of Elizabeth (née Theodore) Bailey.

■ Automobiles became affordable for many Ottawa families and facilitated travel between cities and rural communities where other Ottawas lived. The Saugies, pictured, would pile into the family car to visit friends and family. *In front, left to right:* Ernie Akins, Delores Saugie, and unknown girl. *In the second row:* Marie Saugie, Louis Saugie, unknown girl, Marie Saugie holding baby Carol Saugie, and Dempsey Saugie.

Saugie family. Courtesy of Little River Band of Ottawa Indians Historic Preservation Department.

■ Ottawa girls dressed in 1940s style. Pictured here (*left to right*) are Katie (née Sam) Glocheski, Marie Saugie, and Ruby Akins. Courtesy of Little River Band of Ottawa Indians Historic Preservation Department.

■ The families of Lillian Pete Varney, Elaine Sam Meduna, and Mary Pete were among the Ottawas who continued to live in rural Manistee County. Lillian Pete Varney, Elaine Sam Meduna, and Mary Pete. Private collection of Katherine (née Sam) Glocheski.

■ Ruby Aikins (*left*) and Marie Saugie (*right*). Courtesy of Little River Band of Ottawa Indians Historic Preservation Department.

■ Ottawas at Indian Village contributed to the national baby boom of the 1940s and 1950s. Pictured are General Ledford, Agnes Pete, and their son John. Courtesy of Little River Band of Ottawa Indians Historic Preservation Department.

■ Ruby Aikins and one of her children dressed for a christening at Guardian Angels Church in Manistee. Courtesy of Little River Band of Ottawa Indians Historic Preservation Department.

■ Maude Cogswell and her daughter Delia. Courtesy of Little River Band of Ottawa Indians Historic Preservation Department.

■ Dorothy Medacco and child. Courtesy of Little River Band of Ottawa Indians Historic Preservation Department.

■ Families continued to engage in farm work even after World War II. This photograph was taken during cherry-picking season at Bear Lake. All of the Indians who lived at Brethren drove to Bear Lake together and stayed for about four weeks. After the cherries were picked, they traveled to blueberry fields. At night they would entertain themselves around bonfires. After a day's work, everyone went swimming. *Front row, left to right*: Johnny (Sonnyman) Pete Jr. and Margaret Theodore. *Back row, left to right*: Harold Theodore, John Pete, Mabs Memberto, Ted Theodore, Pete Bailey, and Irving Theodore. Swimmers. Private collection of Rose and Alex Sams.

The most damaging and persistent problems in Ottawa communities were lack of education, welfare services, and money. During the war years, the BIA investigated each of these "Indian problems." In 1945, the superintendent of Indian education for the Lake States area found that the state of Michigan did not provide school books, transportation, or even lunch programs unless Ottawa parents paid for them. Due to their poverty, fewer Michigan Ottawas attended high school than young Ottawas in Wisconsin and Minnesota, but those Little River Ottawa elders who attended public schools during the 1930s and 1940s remember clearly the poor conditions. The superintendent of Indian education launched a formal federal investigation into the educational system meant to serve Michigan Ottawas, and federal investigators' findings confirmed the deficient state of education for Ottawas. While it had determined that education for Michigan Ottawas was, at best, in poor condition, the BIA was unable to decide what to do about it.

■ Johnny Pete and Jim Theodore at a berry camp. Private collection of Rose and Alex Sams.

■ The families of Alex Sams, John Pete, and Julia Theodore have a picnic dinner after a day's work at a berry camp at Bear Lake, Michigan. Berry camp. Private collection of Rose and Alex Sams.

■ Families of Alex Sam, John Pete, and Julia Theodore at berry camp. Private collection of Rose and Alex Sams.

■ After World War II, some Ottawas began buying their own commercial fishing operations. Jim Campeau owned his own fish tug. Jim Campeau. Private collection of Percy Campeau.

Lack of education was only one component of a larger "Indian problem"—the welfare of Ottawa children—which remained unaddressed in the 1940s. In 1946, a BIA study of the economic and social problems the Ottawas faced found that the only state institution that dealt with child welfare was the Committee on Education of Migrants and Indians, an organization that focused mainly on Spanish-speaking migrants. The committee ignored the large number of Ottawa children who moved between truck farms and orchards with their families, working as migrant farm laborers throughout the entire western half of Michigan.

In June 1946, the BIA offered some relief regarding the welfare of Ottawa children when the commissioner of Indian Affairs contracted with the Michigan Children's Aid Society to provide foster care, clothing, medical care, board, home care, and "incidentals" to Ottawa children who were left homeless after the Mount Pleasant Indian School closed in 1934.[2] Ancestors and current members of the Little River Band had once boarded at the Mount Pleasant Indian School, where they were provided with education, clothing, food, health care, and other such necessities of life. During the twelve years since the school had been shut down, Ottawa families simply went without this much-needed assistance.

The Ottawas' problems were exacerbated by the social climate in Michigan. Ottawa efforts to elevate themselves through wage labor were often fruitless in the face of overt racism. Ottawas were passed over for jobs in favor of American or Spanish-speaking migrant laborers, and Americans did little to hide their contempt for local Indians. Throughout Michigan, restaurants and other places of business refused to serve Indians. The Michigan Department of Social Welfare received reports from "various field workers which, quite generally, expressed the opinion that racial discrimination against our Indian people exists. It was mentioned in some places . . . that public eating places displayed signs reading, 'No Indians Served.'" BIA investigators argued in the 1939 Holst Report (discussed in chapter 20) that the Ottawas were highly assimilated, yet citizens and officials in Michigan continued to treat the Ottawas as distinct, separate, and Indian. In 1946, one BIA official agreed that the Ottawas' problems were unique, and that they had to be "dealt with . . . distinctly as Indian problems."[3]

Despite its investigations, the BIA remained indecisive about its obligations and responsibilities towards the Ottawas, and the nature of the relationship between the tribe and the federal government during the 1940s. The Ottawas continued to live without federal services and assistance as BIA officers and agents sat on the fence, not wanting to take charge of the Ottawas' affairs, but also not completely withdrawing from their lives. The BIA denied responsibility for the Ottawas but continued to serve the them, albeit in limited ways. It became quite clear to visiting agents during the 1940s that the Ottawas were not, as the Holst Report claimed in 1939, assimilated. The Ottawas of Mason and Manistee counties continued to face the "distinctly . . . Indian problems" of lack of education, welfare assistance, land, and wealth for much of the twentieth century. While Ottawa men, including many community leaders, were away from home during World War II, Ottawas could do little else but look forward to resuming their fight to overcome the "Indian problems" they faced at home in Michigan.

■ Francis Cogswell and Stanley Cogswell. Private collection of Margaret (née Bailey) Chandler.

■ Robert Hewitt Jr., U.S. Forest Service. Robert was one of many Little River Ottawas who worked to protect their native land as employees of the Forest Service. Courtesy of Patsy (née Hewitt) McPherson.

■ Lee Tyler, Elty Robert Tyler, Elty E. Tyler, Norma Tyler (Melchert), Joanne Tyler (Treml), and Bert Tyler. Courtesy of Terri (née Tyler) Raczkowski.

CHAPTER 22

"An 'Advocate' and 'Attorney for the People'"

World War II abruptly halted the Ottawas' political efforts to obtain repayment for past wrongs or to establish a working government recognized by the United States. Most able-bodied Ottawa men, even married middle-aged men who had fathered several children, enlisted in the United States Armed Forces. The absence of male leaders and the federal government's redirected focus on the war effort created a moratorium on Ottawa political activities. Meanwhile, quibbling continued within the Bureau of Indian Affairs about which level of government—state or federal—should accept responsibility for helping the Ottawas overcome the problems created by a century of dispossession, neglect, and overt racism. The only point of agreement between the Ottawas and the BIA was that the Ottawas needed "an 'advocate' or 'attorney for the people'" who would act on their behalf.[1]

After the war, the Ottawas resumed their political efforts, which focused on creating an organization to coordinate their work, win support for a political agenda, and support leaders to be spokespersons in pursuit of claims. Leaders from communities throughout western

■ Benedict and Alice Kelsey Courtesy of Elizabeth (née Theodore) Bailey.

■ Sarah Baker. Courtesy of Patsy (née Hewitt) McPherson.

■ Cornelius Bailey Private collection of Dorothy (née Wabsis) Bailey. ca. 1960.

■ The White Star Tavern, commonly referred to as "Star Corners," was a popular place for tribal members to socialize. Courtesy of Little River Band of Ottawa Indians Historic Preservation Department.

■ Maria Sam Raymo and Sophia Pete at Indian Village. Courtesy of Little River Band of Ottawa Indians Historic Preservation Department.

■ Theresa, Henry, Louis, and Cornelius Bailey at their homestead in Custer, Michigan. Private collection of Dorothy (née Wabsis) Bailey.

Michigan combined their interests and talents to form a new business committee, much like the one Grand River Ottawa Sampson Robinson had envisioned twenty years earlier. Passage of federal legislation in 1946 creating the Indian Claims Commission (ICC)—an entity that would hear and adjudicate the backlog of Indian tribal claims against the United States—accelerated the Ottawas' political momentum, as the ICC provided Michigan Ottawas with a vehicle to more strongly assert their claims against the United States.[2]

Organization of the Northern Michigan Ottawa Association, most widely known as the NMOA, began in 1947 when Grand River Ottawa leader Levi McClellan and his son-in-law Robert Dominic drafted a constitution and bylaws for their statewide business committee. Under this constitution, each Ottawa community in the state would be considered a discrete "unit" governed by its own committee of elected leaders. The leaders and members of each unit would meet as necessary throughout the year, and also gather annually with the leaders and members of the other units throughout Michigan to elect an organization-wide executive committee comprised of a president, vice-president, treasurer, secretary, interpreter, and councilors. The executive committee would represent the NMOA in its dealings with attorneys and with the ICC. NMOA leaders were charged with educating their constituents, building consensus for decisions, providing funding, and, whenever possible, helping to alleviate hardship in their

■ Ottawas from all over Michigan came together annually at Petoskey for an organization-wide meeting of the Northern Michigan Ottawa Association. There, members discussed issues important to their communities, as well as topics regarding treaties and government relations. Annual NMOA meetings were forums for discussion, as well as community-building events. Many Little River Ottawa leaders attended these meetings while they were growing up. Margaret (née Bailey) Chandler and her husband Dale Chandler are the central figures seated in the front row. Courtesy of the Little Traverse Bay Bands of Odawa Indians.

■ Children participated at NMOA gatherings from an early age. The children seated in the front row (*left to right*) are Martha Micki, the young son of Harold Battice, daughter of Dorothy Battice, Harold Battice Jr., and daughter of Harold Battice. Courtesy of the Little Traverse Bay Bands of Odawa Indians.

■ Milo Smith and sisters Elaine Beaton (Porter) and Velva Jean Beaton, ca. 1940. Private collection of Elaine (née Beaton) Porter.

communities. NMOA leaders quickly won support for their efforts to file ICC claims for wrongs committed against the Ottawas during the treaty era and the reservation years.

The NMOA formed eleven community units, including one that would evolve and become identified as the Little River Band of Ottawa Indians. Cornelius Bailey, who had worked with Sampson Robinson during the 1920s, joined the NMOA and again represented the Ottawas of Mason and Manistee counties, who organized as NMOA Unit Seven. In July 1948, Robert Dominic wrote to Cornelius Bailey asking that Bailey and his community join the NMOA, to work "cooperatively with our claims committee" and to contribute any documents that might help identify or support claims.[3] Bailey responded quickly, and in 1952, the Ottawas of Benzie, Mason, Manistee, and Wexford counties—all descendants of the Indian Town settlement and Ottawas who occupied historic village sites along the Pere Marquette and Manistee rivers—formally became Unit Seven of the NMOA. They elected their officers in December 1953: Albert Micko of Custer, Mr. and Mrs. Nicholas Bailey of Ludington, Irene Bailey of Honor, and Margaret (née Bailey) Chandler of Indian Village. Margaret (née Bailey) Chandler served the community as an elected member of its various governing bodies continuously from 1953 until her death in January 1997.

The founders of Unit Seven joined in 1948 with other Grand River Ottawas who formed Unit Three and Unit Five when the NMOA held its first public council—a meeting attended by approximately three hundred people. The gathered Ottawas sanctioned the NMOA executive committee's plan to hire an attorney who would prepare and file Ottawa claims before the ICC. The BIA took an active interest in the NMOA from its founding, and helped the organization hire its attorney, organize meetings with federal officers, and file claims.

Although many of its aims and functions were political, the NMOA was not only a political organization. The Ottawas' involvement in the organization also gave them reason and opportunity to gather for social events, which strengthened the larger Michigan Ottawa community. The members of the NMOA units organized and held social events to raise money for ICC work; chicken dinners, for example, drew members from all over Unit Seven's range. Even when meetings were political in nature, they were held in members' homes, where the atmosphere was that of a gathering of family and friends. Over the years, all of Unit

■ Paul Pego's First Communion, ca. 1950s. Private collection of George Pego.

■ Martha Smith and one of her grandchildren, ca. early 1950s. Private collection of Elaine (née Beaton) Porter.

■ Genevieve Saugie. August 1958. Courtesy of Little River Band of Ottawa Indians Historic Preservation Department.

Seven's settlements in Mason and Manistee counties hosted NMOA fundraisers and meetings.

Ottawa political structures continued to evolve as the NMOA pursued Ottawa claims during the 1950s, 1960s, and 1970s. Yet even the NMOA—a state- and tribe-wide business committee—was founded and operated on historic Ottawa political processes: within the NMOA, individual communities retained their autonomy while working together. Eventually, these communities identified as entirely separate entities. Throughout the NMOA years, the Ottawas continued to rely upon the principle of face-to-face relations between people who are kin to one another. The claims that Ottawas filed helped a new generation to unite and elect fresh leaders to pressure the federal government for just settlements of past wrongs. The NMOA became the "advocate" and "attorney" the Ottawas needed, and the formation and successes of their organization would pattern Ottawa life and political activity throughout the remainder of the twentieth century.

■ Martha Smith with one of her handmade black-ash baskets, ca. 1950. Private collection of Elaine (née Beaton) Porter.

■ Pete Family Reunion, 1970. *Front row, left to right:* Julia Theodore, Alice Moore, and Helen (née Sam) Wahr. *Back row:* Mabs Memberto, Hank Pete, Helen Pete, and Art Pete. Private collection of Katherine (née Sam) Glocheski.

CHAPTER 23

Decades of Success and Political Evolution

■ Yvonne King (Theodore), granddaughter of Julia Theodore, attended Brethren High School. Ca. 1969. Private collection of Katherine (née Sam) Glocheski.

T he NMOA's influence and reputation grew during the 1950s, 1960s, and 1970s. Under the leadership of Robert Dominic and his wife Waunetta, a Grand River Ottawa who rose to a position of prominence alongside her husband, the NMOA became the representative organization for all western Michigan Ottawa communities. The Dominics traveled throughout the state, visiting Ottawa communities and building an impressive list of contacts who offered services to NMOA member communities. Robert and Waunetta Dominic relentlessly pursued Ottawa claims cases and worked to complete a tribal membership roll that listed every quarter-blood descendant of Ottawas who had received annuities during the last treaty payment in 1870. The Dominics' reputation as representatives of the Michigan bands grew steadily throughout these decades, and the NMOA served as the business committee of every Ottawa community in western Michigan.

In the 1960s and 1970s, when civil rights dominated the national agenda, the NMOA became the vehicle through which Ottawas asserted their distinctiveness and historical rights before the ICC. Alongside all other Michigan Ottawas, the Ottawas of NMOA Unit Seven pressed

223

■ Cornelius and Doris Bailey. Courtesy of Dorothy (née Wabsis) Bailey.

■ Terry Oren, Helen (née Sam) Wahr holding baby Chad Eckhardt, Julia Theodore, and Lavern (née Wahr) Oren, ca. 1972. Private collection of Katherine (née Sam) Glocheski.

■ *Left to right:* Albert Micko, Margaret Bailey (Chandler), Unidentified, Anna Bailey, Elizabeth (née Theodore) Bailey, unidentified, and Jerry Bailey. Courtesy of Elizabeth (née Theodore) Bailey.

■ Family of Mr. and Mrs. Joe Pete. Courtesy of Little River Band of Ottawa Indians Historic Preservation Department.

for financial assistance for Michigan's poorest Indian people, social services in urban and rural communities where such services had been denied, and reclamation of treaty-preserved properties. The Ottawas, however, faced substantial roadblocks, as they had not been granted the opportunity to create a federally sanctioned constitutional government under the IRA during the 1930s. At the same time that Bureau of Indian Affairs officials praised the NMOA for its effective political actions and encouraged the organization to pursue its goals, they refused to recognize the NMOA as the official government of the Michigan Ottawa people. As a result, the federal government continued to deny the Ottawas the same level of federal protections and services that were granted to "federally recognized" tribes. The BIA frequently cited the Ottawas' official federal status as "unrecognized" descendants of a tribe, to ignore NMOA demands, and to continue withholding services to Ottawas.

The Dominics and the members of the NMOA's constituent units were not derailed, despite these challenges and the BIA's mixed messages. By 1962, the Dominics were in the process of compiling a roll of nearly five thousand modern members of the Ottawa Tribe. The BIA interacted with the NMOA consistently as the Ottawas' representative organization, accepted the NMOA's blood-quantum certification as proof of its members' Indian ancestries, and regularly encouraged Ottawas to contact the Dominics to investigate eligibility for services. By the end

■ Medacco and Saugie families come together for Christmas dinner in 1956. Courtesy of Little River Band of Ottawa Indians Historic Preservation Department.

of the 1960s, Michigan Ottawas—based on the NMOA's blood-quantum certification—became eligible for a wide range of services, including financial aid for education, employment, and medical care. The BIA even accepted the NMOA's certification as sufficient genealogical evidence of heirship in trust land cases. The NMOA achieved all of this in spite of,

■ Jerry, Roxanne, and Marilyn Koon. Courtesy of Jim Koon.

and in contradiction to, the BIA's claim that neither the NMOA nor any Michigan Ottawa community were federally recognized—a requirement for receiving federal services. NMOA leaders and their constituent communities refused to listen to the federal government's excuses and accept its ever-shifting policies regarding Michigan Indians.

Treaty-reserved hunting and fishing rights moved to the forefront of the Michigan Indian political agenda during in the 1960s. The Ottawas of Unit Seven who had continued to hunt, fish, and gather—claiming a right to do so under the 1836 Treaty of Washington—were among the most active hunting-and-fishing-rights proponents. In 1965, William Jondreau of the Keweenaw Bay Reservation brought the issue of treaty-protected Indian fishing into state court, and in 1971, the Michigan Supreme Court validated the hunting and fishing rights of all Indians party to the 1854 Treaty of LaPointe. Unit Seven officers watched progress on this case closely and discussed their own pursuit of hunting and fishing rights in the courts as early as 1965.

State of Michigan officials, however, strongly opposed Ottawa interpretations of 1836 treaty language regarding hunting and fishing rights. Tensions heightened as Michigan's legislators and conservation officers more vocally opposed Ottawa and Chippewa claims between 1971 and 1975. In 1970, the Michigan Department of Natural Resources (DNR) and the Michigan Ottawas and Chippewas attempted

■ Henry Lewis Jr., ca. 1972. Private collection of George Pego.

■ Pego family gathering. *Front row, left to right*: Darlene (née Pego) Pineda, Allen Pego, and Sally (née Pego) Jobes. *Back row:* Mary (née Pego) Sherman, George Henry Pego, Lucille Pego, Paul Pego, and Georgianna (née Pego) Adamczak. Private collection of George Pego.

■ Pamela and Virginia Medacco with Michael Landon at Buck Lake Ranch in Indiana, where the Medacco girls were in a show with Landon in 1964. Private collection of Steve and Dorothy Medacco.

to reach a negotiated settlement. DNR officials led the NMOA and Michigan Ottawas to believe that those who held proper identification cards—which the NMOA issued as proof of one-quarter or more blood quantum—could hunt and fish on lands the Ottawas ceded in 1836. However, private landowners and the state of Michigan blocked the Ottawas' access to many resource sites and to the Great Lakes. Ottawas in Mason, Manistee, and Oceana counties had been arrested for hunting and fishing since the 1920s, but had few financial, political, or legal resources to protect their rights. The Ottawas had little recourse but to buy hunting and fishing licenses or risk incarceration and fines; some chose to buy state licenses, while others flatly refused. Even in the face of arrest, the Ottawas continued to assert throughout the 1960s and 1970s that they retained their hunting and fishing rights under provision of the 1836 treaty.

Meanwhile, the NMOA also pursued land-claims cases on behalf of Michigan Ottawas. Unit Seven participated in these cases, which the NMOA brought against the United States through the ICC. Ottawas claimed that the United States had paid their ancestors an unconscionably low price for the Michigan lands ceded to the United States during the nineteenth century, giving the Ottawas a few cents per acre and selling the same land for a much higher price. Docket 40-K was centered on the undervaluation of Grand River Ottawa lands lying south of the Grand River, which the Ottawas sold to the United States by the 1821 Treaty of Chicago. Cornelius Bailey and the Unit Seven community raised money to help pay the NMOA's attorney, kept members abreast of case developments, and compiled lists of descendants eligible for payment when, in the late 1960s, the ICC ruled in favor of the Grand River Ottawas' Docket 40-K claims.

The Ottawas won another battle in 1970 when the ICC ruled in their favor on Dockets 58 and 18-E. These cases were also land claims, this time based on the 1836 Treaty of Washington, that charged the United States with purchasing most of Michigan's Lower Peninsula for a few thousand dollars and then selling the land for millions. When the ICC awarded the Ottawas and Chippewas of Michigan over $10.5 million, the Ottawas were invigorated. These victories were the first the Ottawa people had seen in nearly seventy years, and NMOA members increasingly viewed their organization as the legitimate and sovereign government of the Ottawa Tribe.

However, BIA officers continued to see the NMOA otherwise. When it came time to collect payment for the Docket 40-K reward, the BIA decided that because the Ottawas were not federally recognized, payment would only be made to descendants of signatories to the 1821 Treaty of Chicago, regardless of blood quantum. This meant that many individuals with very little Indian ancestry and who did not take part in NMOA or Ottawa community events would receive payment for a claims case in which they had not participated. Had the BIA's decision been implemented, a large percentage of the cash award would have been taken from Ottawa people who continued to see themselves as active members of the Ottawa Tribe.

In response to the BIA's proclamation, NMOA members unanimously asserted that only persons of one-quarter or more Ottawa parentage should receive payment from the ICC judgment fund. Rather than con-ceding to the Ottawas' position, the BIA declared that only "recognized" tribes had the right to determine their membership. Therefore, because the Ottawas had been denied the opportunity to create a constitutional government under the IRA, the BIA determined that it—not the tribe represented by the NMOA—could determine who would receive payment and how much each individual would receive. BIA officers continued to demand that the judgment be divided among every

■ Country-music singers Kathy and Virginia Medacco performed under the stage name "The Gaye Sisters." They are pictured here in a promotional photograph taken by WKZO TV and Radio. Private collection of Steve and Dorothy Medacco.

■ Virginia Medacco poses with Johnny Cash, ca. 1960s. Private collection of Steve and Dorothy Medacco.

■ Jim Koon Sr. and his sons Jim Jr. and Donald at their mother's house in Filer City, ca. 1960s. Private collection of Jim Koon.

Ottawa descendant throughout the 1960s, fueling NMOA opposition and enlivening the political participation of Ottawas through Michigan.

The Ottawas undertook a two-part strategy to thwart BIA efforts to divide their judgment fund with persons not counted as members of the Tribe. The NMOA created a committee charged with enrolling quarter-blood descendants of nineteenth-century Ottawa band members, and then lobbied federal legislators to pass a law that would divide the money among only those persons whose names were on the enrollment list, known in Michigan and Washington as the Dominic Roll or the Grand River Roll. Ottawa leaders wrote letters to their congressional representatives, the secretary of Interior, and the commissioner of Indian Affairs. The NMOA's organized protests and efforts led to the end of BIA retaliation against the organization and payment of the Docket 40-K judgment fund to only the Grand River Ottawas of one-quarter or more blood quantum. This 1976 victory further elevated the NMOA's standing in Ottawa communities.

To increase their political clout, solidify their community, and provide for the special needs of their rural communities, NMOA Unit Seven members formed a state-chartered corporation called the Thornapple Band of Indians, Inc., in 1971. The members of the Thornapple Band, which evolved from the political foundation of the NMOA, chose this name to emphasize their descendancy from Grand River Ottawas who had emigrated in the 1850s from the Thornapple River villages to the Grand River reservations. The Thornapple Band's mission was "to encourage the residents of the area to become involved in the Indian community as a whole, and to deal with the problems of the neighborhood in a constructive and effective manner."[1] For a time, the Ottawas of Mason and Manistee counties functioned simultaneously as the Thornapple Band and NMOA Unit Seven. They elected officers, with Katherine (née Sam) Glocheski as president, and immediately pressed their first order of business: higher-quality education for Ottawa children in Manistee public schools.

The issue of federal recognition for an Ottawa tribal government remained a potent and central issue for the Thornapple Band/NMOA Unit Seven and the other NMOA units throughout the 1970s. A number of Ottawa communities observed the progress made by Michigan tribes that functioned under IRA governments. The Saginaw Chippewas, Bay Mills Chippewas, Keweenaw Bay Indian Community (Chippewas), and

■ Beatrice Hall Koon and Jim Koon Sr., ca. 1975. Private collection of Jim Koon.

the Hannahville Potawatomis were building housing for their tribe members, opening health clinics, and offering social programs—all of which could not be achieved or accessed by an unrecognized tribe. Part of the Ottawa community opposed federal recognition no matter what benefits it might bring; these Ottawas equated federal recognition with a return to reservation life and the failed federal policies of the nineteenth century. The NMOA executive committee, however, saw federal recognition as a prerequisite for the full exercise of the governmental functions they had fulfilled since the 1940s.

In 1975, Robert Dominic and the NMOA began seeking federal recognition. BIA officers discouraged NMOA efforts to obtain federal recognition, arguing that the modern business committee was not equivalent to a tribe. If the Ottawas were to obtain federal recognition, BIA officers argued, they stood a better chance of meeting federal criteria if individual communities represented by local NMOA units petitioned the federal government for recognition apart from the NMOA. The NMOA did not achieve federal recognition before Robert Dominic died the following year, in 1976. His wife Waunetta became the NMOA president in March 1976, and debates about the benefit of pursuing recognition and the political entity that should be granted federal status continued until her death in 1980. During the 1970s and early 1980s, NMOA Unit Seven members continually discussed federal recognition for their communities in Mason and Manistee counties.

The formation of the NMOA and its constituent units, and the victories the Ottawas achieved through this organization in the 1950s,

■ Jerry Koon in his paratrooper uniform, ca. 1950s. Private collection of Jim Koon.

1960s, and 1970s revitalized Ottawa communities after World War II and strengthened Ottawa polity. During the 1980s, changes in the NMOA's leadership would diminish the organization's influence and shift political focus to individual Ottawa communities. Unit Seven of the NMOA, or the Thornapple Band, would evolve yet again into the Little River Band of Ottawa Indians in the coming decades. Although the names by which the Ottawas of Mason and Manistee counties identified themselves changed over the years, their community remained constant. Based on their involvement in the NMOA and their actions on issues specific to their community, the members of the Little River Band would obtain federal reaffirmation of their sovereign status, functioning as the autonomous Ottawa community they had been since the treaty era to build a modern, constitutionally governed tribe in the 1990s.

■ *Left to right*: Mary Gillespie Clearing-Sky (with her two children), Anna (née Sam) Lempke, and Katie (née Sam) Glocheski out spear fishing on Pine Creek (between Wellston and Irons) in July 1971. The NMOA had recently issued Michigan Indians cards granting them permission to fish at anytime, anywhere—a right often contested by state game wardens. Private collection of Katherine (née Sam) Glocheski.

CHAPTER 24

Distinct, Separate, and Sovereign

T he events of the mid-to-late 1980s and early 1990s drew on the Ottawas' ability to adapt to changed circumstances. Encouraged by NMOA victories in the 1960s and 1970s, the Ottawas continued to push for restitution for over a century of injustice. The 1980s saw the breakup of the NMOA, the evolution of the Thornapple Band into the Little River Band, and federal reaffirmation of the Little River Band's tribal sovereignty. Since their ancestors moved from their Grand River villages to reservations in the late 1850s, the Ottawas of Mason and Manistee counties identified themselves by several different names. However, the community remained the distinct, separate, and sovereign band it had always been.

The path to reaffirmation began during the NMOA years. In 1973, the Ottawas filed a lawsuit regarding their rights to hunt and fish on the lands their ancestors ceded to the United States in 1836. In 1979, a United States district-court judge ruled in the Ottawas' favor, restoring their right to fish in the Great Lakes without state regulation. The judge overturned over 130 years of error by ruling that the 1855 Treaty of Detroit did not terminate the Ottawas' government-to-government relationship

■ Anna (née Sam) Lempke and Katie (née Sam) Glocheski on a fishing trip in May 1983. These two women have been fishing companions for nearly thirty years, and, now in their seventies, still go on fishing trips together. Private collection of Katherine (née Sam) Glocheski.

■ Julia Theodore's home was the last house remaining at Indian Village when it was torn down in the mid-1970s. Julia and her children built the house in the late 1930s, and she lived there until the late 1960s. Katie (née Sam) Glocheski and two neighbors are walking towards the house in this photograph, taken in 1968. Private collection of Katherine (née Sam) Glocheski.

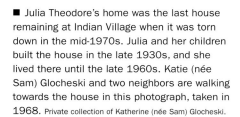

■ The first Tribal Council under the Tribe's new constitution. 1999. *Front row, left to right*: Connie (née Sam) Waitner, Kathy (née Koon) Berentsen, Joan Spalding, Elaine (née Beaton) Porter, and Carol (née Wahr) Bennett. *Back row:* Lisa McCatty, Chuck Fisher, Bill Willis, and Don Koon Sr. Courtesy of Little River Band of Ottawa Indians Historic Preservation Department.

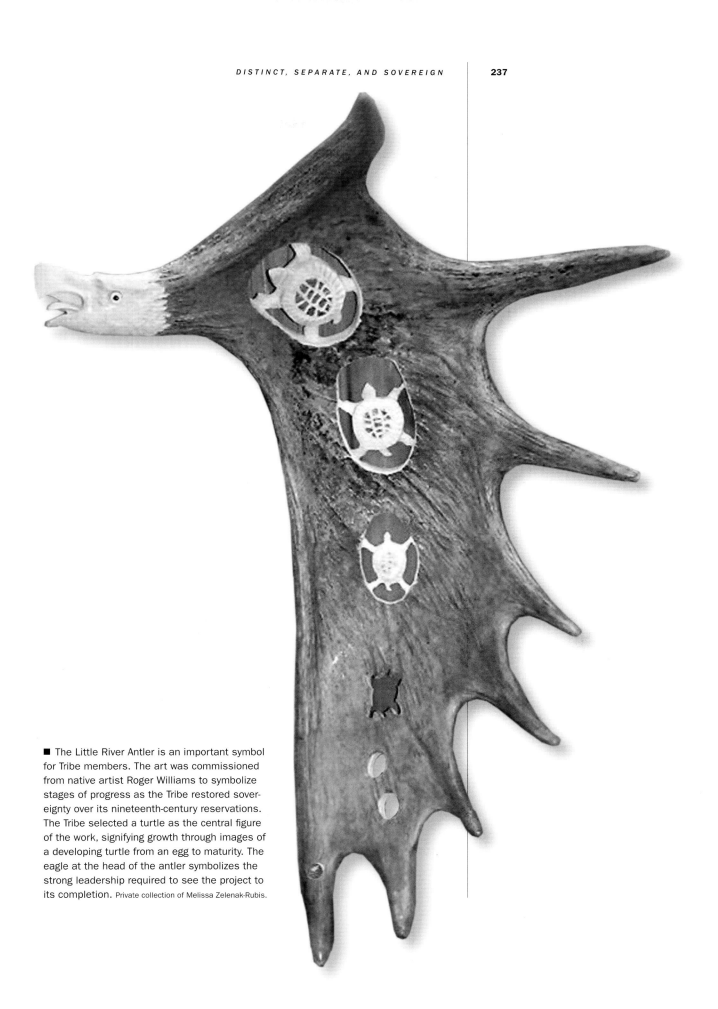

■ The Little River Antler is an important symbol for Tribe members. The art was commissioned from native artist Roger Williams to symbolize stages of progress as the Tribe restored sovereignty over its nineteenth-century reservations. The Tribe selected a turtle as the central figure of the work, signifying growth through images of a developing turtle from an egg to maturity. The eagle at the head of the antler symbolizes the strong leadership required to see the project to its completion. Private collection of Melissa Zelenak-Rubis.

■ On October 16, 1994, the Little River Ottawas held a formal celebration in honor of their federal reaffirmation. The event featured a processional, of which Steve Medacco—pictured here in full regalia—was part. Courtesy of Little River Band of Ottawa Indians Historic Preservation Department.

■ In honor of federal reaffirmation of their tribal status, the Little River Ottawas were named grand marshals of the 1995 Manistee National Forest Festival Parade, which travels through historic downtown Manistee. On the float are Lavern (née Whar) Oren, Elizabeth Bailey, Katie (née Sam) Glocheski, Jonnie Sam Sr., Ruth (née Koon) Dean, Margaret (née Bailey) Chandler, John Koon, and Anna (née Sams) Lempke. Courtesy of Little River Band of Ottawa Indians Historic Preservation Department.

with the United States after the allotment of reservation lands in the 1870s.[1] The federal government's mistaken belief that the Ottawas had ceased to be a sovereign and distinct tribe in 1855 had denied the Ottawas desperately needed assistance for over a century—a need paradoxically created by unfulfilled treaty stipulations.

In the mid-1970s, the federal government once again investigated and assessed the Ottawas' social and economic circumstances, beginning in 1975 when Congress created the American Indian Policy Review Commission (AIPR) to investigate the condition of Indian tribes throughout the United States. In the AIPR's *Final Report*, the commission made 206 specific recommendations regarding issues of importance to American Indian tribes. The commission specifically reported on the status of tribes like the Ottawas, who were excluded from federal services and prevented from exercising their governmental prerogatives—not because their tribes had ceased to exist, but due instead to the "accidents and vagaries of history."[2] On its list of tribes unjustly denied the status of federal recognition, the AIPR noted the Thornapple Band specifically. Under the umbrella of the NMOA, the Ottawas could have capitalized on the findings of the AIPR and the 1979 district-court ruling by immediately pressuring the federal government to reaffirm the sovereignty of the Ottawa Tribe. However, this did not happen—at least not right away.

The question of which form Ottawa government would next take—whether all of the Michigan Ottawa communities would be recognized as a single tribe represented by the NMOA, or as individual entities—was debated throughout the 1970s. The Grand Traverse Band of Ottawa and Chippewa Indians (NMOA Unit Two) ended this debate in 1980. That year, the Grand Traverse Band petitioned the United States for federal recognition, separate from the NMOA, and received the status of a federally recognized tribe. This success upset the political balance and unity that the NMOA member communities had enjoyed since 1948. NMOA leaders attempted to follow the Grand Traverse Band's lead by beginning the paperwork necessary to participate in the Federal Acknowledgment Process (FAP) in 1979, but the organization's founder and president, Waunetta Dominic, died before the petition was completed. After her death in 1980, the NMOA's leadership did not follow through with the FAP petition. These events changed the course of Ottawa politics: if the NMOA could not represent all of the Ottawa bands, each band would have to be acknowledged separately.

■ The Little River Ottawas participated in the Manistee National Forest Festival since its inception in the early 1930s. Here, Daniel McGowan, Yvonne Theodore King, Sandy Renner, Julia Theodore, Jonnie J. Sam II, Chief James Koon Sr., Helen Wahr, Millicent (née Skocelas) Biers, and an unknown woman, boy, and girl ride the Tribe's float in the 1971 festival parade. Courtesy of Jonnie J. Sam II.

■ Little River Ottawas (*left to right*) Lavern (née Wahr) Oren, Anna (née Sams) Lempke, Elizabeth (née Theodore) Bailey, and Ruth (née Koon) Dean participate in the 1995 Manistee National Forest Festival. Courtesy of Little River Band of Ottawa Indians Historic Preservation Department.

■ *Left to right:* Katie (née Sam) Glocheski, Jonnie Sam Sr., and his grandsons Ryan and Zach Szpliet at the 1995 Manistee National Forest Festival. Courtesy of Little River Band of Ottawa Indians Historic Preservation Department.

■ Elizabeth (née Theodore) Bailey and John Koon (*in front, left to right*), and Lavern (née Wahr) Oren, Anna (née Sams) Lempke (holding one of her great-grandsons), and Margaret (née Bailey) Chandler (*in back*) ride the Tribe's float at the 1995 Manistee National Forest Festival.
Courtesy of Little River Band of Ottawa Indians Historic Preservation Department.

The issue of Great Lakes fishing resurfaced in 1983 when Bay Mills Chippewa fishermen dropped gill nets into Lake Michigan between Muskegon and Manistee and the Little River Ottawas became the target of hostility in the local non-Indian community. The Little River Ottawas wanted to combat this animosity, make their distinct identity known, and voice their disagreement with the Chippewas' use of gill nets in Lake Michigan. However, internal political divisions among the members of the Thornapple Band prevented them from organizing clear representation on these matters. The Thornapple Band was, like the Grand Traverse Band, eligible to apply for acknowledgment through the FAP, but lack of access to federal records and the financial resources to obtain them slowed the process.

The leaders of the Thornapple Band used the joint issues of responding to local matters created by Great Lakes fishing and the exercise of tribal sovereignty to focus community awareness and reinvigorate their political organization. To help overcome the factional disputes in the Thornapple River Band organization, leaders created a second state-chartered corporation: the Little River Band of Ottawa Indians, Inc. Anna Mae (née Sams) Lempke, her sister Anna Jean (née Sams) Guenthardt, and Lavern (née Wahr) Oren (all great-granddaughters of William Paquodush), as well as Anna Mae (née Sams) Lempke's daughter Connie (née Lempke) Waitner, and Connie's cousin Millicent (née Skocelas) Biers, chartered the Little River Band of Ottawa Indians, Inc., in 1983. They chose this

■ Tribe members gathered at Horseshoe Bend on May 15, 1994, to clean up the property. This parcel was the first land returned to the Tribe after its federal reaffirmation. *Left to right:* John Pete, Margaret (née Bailey) Chandler, Anna (née Sams) Lempke, Theresa Koon, John Koon, Jean Guenthardt, Ruth Dean, Percy Campeau, and Gordon Guenthardt. Courtesy of Little River Band of Ottawa Indians Historic Preservation Department.

■ Little River Ottawas were among the Native American dancers who performed at the Celebrate! Woodland Heritage event at Manistee's Ramsdell Theatre in September 1992. *Front row, left to right*: Elizabeth Gonzales, unidentified girl, unidentified boy, Spring Hugo, and Doug Wilson. *Back row:* Martha Brushman, Jeremy Wilson, and unidentified man. Center child: Shianne Gonzales. Courtesy of Little River Band of Ottawa Indians Historic Preservation Department.

name for their organization because a local utility company had donated to the Tribe a small parcel of land on the shore of the Little Manistee River, which was a piece of the reservation that their families had used and occupied since the mid-nineteenth century.

The Ottawas of Mason and Manistee counties quickly came together in support of the Little River Band. A local Indian pastor of the Nazarene Church, Reverend David Wolf, helped to recruit local families to form a board of directors. Officers of the newly formed corporation included the children, grandchildren, and great-grandchildren of the leaders who had served the historic band for the nearly 130 years since the final treaty between the Ottawas and the United States was signed in 1855. By 1984, the Little River Band began the work of educating the non-Indian people in the communities of Mason and Manistee counties about the Ottawa Indians who lived in the area, and the Little River Band also began to exercise the prerogatives of tribal government.

The Little River Band, as a tribal government, worked with National Forest Service employees to administer land within the Manistee Reservation throughout the 1980s. The National Forest Service relied on the Little River Ottawas to guide its efforts to repatriate remains taken from Indian burial sites within the reservation boundaries. The Little River Band also applied for and received a grant from the United States Department of Health and Human Services to begin a tribal business.

■ *Left:* Torreano Lewis, son of Henry and Marsella Lewis. 1985. Private collection of George Pego.

■ *Center:* Edward (Chuck) Sherman Jr., son of Mary (née Pego) and Ed Sherman. 1989. Private collection of George Pego.

■ *Right:* Paul Cooper, ca. 1980s. Cooper is the grandson of Paul Lewis, who was killed at Normandy during World War II. Private collection of George Pego.

■ Steve Medacco is dressed in regalia to dance at a Girl Scouts jamboree in north Muskegon. 1985. Private collection of Steve and Dorothy Medacco.

Ottawa Sign and Design operated on the grounds of a National Forest Service compound on the Manistee Reservation; one of its first jobs was a Forest Service commission. Within five years, the leadership of the Little River Band drew a significant number of Mason and Manistee county Ottawas into the organization, and in the late 1980s, Little River Band members began to work towards reaffirmation of federal recognition of their community.

The Little River Ottawas began this work in 1988 by joining with the Little Traverse Bay Bands of Odawa Indians, the Pokagon Band of

■ Tom Chandler and his handmade black-ash baskets, 1988. Tom learned his art from his grandmother Elizabeth (née Theodore) Bailey. Many of his baskets are housed in museum collections. Private collection of Margaret (née Bailey) Chandler.

■ Wabsis-Bailey family portrait, 1990. *In front, left to right*: Zachary Wabsis and Ronald Sell. *Second row:* Brandy and Susan Wabsis. *Third row:* Niki and Doris Wabsis. In back: Daniel Bailey. Private collection of Dorothy (née Wabsis) Bailey.

Potawatomi, the Huron Band of Potawatomi, the Burt Lake Band of Ottawa and Chippewa, and the Gun Lake Band of Potawatomi Indians as members of the Confederated Historic Tribes, Inc. (CHTI). CHTI's mission was to help restore federal recognition to the many unrecognized Indian tribes in the State of Michigan. Soon after joining CHTI, the Little River Ottawas began working cooperatively with the Little Traverse Bay Bands (NMOA Unit One) to pursue, through federal legislation, restoration of the federal-trust status they had been denied since the 1880s. The Little River Ottawas received funding to hire a historian to begin research on their tribe's ethnohistory in 1989, and the next year, they filed a letter of intent to submit an FAP petition to the Bureau of Indian Affairs' Branch of Acknowledgment and Research. In 1991, the Little River Band received a $75,000 grant from the Administration for Native Americans (ANA) to hire and employ a director, enrollment officer, and secretary to initiate the work required to pursue reaffirmation. The Little River Ottawas immediately began registering members and their descendants.

The Little River Band and the Little Traverse Bay Bands began to educate congressmen and senators about the history of their tribe and bands. The Little River Ottawas began their story with the pretreaty

■ Beginning in 1989, the Little River Band of Ottawa Indians joined with the Little Traverse Bay Bands of Odawa Indians and petitioned Congress to restore their treaty-based relationship with the United States. In February 1994, representatives of the tribes testified in hearings before the U.S. Senate Select Committee on Indian Affairs. The testimony presented that day persuaded federal legislators to enact Public Law 103-324 on September 21, 1994, which restored federal recognition to the tribes.

Witnesses for the tribe were: (*left to right*) Hon. Frank Ettawageshik, Hon. Shirley Naganashe-Oldman, Hon. Daniel Bailey, Hon. Katherine Glocheski, William J. Brooks, and James M. McClurken. Collection of the Little River Band of Ottawa Indians.

hunting, fishing, and gathering bands on the Grand River and its tributaries through their merging with the Ottawa bands on the Pere Marquette and Manistee rivers when their ancestors moved to reservations in the late 1850s. They narrated events about their dispossession during the allotment years; the impoverishment of their bands as American speculators, squatters, and settlers claimed title to reservation lands; and their gradual migration north and concentration on the Manistee Reservation during the early twentieth century. Little River elders told of the poverty of the 1930s as a product of their ancestors' dispossession and the local racism they had faced, and that through all of these years, their great-grandfathers, grandfathers, and fathers had continuously pressed the United States to live up to the intentions of the 1855 Treaty of Detroit.

In 1991, the Little River Band and the Little Traverse Bay Bands requested that federal legislation reaffirm their government-to-government relationship with the United States, to be introduced in Congress. During the next two years, the Little River Ottawas traveled to Washington, D.C., to meet with congressmen and to deliver testimony in support of their tribe. The State House of Representatives, the Saginaw Chippewa Tribe, the Sault Ste. Marie Band of Chippewa, the Bay Mills Indian Community, the Hannahville Indian Community, and the Manistee

County Commission also supported the Tribe by submitting resolutions of support for the Little River Band's reaffirmation. The House Interior and Insular Affairs Committee held hearings regarding the legislation, and soon after, Michigan's senators also introduced reaffirmation legislation in the Senate. In 1993, the reaffirmation legislation was reintroduced to a new Congress, and members of the Little River Band and the Little Traverse Bay Bands again traveled to Washington, D.C., to speak once again before the House Interior and Insular Affairs Committee. In 1993 and 1994, the House Interior and Insular Affairs Committee and the Senate Committee on Indian Affairs conducted more hearings and heard testimony in support of the tribes, delivered by nationally respected Native American leader Vine Deloria.

Perhaps the most poignant testimony was delivered by the Little River Band's chairman, Daniel Bailey, in his speech to Congress in February 1994. Before the Senate Committee on Indian Affairs, Bailey confidently stated:

> The Little River Band of Ottawa Indians has continued to act as a
> tribe from treaty times to the present. We are a kin-based community

■ The 1994 Senate hearing was also attended by delegations from the Pokagon Potawatomis, who, in this photograph, are seated in the audience immediately behind the witness table. They are (*left to right*) Tom Topash, Rae Daugherty, James Keedy, Mike Daugherty, and Joseph Winchester. Burt Lake Band of Ottawa and Chippewa Indians chairman Carl Frazier and tribal manager Gary Shawa are seated behind the Pokagon delegation. Collection of the Little River Band of Ottawa Indians.

■ Little River Band chairman Daniel Bailey testified that day about the six generations of his family members who had dealings with the United States, including Chief Cobmoosa, Wabsis, and Francis Bailey, all of whom signed the 1836 Treaty of Washington. Bailey shared his thoughts about tribal history and asked for a restoration of the Tribe's rights as a gift that his generation would leave to the generations that followed. Tribal council member Katherine (née Sam) Glocheski, in this photograph, reads her testimony about her early life at Indian Village. She spoke of the difficulties the Indian Village residents faced, and the efforts that her tribe had made to assert its treaty rights during her lifetime. Witnesses for the tribe were: (*left to right*) Hon. Shirley Naganashe-Oldman, Hon. Daniel Bailey, Hon. Katherine Glocheski, William J. Brooks, and James M. McClurken. Collection of the Little River Band of Ottawa Indians.

who make decisions about our common issues by the consensus of our members. For more than a century our members have worked to protect our treaty-based rights. We have passed the knowledge of who we are and the record of our rights from generation to generation from before the Americans came to our land to this day. . . . We have reminded the federal government of its responsibilities through Congress, the courts, and through the Bureau of Indian Affairs, and we have no plans to stop.

I am now a grandfather. . . . My tribe does not have the means to maintain tribal economic programs that will allow my children and grandchildren to remain in our community. We no longer own any common property that we can use to house our people or generate income. We lack basic health and human services that would help us overcome social problems that rob us of our human potential. I want my children and grandchildren to know that they are Ottawa Indians and to exercise the rights my grandparents have worked so hard to preserve. We have overcome these problems as our ancestors did—using our own initiative working together with the federal government as a tribe.[3]

■ Pearl Smith demonstrating basketry, ca. 1980s. Private collection of Elaine (née Beaton) Porter.

■ Elaine (née Beaton) Porter with one of her handmade split-black-ash baskets, ca. 1990. Private collection of Elaine (née Beaton) Porter.

■ Ruth (née Koon) Dean sits making baskets during the 1971 Manistee National Forest Festival. Private collection of Jim Koon.

■ Bridget (née Brushman) Cole. Courtesy of Little River Band of Ottawa Indians Historic Preservation Department.

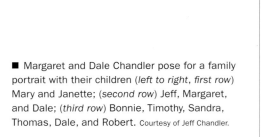

■ Margaret and Dale Chandler pose for a family portrait with their children (*left to right*, *first row*) Mary and Janette; (*second row*) Jeff, Margaret, and Dale; (*third row*) Bonnie, Timothy, Sandra, Thomas, Dale, and Robert. Courtesy of Jeff Chandler.

The story the Little River Ottawas told to Congress showed that they and their ancestors had contended against nearly overwhelming odds to maintain their Ottawa identity. Based on the Little River Ottawas' story, the evidence they marshaled, and the support of their local communities, legislation was introduced in Congress to reaffirm the Little River Band as a distinct community. The reaffirmation legislation passed in the Senate in May 1994, in the House of Representatives in August 1994.

On September 21, 1994, the president of the United States signed into law Senate Bill 1357, *To Reaffirm and Clarify the Federal Relationships of the Little Traverse Bay Bands of Odawa Indians and the Little River Band of Ottawa Indians as Distinct Federally Recognized Indian Tribes.* After over 150 years of dispossession, injustice, and outright denial of their indigenous identity, the Little River Band of Ottawa Indians received legislative reaffirmation of their standing as a sovereign Indian tribe within the United States. Back home, the newly reaffirmed Little River Band celebrated by holding its first annual Reaffirmation Feast on October 16, 1994, at the Knights of Columbus Hall in Manistee.

The Little River Ottawas have identified themselves in many ways throughout their history—the Grand River Bands, the Indian Town community, NMOA Unit Seven, the Thornapple Band, and the Little River Band—but their community has remained constant. The Little

River Ottawas have not assimilated, and their history is not a narrative of cultural decline. The changes they underwent represent the adaptations of a vital community to new sets of circumstances, which they navigated by relying on their historic patterns of subsistence and governance. They are members of an independent, kin-based band, who continue to practice and rely upon hunting, fishing, gathering, gardening, and reciprocal sharing. They join with their tribesmen in councils, which now take the form of business committees and organizations with elected officers in lieu of confederacies of ogemuk and headmen. Evolution and change mark any human community over time, and the Little River Ottawas are no exception. Still, the society that the Little River Ottawas and their ancestors created through ancient Ottawa political, economic, and social patterns has always been—and remains—distinct, separate, and sovereign.

■ Jonnie Sam Sr. on the steps of the U.S. Capitol. This photograph was taken on August 24, 1974, during one of the Tribe's early visits to Washington, D.C., to discuss federal reaffirmation. Collection of the Little River Band of Ottawa Indians.

■ Westward view of the Tribe's casino property at the corner of US 31 and M22 in Manistee, Michigan. Courtesy of Little River Band of Ottawa Indians Historic Preservation Department.

Constructing a New Government

F ederal reaffirmation of the Little River Ottawas' government-to-government relationship with the United States has allowed the modern Tribe opportunities for which they and their ancestors had worked and hoped for more than a century. After reaffirmation, the Little River Ottawas could not have foreseen the degree of success they would achieve in a few short years. From the mid-1990s to the turn of the twenty-first century, the Little River Ottawas created the constitutionally guided tribal government that Sampson Robinson had envisioned eighty years earlier. Though they waited for two years to receive federal cash appropriations due to them as a tribe newly restored to the list of federally recognized tribes, the Little River Ottawas spent the final years of the twentieth century constructing their new, sovereign tribal government. They worked to create the offices, departments, committees, and commissions that would form their government, and to establish the Little River Band's relationship with other communities, governments, and tribes in the Great Lakes region. The committees and commissions of the Little River Band's tribal government serve the tribal

■ Chief Judge Daniel Bailey swore in the Tribe's first ogema, Robert Guenthardt, on April 8, 2000. Courtesy of Little River Band of Ottawa Indians Historic Preservation Department.

■ Ghost Suppers have long been a tradition among Little River Ottawas, and are now regularly scheduled annual events in the Little River community. At this 1994 Ghost Supper, attendees feast on a large potluck-style meal. Courtesy of Little River Band of Ottawa Indians Historic Preservation Department.

community and membership in diverse ways and uphold values that have transcended the entire history of the Ottawa people.

In order to establish this government, the Little River Ottawas had to complete the tribal constitution that they had begun drafting in 1994. Their constitution would establish the Tribe's government-to-government relationship with the United States, determine the rules by which the Little River Ottawas would govern themselves, and provide legitimacy for the Tribe's interaction with other governments at the local, state, and federal levels. One of the first advisory committees created by the Little River Band's newly reaffirmed Tribal Council was the Constitutional Review Committee. The members of this committee helped the Tribal Council to revise the 1994 draft constitution by soliciting input from the membership during public hearings. In 1997, the Little River Band completed its revised constitution, which was adopted by the Tribal Council, ratified by the tribal membership by majority vote, and submitted for approval to the federal government. On July 10, 1998, the United States approved the Little River Band's Tribal Constitution, which is the formal governing document of the Tribe.

The Little River Band's Tribal Constitution created a democratically elected government patterned after that of the United States, with three branches—legislative, executive, and judicial—guided by a system of checks and balances. A nine-member Tribal Council, elected every four years by the voting membership, makes up the legislative branch of the Little River Band's government, and it functions much like the United States Congress. The Little River Band Tribal Council is obligated by the constitution

1. to govern the conduct of members of the Little River Band and other persons within its jurisdiction;
2. to promote, protect and provide for public health, peace, morals, education and general welfare of the Little River Band and its members;
3. to provide by ordinance for the jurisdiction of the Tribe over Indian Child Welfare matters, and all other domestic relations matters; [and]
4. to provide for the manner of making, holding and revoking assignments of the Little River Band's land or interests therein.[1]

■ Jerry Ramsey attends the Tribe's 2004 *Jiing-tamok* garbed in handmade regalia, including an otter turban. Private collection of Melissa Zelenak-Rubis.

■ Ruth (née Koon) Dean attends a dedication ceremony at Highbridge, 1996. Courtesy of Little River Band of Ottawa Indians Historic Preservation Department.

The Tribal Council is also charged with ratifying agreements and contracts made by the executive branch with other governments, acquiring and disposing of property and assets for the Tribe, hiring legal counsel, creating regulatory commissions, delegating the work of managing tribal properties, holding meetings, and approving judiciary appointments. In short, the Tribal Council is mandated to "take action, not inconsistent with this Constitution or Federal law, which shall be necessary and proper to carry out the sovereign legislative powers of the Tribe."[2]

The Tribe's executive branch is headed by an ogema, who is elected by Tribe members to a four-year term and fills a role much like that of the president of the United States. The ogema enforces and executes the laws, ordinances, and regulations passed by the Tribal Council; consults with the Tribal Council; and, under some circumstances, can veto actions of the Tribal Council. The ogema's office oversees the management of the tribal government, makes agreements with other governments, appoints judges to the Tribal Court, and prepares budgets. Since reaffirmation, four ogemuk have served the Tribe, and each descend from individuals who have had important leadership roles in the Tribe in the past: the Honorable Daniel Bailey (grandson of Cornelius Bailey), the Honorable Robert Guenthardt (great-great-grandson of William Sam), the Honorable Jonnie J. Sam II (great-grandson of William Sam), and the Honorable Lee Sprague (great-grandson of Joseph Medawis). The Honorable Patrick Wilson, ogema, traces his ancestry to treaty signatories Wabsis and Nekeyosay, whose descendants have long served the Tribe. The current ogema, the Honorable Larry Romanelli, is a descendant of Grand River ogema and treaty signatory Opego.

The Little River Ottawas have created their own Tribal Court and Court of Appeals—the judicial branch of the tribal government—which is charged by the Tribe's constitution to adjudicate civil and criminal matters involving Tribe members. Judges are elected by the tribal membership and serve six-year terms. Judges may be asked to review acts of the Tribal Council to ensure consistency with the stated authority of the legislative branch. As well, judges can charge fines and penalties for violations of tribal law, grant search warrants to the Tribal Police, and issue injunctions and orders. All Tribal Council members and the ogema are given their oath of office by a tribal judge.

The value of supporting one's family guides the Little River Band's tribal government in establishing social and political priorities. To

help them meet their constitutional mandates, the Tribal Council has appointed a number of commissions and committees, most of which were established immediately following reaffirmation. These entities were (and are) charged with considering community issues and making recommendations to the Tribal Council. Several of these committees and commissions grew out of a series of "strategic planning" meetings held between January and March 1995. Tribe members gathered at Stronach Township Hall in Manistee County to discuss the short- and long-term social, cultural, economic, and governance goals and values of their tribal organization and determine the needs of their community. Since March 1995, the Tribe has established ten advisory committees/ commissions to carry out the Tribe's goals and plans, and to provide an ongoing mechanism for community input and advice to the Tribal Council. Volunteers—many of whom also had full-time jobs and families

■ Little River Ottawa children attend a tribal Christmas party in 1995. Some of the children pictured here include Tim (Buddy) Oleniczak (*on floor by the tree, wearing blue*), Justin Gumieny (*in overalls*), Shawn Davis (*wearing geometric sweater*), Jonah Gumieny (*next to Shawn, on right*), and Zach Szpliet (*in white shirt on right*).
Courtesy of Little River Band of Ottawa Indians Historic Preservation Department.

■ Setup crew for the Tribe's first Pow Wow, which was held at the Onekama fairgrounds in 1995. Courtesy of Little River Band of Ottawa Indians Historic Preservation Department.

to care for—organized themselves into the Tribe's first commissions and committees: Constitutional Review (discussed above), Enrollment, Health, Cultural Preservation, Child Welfare, Economic Development, Natural Resources, Education, Housing, and Land Use/Management. These would become the building blocks and mainstays of the Little River Ottawas' tribal government. One in particular, the Enrollment Commission, was formed before the Tribe was reaffirmed, and has continued its work of reviewing applications for tribal membership to determine whether applicants meet the criteria outlined in the Tribal Constitution.

All governments have physical boundaries within which they exercise their sovereign authority. The Little River Ottawas directly govern within the territory defined in their constitution as

all lands which are now or hereinafter owned by or reserved for the Tribe, including the Manistee Reservation in Manistee County (Michigan), Custer and Eden Townships in Mason County (Michigan) and all lands which are now or at a later date owned by the Tribe or held in trust for the Tribe or any member of the Tribe by the United States of America.[3]

■ The Little River Band Tribal Council in session. Courtesy of Little River Band of Ottawa Indians Historic Preservation Department.

■ The grand opening of the Little River Casino Resort in July 1999 was cause for celebration in the tribal and local communities. Courtesy of Little River Band of Ottawa Indians Historic Preservation Department.

■ Ogemuk are sworn in by tribal judges. Here, tribal judge Daniel Bailey performs the swearing-in ceremony for Ogema Jonnie J. Sam II. Courtesy of Little River Band of Ottawa Indians Historic Preservation Department.

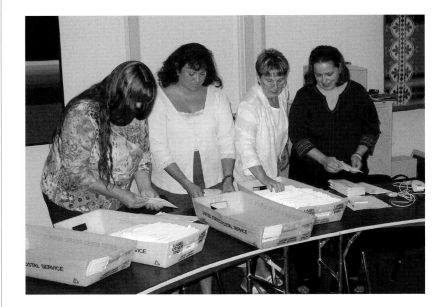

■ The Little River Band's tribal officers are elected by its members. After tribal elections, members of the Election Board sort and count ballots, as shown here. Courtesy of Little River Band of Ottawa Indians Historic Preservation Department.

■ One of the newly reaffirmed Little River Band's priorities was to reacquire lands important to the Tribe and its history. In 1996, as part of a legal settlement, Consumers Power Company signed over a 99-acre parcel of land that included part of historic Indian Village. Elders (*in back, from left to right*) Jonnie Sam, Robert Theodore, Margaret (née Bailey) Chandler; (*seated in front, from left to right*) Judy Schultz, Lavern (née Wahr) Oren, Ogema Robert Guenthardt, Tom Bowes, and Dick Gerkowski. Lavern Oren and Ogema Robert Huenthardt were the tribal representatives who attended the signing over of the land. Courtesy of Little River Band of Ottawa Indians Historic Preservation Department.

The Tribal Council and the great majority of Tribe members have made protection of the reservation boundaries and acquisition of land within these boundaries a priority. Ancestors of the Tribe lost title to land within their 1836 and 1855 reservations in a number of ways (see chapters 6 through 12), and the Tribe's contention that the reservation boundaries—the external lines described in their treaties with the United States—have never been extinguished by an act of Congress is important to the Little River Band. The lands within the boundaries of a reservation are defined by the United States as "Indian Country"; as such, under federal law, the Little River Ottawas retain the legal right to govern themselves within the boundaries of their treaty-preserved reservation.

■ The Tribe's first housing project—*Aki Maadiziwin*—began almost immediately after reaffirmation. *Aki Maadiziwin* was first comprised of eleven units built specifically for tribal elders. Shown here (*left to right*) are John Ross, Josephine Schondelmayer, Percy Campeau, Ruth Dean, and Phil Memberto at the groundbreaking ceremony. Courtesy of Little River Band of Ottawa Indians Historic Preservation Department; Melissa Zelenak.

One of the Little River Band's endeavors, which began immediately after reaffirmation, has been to restore reservation land to the ownership of the Tribe. The Tribal Council established the Land Use/Management Committee to carry out the work of developing a comprehensive plan for land acquisition, as well as standards and policies for the development of tribal lands. The first property restored to the Tribe's ownership was a 99-acre parcel lying ten miles east of Manistee on the Manistee River. The parcel included part of historic Indian Village, where Little River Ottawas congregated after their land had been taken by settlers. The land was returned to the Little River Band in 1996 by Consumer's Power Company as a result of a legal settlement. Several more parcels of reservation land were returned to the Tribe in 1999, also as part of this settlement.

Beginning in 1997, the Tribe began purchasing properties and buildings in the Manistee area for the operation of its government. In 1998, the Little River Band purchased several large parcels of land in and around Manistee, including Manistee's former Newland Academy, which became the Tribe's Justice Center. As well, the Tribe has purchased a restaurant in downtown Manistee, and land and buildings in nearby Eastlake. By 2000, the Little River Ottawas had already returned thousands of acres of reservation land to tribal ownership, including 580 acres along the Pere Marquette River in Custer Township—a piece of land that was known as the "Indian Town" reservation community in the nineteenth

■ The Little River Ottawas celebrated the resto-ration of their tribal status with a Reaffirmation Feast, the first of which was held on 16 October 1994 at the Knights of Columbus Hall in Manistee, Michigan. Jerry Koon Sr., Anna (née Sams) Lempke, and Don Koon Sr., pictured here, were just a few of the attendees. Courtesy of Little River Band of Ottawa Indians Historic Preservation Department.

century. The Tribe continues to search for land, office space, homes, and other properties—including places important to the Tribe's history and identity—to accommodate the services, housing, and other developments that have accompanied the Tribe's increasing membership. The lands returned to and purchased by the Tribe will provide Little River Ottawa families with a homeland for generations to come.

As in times past, tribal elders are respected and recognized for their knowledge, and their authority is acknowledged through the Elders Committee. The tribal officers who constitute the Elders Committee arrange and hold meetings for elders which are forums for discussion of issues of importance to the Tribe. Elders meet regularly for luncheons, organize trips to visit other Michigan tribes, and host dinners and programs for elders of other tribes—all activities that foster good relations among tribal communities in the Great Lakes area. The Little River Band has been—for all of its history—a community of people linked by kinship. Promoting understanding of the Tribe's history is so important to elders and Tribe members that they created the Department of Historic Preservation to preserve the Tribe's history, and to educate members about tribal history, language, and culture. The Cultural Preservation Committee, too, promotes culturally based community education activities, one of which was organizing the Tribe's first powwow in many years in July 1996.

Educating Little River Ottawas in subjects that promote the welfare of members and provide them with knowledge and skills necessary for citizenship in the modern Tribe is a high priority. Much responsibility of providing educational services to the tribal community falls to the Education Committee. Specifically, the level of education that Little River Ottawa children obtain has increased greatly since the Tribe began providing members with housing and other essential resources. A 1980 national survey reported that 17 percent of American Indian tenth-graders thought that they would complete a bachelor's degree; by 2002, this number rose to 36 percent. Comparatively, in 2006, 34 percent of Little River Ottawa high school graduates registered for college, signifying that—for the first time in a century—Tribe members are being educated in numbers comparable to those of other Indian tribes in the United States. To facilitate and promote educational achievement, the Education Committee provides scholarships for vocational and higher education.

The Tribe provides cultural education for youth, as well as educational opportunities for its children beyond those offered in public schools. Some of these include sponsoring students to pursue instruction in singing, dancing, and the arts, and to attend national seminars on subjects such as environmental awareness, issues of leadership, small-business creation and operation, and wildlife and ecosystem management. The Tribe supports activities and endeavors of this nature through its students, as well as tribal departments, programs, and projects. In addition, the Education Committee sponsors adult community-education programs.

Some of the events and conditions that make up the Little River Ottawas' story have led to the creation of other departments, programs,

■ Valerie Chandler, with her great-grandmother Elizabeth (née Theodore) Bailey and grandmother Margaret (née Bailey) Chandler, relax at one of the Tribe's first Pow Wows. This event was held at the Manistee County fairgrounds in Onekama, July 1996. Courtesy of Valerie Chandler.

■ Health care for Tribe members was one of the primary concerns discussed at the Little River Band's strategic-planning meeting, held immediately after reaffirmation in January 1995. Health care remains a central service and concern in the tribal community. Within the first few years after reaffirmation, the Little River Band's Health Center, located at 310 Ninth Street in Manistee, Michigan, was providing health care to Tribe members. Private collection of Melissa Zelenak-Rubis.

and projects. Several of these are designed to reunite families separated during the dispersal of the Ottawas in the difficult years of the early twentieth century, and to improve the quality of life within the tribal community. Among these are the Housing, Family Services, and Members Assistance departments, which are charged with providing for the most basic physical needs of the community. The Tribe's committees and commissions work together to oversee department services and projects meant to benefit the Little River community. For example, the Housing Commission, the Muschigong Construction Board, and the Elders Committee all influence the workings of the Housing, Family Services, Members Assistance, and Utilities departments.

Housing, in particular, quickly became an important concern in the tribal community. The Housing Committee established shortly after reaffirmation evolved into the Housing Commission by 1996, a shift that has enabled the Tribe to access funds for housing developments. To address housing concerns in the Little River community, the Housing Department acquires land, builds housing, and rebuilds or restores homes already standing in the community; these homes are then allocated to elders and low-income members and their families. Plans for the Tribe's first housing project, called "Aki Maadiziwin," were set in motion immediately after reaffirmation. By spring 2002, the twelve-home

■ The Tribe's Justice Department building and water tower stand just east of the Little River Casino Resort. The water tower provides water to the Tribe's casino and to its housing project. The Tribe's Justice Department building houses the Tribal Court, Tribal Police, Tribal Prosecutor's Office, and Tribal Peacemaking Office. Private collection of Melissa Zelenak-Rubis.

housing unit, built specifically for tribal elders, was completed, as were a sewer lift station and water-well house that service the housing project. The Tribe employs its own workers, who are responsible for the repair and maintenance of these homes, and the Tribe's Utilities Department provides safe drinking water and sanitation services to the community. Future development plans for Aki Maadiziwin include a community center. Because of community development projects like this one, Tribe members from locations all over the country have returned to the Ottawa homeland and rejoined their tribal community.

The Tribe invests in the well-being of its members in other ways as well. The Child Welfare Committee, for example, oversees tribal intervention in court proceedings that involve child-welfare matters among Tribe members. For many years, Little River Ottawa children were taken away from their parents by state social workers to be sent out for adoption, often to non-Indian homes. Many tribal elders have shared their experiences of being taken away from their homes and families, sent to schools in unfamiliar communities, and being placed in homes where they were unhappy. Through the Binojeeuk Commission, the Tribe works with state agencies to assure that children born to Tribe members are cared for by Indian families, in the event that foster care is required. The Tribe's Health Committee, which has since become the Health Board, instituted a health-care contract system, provides outreach services to the tribal community, and conducts health assessments. In more recent years, the Health Board established and operates a clinic that provides health and dental care to members of the Little River Ottawa community.

■ Neva and Jim Berry. Courtesy of Little River Band of Ottawa Indians Historic Preservation Department.

Restoring the Manistee-area environment and resources after years of depletion and degradation by lumbering and industry is another ongoing project of the Tribe. Caring for the natural world and the responsibilities of conservation fall to the Natural Resources Commission, which regulates the natural resources and protects the environment within the Tribe's jurisdiction. Initially, the Natural Resources Committee drafted regulatory codes for hunting, fishing, and gathering, and has since evolved into a commission that enforces these codes on the reservation. The Little River Band's Natural Resources Commission also maintains a full-time professional staff, including a wildlife biologist, a fisheries biologist, technicians, and water-quality specialists. Together with Tribe members, these individuals have conducted important research about populations of birds, deer, bear, bobcats, and fish in the area. They monitor species population numbers and the health of wildlife, and work to enhance the native plant species on which Little River Ottawas still rely, including wild rice, maple trees, and ash trees.

The Little River Band is responsible for funding its departments, programs, and projects, such as those mentioned above. An important source of funding for the Little River Band comes from the Little River Casino Resort. The Economic Development Committee initiated plans to build the casino, and oversaw state-tribal negotiations surrounding this economic venture. The Tribe unveiled plans to build the Little River Casino Resort on a large property it purchased along U.S. 31, just outside

■ After a long struggle against opposed parties, the Little River Band, along with the Little Traverse Bay Bands and the Pokagon Band of Potawatomi, the state of Michigan finally approved and signed a gaming compact with the tribes. Governor John Engler signing gaming compact. Courtesy of Little River Band of Ottawa Indians Historic Preservation Department.

of the City of Manistee. Faced with ardent, organized opposition to a gaming compact (signed between the Little River Band, Little Traverse Bay Bands, the Pokagon Band of Potawatomi, and the state of Michigan) kept those plans from coming to fruition until 1998, when the Michigan state legislature finally approved the agreement. In December 1998, the Tribe held a blessing ceremony and officially broke ground to begin construction of the casino. Anticipating the eventual materialization and operation of this facility, the Tribal Council established a Gaming Commission in 1997 to oversee the operation of the Little River Casino Resort. The facility opened to the public on July 23, 1999. Within just six months, the Little River Band built and opened an expansion. The Tribe has used income from the casino to build, open, and expand an adjacent hotel, making a resort destination for visitors to Manistee County.

To provide additional funding for the operation of their tribal government, the Little River Band also employs a staff of grant writers

■ On September 21, 1994, the tribal status of the Little River Band of Ottawa Indians was reaffirmed by the federal government when President Bill Clinton signed Senate Bill 1357 into law during a ceremony held in the Oval Office. Clinton signing. Courtesy of Little River Band of Ottawa Indians Historic Preservation Department.

who seek funds, especially from agencies and foundations that work to preserve the environment, promote sustainable communities, and tend to the welfare of community members. In addition, the Tribe provides resources that help members create their own businesses—enterprises that add to the financial stability of the Little River community.

In the years since reaffirmation, the Little River Ottawas have been rebuilding their community. Their leaders have crafted governing documents that define the tribal government's role and mission in community life, and tribal officers work hard to meet their constitutionally defined goals of governing, promoting, protecting, and providing for public health, peace, morals, education, and the general welfare of the Little River Ottawas. However, the work of the Little River Band's Tribal Council and government could not have succeeded if the members of the Tribe did not share their leaders' goals. Little River Band members, too, have continued to work hard to strengthen their Tribe's hold on treaty-preserved properties, enhance community relationships among their kin, and move the Little River Band forward into a new century and a successful future.

CHAPTER 26

An Ancient Community, a New Century

Reaffirmation has helped the Little River Ottawas to ensure the continuity of their distinct culture and society for generations to come. Under its new, federally recognized tribal government, the Little River Band has grown quickly and worked hard to rebuild a community damaged by state and federal assimilation policies aimed at destroying Ottawa culture, years of disenfranchisement and racial discrimination, and a century of economic hardship. The modern Little River Band's tribal government manages the Tribe's various responsibilities to its members, the local and tribal communities, and the natural world. Since reaffirmation, the Tribe has reacquired thousands of acres of land, become a leader in environmental protection and conservation, developed welfare services, undertaken economic and community development, and worked to preserve and promote Ottawa culture among members and in the local community. In the first years of the new century, the Little River Ottawas have remade their community once again, entering the twenty-first century as a productive, modern tribe.

■ The Stone family held their reunion at the Little River Band's Pow Wow in 2004. Private collection of Melissa Zelenak-Rubis.

■ Jingle dancers are lined up for the 2004 *Jiingtamok* Grand Entry. Jingle dresses are made with 365 cones, one sewn on each day of the year as the seamstress says a prayer. The jingle dance is a healing dance. Private collection of Melissa Zelenak-Rubis.

Today, the Little River Ottawas number over three thousand individuals—all of whom can trace ancestry to the Grand River Ottawas who lived in, or moved to, Mason and Manistee counties during the mid-nineteenth century. Half of the members of the modern Tribe live in nine Michigan counties—Kent, Lake, Manistee, Mason, Muskegon, Newaygo, Oceana, Ottawa, and Wexford—which constitute the territorial range, or what federal officers call the "service area," within which the Tribe provides health and welfare services to its members.[1] Roughly a quarter of the Little River Band members live in other Michigan counties, and

■ In summer 2004, the Tribe's Natural Resources Department released into the wild, on the Manistee River, two pairs of trumpeter swans. Since then, many more have been released in an effort to repopulate the river with this species. Private collection of Melissa Zelenak-Rubis.

■ Tribal ogema Patrick Wilson performs a men's traditional dance at the Little River Casino Resort. Private collection of Melissa Zelenak-Rubis.

■ Linda (née Moore) Hoover holds a handmade tobacco pouch. Hoover is a well-known tribal artist who sells her work all over the country. Private collection of Melissa Zelenak-Rubis.

another quarter live outside of Michigan—many in Wisconsin, where their grandparents moved to cut timber during the early twentieth century.

Although the Tribe has grown substantially since reaffirmation, it is a relatively small political entity, even when compared to the number of citizens in most small cities. The Little River Ottawas form a small, kin-based community of members with whom tribal officers often come into direct contact. At regularly scheduled membership meetings, tribal

■ Little River Ottawa women attend a class on black-ash basket making in 2004. Private collection of Melissa Zelenak-Rubis.

officers address and discuss issues with Tribe members themselves. Tribal officers are accountable to the people who elect them, and are specifically charged by the Tribe's constitution to work in the best interest of their constituents. Despite the personal nature of the Little River Band's tribal government, the Tribe's political processes have not been without challenges and conflicts, all of which are met and overcome through their own constitutionally governed initiatives.

Externally, the Little River Band has worked to create, negotiate, and maintain its relationships with local, state, and federal governments, as well as with other Indian tribes. The Little River Ottawas, along with the twelve other recognized tribes in Michigan, attended a Grand Council of the Three Fires in Mount Pleasant, Michigan, in March 2000, where Ottawa, Chippewa, and Potawatomi peoples discussed restoring the historical relationship between these three tribes. The Little River Band has joined with several of these tribes to pursue common goals, such as Great Lakes and inland fishing rights, tribal inclusion in efforts to protect and preserve water resources in the Great Lakes Basin, and issues regarding state gaming rights, agreements, and revenues. When issues arise that involve the larger Manistee/Ludington local communities, the Little River Band has forged alliances with community organizations to pursue common goals. For example, in recent years the Tribe joined

■ Little River Ottawas attend a reservation workshop in Grand Rapids in fall 2004. Private collection of Melissa Zelenak-Rubis.

■ In early 2004, Tribe members attended the first in a series of Gdoshkwaanagana Reservation workshops, programs designed to educate Tribe members about their tribe's reservation history. At this workshop, held in Milwaukee, Wisconsin, Tribe members learned about reservation history and read historical documents written by their ancestors regarding the Tribe's land. Among the attendees at this workshop were Ogema Lee Sprague, Tribal Council members, and other tribal staff members. Private collection of Melissa Zelenak-Rubis.

■ The Snow Snake Tournament (*Goonignebig*) is an annual event in the Little River tribal community. Everyone makes his or her own snow snake. Participants put lead weights in their snakes and decorate them, sometimes with clan symbols. The snakes are thrown down long tracks made of snow. Here, Carson Rubis participates in this traditional contest. February 2004. Private collection of Melissa Zelenak-Rubis.

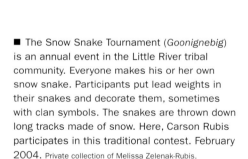

with a Manistee-area community group and successfully opposed an environmentally dangerous coal-burning plant proposal for Manistee, commonly referred to as the Tondu "Northern Lights" Project. The Little River Ottawas have also worked with the Manistee city council to administer grants received in 2002 by their separate governments for the benefit of the whole community—tribal and local.

Some of the Tribe's most significant and complex relationships—those with the state of Michigan and the city of Manistee—center around the Little River Band's most visible economic development project:

the Little River Casino Resort. Since the casino opened in 1999, it has undergone three expansions, which have added gaming space, new hotel wings, restaurants, an entertainment area, and a garden atrium. In 2004, the Little River Ottawas took over full management of the casino, an event that was cause for a large, tribe-wide celebration. Throughout its existence—from its grand opening in 1999 until 2006—the Tribe has used income from the casino to support the local community, to which the Tribe contributes 2 percent of its electronic-gaming revenue

■ Little River Ottawa attendees at the 2004 Muskegon Reservation workshop. Private collection of Melissa Zelenak-Rubis.

■ Ogema Lee Sprague speaks from the steps of the State Capitol in Lansing, Michigan, on April 28, 2004, to participants in a rally organized by the United Tribes of Michigan to oppose a bill that would break the gaming compact between the state and Michigan tribes. Private collection of Melissa Zelenak-Rubis.

■ Tribal artist Tim Gibson's paintings hang in many of the tribal buildings. Private collection of Melissa Zelenak-Rubis.

■ Tribal representatives attended a 2004 rally at the State Capitol in Lansing, Michigan, where Michigan Indian tribes voiced their opposition to a house bill affecting the gaming compact between Michigan tribes and the state of Michigan. *Left to right:* Ogema Lee Sprague; Tribal Council Speaker Steve Parsons; assistant tribal manager Lynn Moore; councilwomen Tammy Kleeman, Pamela Medahko, and Pat Ruiter; tribal elder Roger Sprague; and tribal councilman Brian Medacco (*crouching in middle*). Private collection of Melissa Zelenak-Rubis.

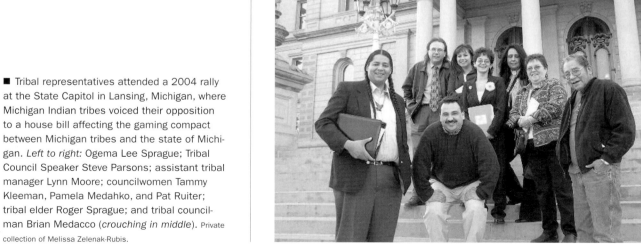

each year. Between 1999 and 2006, the Tribe's contribution has totaled over $10 million. The Little River Band has also become the largest employer in Manistee County, generating about 1,200 support jobs since reaffirmation.

The Little River Band also contributes to the entire Great Lakes region through its focused efforts to preserve and protect the environment and wildlife. Together, the Little River Band, the Little Traverse Bay Bands of Odawa Indians, and the Grand Traverse Band of Ottawa and Chippewa Indians joined with the Northwest Michigan Governmental Alliance to oppose the selling of Great Lakes water and slant-drilling in the Great Lakes, to control exotic species in the Great Lakes, and to place limits on land use, solid waste, and sanitation systems in the region. These same three tribes have also attempted to preserve Great Lakes water by suing Perrier (a brand owned by the Nestle Corporation) for violating the Water Resources Act of 1986, whose terms state that water taken from the Great Lakes Basin should not be sold outside of that region. The Little River Band allied with the United States Environmental Protection Agency (EPA) to challenge the Mercury Emission Credit Program, by which factories could avoid reducing mercury emissions by purchasing credits from cleaner plants and factories. Recently, the U.S. Forest Service signed an agreement with four tribes that were signatories to the 1836 Treaty of Washington to protect tribal people who gather medicines, transitional handicraft material, and cedar boughs from the Huron,

■ Ruth (née Koon) Dean signs a reservation workshop petition in 2004. Ruth is the only living signatory of the Tribe's 1937 petition for reorganization under the Indian Reorganization Act. *Private collection of Melissa Zelenak-Rubis.*

■ More than forty Little River Ottawas attended one of the reservation history educational workshops held in Watersmeet, Michigan, in 2004. *Private collection of Melissa Zelenak-Rubis.*

■ Raven and Kareen Lewis and Wabanung Bussey attend the Tribe's annual *Jiingtamok* in their handmade regalia. Kareen Lewis is wearing a jingle dress. Courtesy of Little River Band of Ottawa Indians Historic Preservation Department.

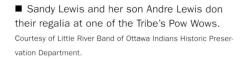

■ Sandy Lewis and her son Andre Lewis don their regalia at one of the Tribe's Pow Wows. Courtesy of Little River Band of Ottawa Indians Historic Preservation Department.

Manistee, and Hiawatha forests, and waives camping fees for members of these tribes in a number of federal forest campgrounds within the ceded territory.

Through its environmental and conservation efforts, the Little River Ottawas have established relationships with government agencies such as the EPA, the Department of Environmental Quality (DEQ), and the United States Department of Fish and Wildlife. In July 2001, the

■ Tribe members gather at membership meetings, held twice yearly, to learn about and discuss issues important to the tribal community. Often a potluck dinner is held, at which Little River Ottawas socialize and build community cohesiveness. Courtesy of Little River Band of Ottawa Indians Historic Preservation Department.

■ In 2004, the Tribe took over full management of the Little River Casino Resort, which was cause for a large celebration. Pictured here are (*left to right*) Tammy Kleeman, Pam Medahko, Steve Parsons, unidentified boy, Lisa McCatty, Ogema Lee Sprague, Israel Stone, and Pat Ruiter at the commemorative ribbon-cutting ceremony. Courtesy of Little River Band of Ottawa Indians Historic Preservation Department.

Little River Band received one of a total of ten EPA grants intended for efforts to reduce vehicle air emissions and promote energy efficiency. The Tribe later received an EPA Brownfield Assessment grant to clean up contamination sites at the Tribe's Gathering Grounds and Eastlake properties. The Department of Fish and Wildlife granted the Tribe funds to collect and analyze information on the bobcat populations in the Manistee area in 2004. The Little River Band has also brought air-quality monitoring to Manistee County in cooperation with the EPA and the DEQ, when, in 2006, the Tribe set up a station to monitor ground-level ozone and particulate matter.

Many of the Tribe's environmental protection and conservation efforts have been focused on Manistee's lakes and rivers, and their

■ Each year, the Little River Band hosts a Language and Culture Camp where tribal families gather for a weekend of camping, learning, and celebration of Ottawa culture. Programs include culture classes; instruction in traditional Ottawa arts and crafts such as hide tanning, basket making, and drum making; presentations on topics such as hoop dancing, flute playing, and natural medicines; and, of course, instruction in the Ottawa language, *Anishinaabemowin*. Presentations are in both English and *Anishinaabemowin*. Here, Ottawa language instructor Kenny Neganigwane Pheasant addresses the crowd of language-camp participants. Courtesy of Little River Band of Ottawa Indians Historic Preservation Department.

associated wildlife. The Tribe oversees the administration of fishing permits for waterways within the reservation borders, such as permits for salmon spearing and commercial fishing. The Little River Ottawas, along with other Michigan tribes, took part in a 2000 study of spawning reefs for lake trout restocking efforts. In 2003, the Tribe made a donation to the Conservation Resource Alliance to be used specifically for improving and preserving the Manistee, Little Manistee, and Pere Marquette rivers.

The Little River Band has monitored sturgeon populations in the Manistee River and its connecting waterways. Sturgeon—ancient inhabitants of the Manistee River—were declared endangered in 2002. In 2003, the EPA awarded the Tribe a grant to protect the Manistee River and document sturgeon activity within the watershed. The Tribe used the money to establish a stream-side rearing facility in June 2003, where the

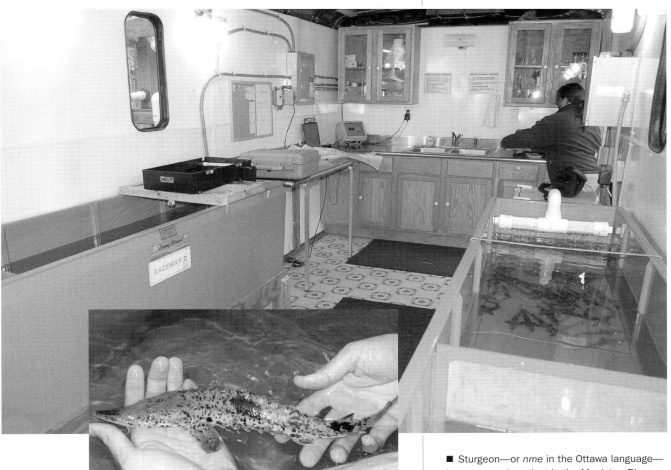

■ Sturgeon—or *nme* in the Ottawa language—became nearly extinct in the Manistee River due to the disruption of the natural environment that accompanied settlement of the area. One of the most significant projects of the Tribe's Natural Resources Department was to repopulate sturgeon in the Manistee River by breeding the fish in a streamside-rearing facility and releasing them into the wild. For the first time in over a century, sturgeon are spawning naturally in the Manistee River. Natural Resources Department.

■ Marty with kids and sturgeon. Natural Resources Department.

■ Each year, the Little River Ottawas participate in the Indian Family Olympics, held in Mount Pleasant, Michigan. Courtesy of Theresa Keshick.

■ LRBOI language instructor Kenny Pheasant teaches the Ottawa language in local-area schools in Manistee County, as well as coordinates and instructs the Tribe's annual Language and Culture Camp. Here, Pheasant stands before a Kennedy Elementary classroom. Courtesy of Little River Band of Ottawa Indians Historic Preservation Department.

■ Migizi Business Camp. The program is sponsored by the LRBOI Education Department and has been recognized by Harvard University. Teachers introduce students to business procedures and entrepreneurial endeavors. Courtesy of Little River Band of Ottawa Indians Historic Preservation Department.

Natural Resources Department raises sturgeon. The Tribe held its first annual release of streamside-reared sturgeon into the Manistee River in 2004. After only a few years of tribal intervention, the Little River Band Natural Resources Department has documented the natural spawning of sturgeon in the river for the first time in nearly one hundred years.

Apart from its joint efforts with state and other local authorities, the Little River Band has undertaken its own environmental and conservation efforts in the Manistee area. The Tribe opened its own wastewater treatment plant in 2002. Between 2004 and 2006, the Tribe's Natural Resources Department has reintroduced approximately 3,000 pounds of wild rice into the Manistee Marsh at the mouth of the Manistee River and at the Red Bridge Marsh above tribal land near Tippy Dam. In 2006, the Tribe released eight trumpeter swans into the wild, as part of its ongoing effort to rehabilitate the species' population on the Manistee River. The Natural Resources Department has orchestrated the rehabilitation of several injured red-tailed hawks and other birds of prey, which have been released back into the wild at the places where they were found.

The Little River Ottawas come together to recognize these and other accomplishments of their tribal government's departments, and they also gather to socialize and celebrate. The growth and vitality of the reaffirmed Little River Ottawa community is evident in a number of membership-wide events. Each year, for example, the Tribe commemorates the day that President Bill Clinton signed the act reaffirming the Tribe's relationship to the United States (on September 21, 1994) by

■ Little River Ottawa elder Alyce Giltz, dressed in traditional regalia. Courtesy of Little River Band of Ottawa Indians Historic Preservation Department.

■ Many Little River Ottawas served in the U.S. Armed Forces in all of the major wars. The Tribe honored its veterans by holding a special feast commemorating the creation of the Veterans Warrior Society on November 4, 2000. Shown here are its members, ca. 2000. Courtesy of Little River Band of Ottawa Indians Historic Preservation Department.

■ Chief tribal judge Daniel Bailey. Private collection of Melissa Zelenak-Rubis.

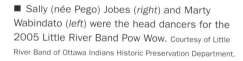

■ Sally (née Pego) Jobes (*right*) and Marty Wabindato (*left*) were the head dancers for the 2005 Little River Band Pow Wow. Courtesy of Little River Band of Ottawa Indians Historic Preservation Department.

holding a Reaffirmation Feast. The first of these was held on September 24, 2001. That year, the Little River Band's Natural Resources Department held its first Fall Feast on September 8. The Tribe hosts an annual powwow—called *Jiingtamok*—each July that draws participants from throughout the nation. The *Jiingtamok* is held at the Gathering Grounds, a place where Tribe members come together for feasts, camps, celebrations, and even weddings. Over the years since reaffirmation, the Tribe has continually improved the Gathering Grounds by adding such things

■ Tribe member Michelle Wellman performs a traditional dance at the Tribe's *Jiingtamok*. Courtesy of Little River Band of Ottawa Indians Historic Preservation Department.

■ Tribal councilwomen (*left to right*) Pam Medahko, Elaine Porter, Pat Ruiter (*in back*), Tammy Kleeman, and Lisa McCatty pause for a photograph during their visit to the 2004 Tribal Summit meeting held at the Little River Casino Resort. Private collection of Melissa Zelenak-Rubis.

as a bath house, handicap-accessible deck, a pavilion, an elders' seating area, a permanent arbor, an emcee stand, and fencing.

On Memorial Day, Tribe members gather to clean and repair markers in cemeteries where their ancestors rest. The Tribe's Veterans Warrior Society—comprised of men and women who served in the United States Armed Forces—also holds events on Memorial Day and at other times during the year. The Tribe commemorated the creation of the Veterans' Warrior Society by holding a special feast on November 4, 2000. To

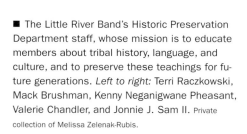

■ The Tribe's Natural Resources Department staff. *Front row, left to right*: Teresa Romero, Stephanie Ogren, Bonnie Harnish, Justin Chiotti, and Darin Griffith. *Back row:* Grant Poole, John Bauman, Archie Martell, Mike Snyder, Ken Le-Haye, Mark Knee, Jeremy Howe, Bob Sanders, and John Grocholski. (Absent: Marty Holtgren, Nate Svoboda, Frank Beaver, Israel Stone, Jimmie Mitchell, and Rochelle Rollenhaggen.) Private collection of Melissa Zelenak-Rubis.

encourage its members to live healthfully, the Tribe holds a Wellness Walk, participates in the Michigan Indian Olympics, and offers classes on various topics related to a healthy lifestyle. As well, symposiums on wildlife and environmental issues are well attended by Tribe members. The many more events that Little River Ottawas host and attend each provide opportunities to strengthen relations that contribute to the rebuilding of the Tribe.

Many events in the Little River Ottawa community focus on preserving the Tribe's unique culture and history. In particular, perpetuating

■ The Little River Band's Historic Preservation Department staff, whose mission is to educate members about tribal history, language, and culture, and to preserve these teachings for future generations. *Left to right:* Terri Raczkowski, Mack Brushman, Kenny Neganigwane Pheasant, Valerie Chandler, and Jonnie J. Sam II. Private collection of Melissa Zelenak-Rubis.

the Ottawa language is of critical importance to the Little River Ottawas, because the words of their ancestors convey a unique worldview that is the center of Ottawa culture. The Tribe offers year-round weekly language instruction to members, and sponsors an annual Language and Culture Camp, where students of all ages spend several days in workshops with Ottawa-language speakers, who facilitate students' immersion in the language. The Tribe's language-instruction efforts have extended into the local community as well; in 2002, tribal language instructor Kenny Pheasant began working with the public school board to develop and offer Native language classes at Manistee's Kennedy Elementary School. The Tribe has since developed and distributed two CD-ROMs to promote the *Anishinaabe* language, and has created the first and only Ottawa

■ Ogema Patrick Wilson. Private collection of Melissa Zelenak-Rubis.

■ Tribal Court staff (*left to right*): Sandy Walters, Steve Lewis, Deborah Miller, and Kris Peterson. Daniel Bailey in front. Private collection of Melissa Zelenak-Rubis.

■ The Bailey family celebrated the ninetieth birthday of their matriarch—Elizabeth (née Theodore) Bailey—in May 2000. Elizabeth, sitting in a wheelchair in the center of the picture, is surrounded by her entire family. Courtesy of Elizabeth (née Theodore) Bailey.

■ Kleeman and Deverny family. Private collection of
Melissa Zelenak-Rubis.

■ Employees in each department of the Little
River government take turns serving a monthly
luncheon for their fellow workers. Little River Band
employee luncheon. Private collection of Melissa Zelenak-Rubis.

■ The Little River Band takes its stewardship of
the natural environment seriously. The Natural
Resources Department has undertaken the
rehabilitation of several injured red-tailed hawks
and other birds of prey found in the area. Here,
Teresa, a department employee, holds a baby
red-tailed hawk about to be released back into
the wild. Red-tailed hawk with Teresa. Courtesy of Little River
Band of Ottawa Indians Historic Preservation Department.

language website, called *Anishinaabemowin*, currently ranked as one of the top-rated language sites on the Internet.

The Little River Band holds educational workshops to help restore lost cultural and historical knowledge. Ancestors of today's Little River Ottawas who dispersed across the Michigan landscape had few resources with which they could convey tribal history. Family stories passed from individual to individual, but the cultural and historical accounts of the Ottawa Tribe were often forgotten. At some workshops, Tribe members teach and learn black-ash basketry and porcupine-quill work. These arts convey important cultural meanings to Tribe members, and elicit discussions about earlier times when whole families exercised these artistic skills and sold their work simply to earn enough money to survive. Historical seminars focus directly on documenting and conveying historical details (like those presented in this book), specifically to help people

■ Since 2004, the Tribe's Natural Resources Department has reintroduced approximately 3,000 pounds of wild rice into the Manistee Marsh at the mouth of the Manistee River, and at the Red Bridge Marsh above tribal land near Tippy Dam. Private collection of Melissa Zelenak-Rubis.

■ The Little River Band is now the largest employer in Manistee County, generating about 1,200 support jobs since reaffirmation. Many Tribe members and residents of the Manistee area are employed at the Little River Casino Resort. Shown here are some of the Tribe members on the casino resort staff. Private collection of Melissa Zelenak-Rubis.

■ The Little River Band of Ottawa Indians Tribal Council, 2007. Front (*left to right*): Janine Sam, Elaine (née Beaton) Porter, Pat Ruiter, Kim (née McClellan) Alexander. Back (*left to right*): Norbert Kelsey, Don Koon Jr., Shannon Crampton, Israel Stone, and Steve Parsons. Department of Public Information.

■ The newly restored Tribe welcomed those descendants of people who had left the community during the difficult years after the Great Depression. Here, the grandchildren of Moses Bailey gather for a family reunion in 1997. *Front row, left to right*: Linda Parham, Lolita Ivory, Tonka Lones. *Second row*: James Lones, Helen Price, Delia Ross, Roberta Tate, Renetta Barnette. *Third row*: Allen Lones, Timmy Lones, Glen Lones, Wayne Lones, Dale Lones, and Robert Lones. Family reunion. Courtesy of the Lones Family.

who have been estranged from the Tribe during the twentieth century learn how and why their community dispersed throughout Michigan and neighboring states. All of these events attract large numbers and are valuable to the tribal community. In addition, the Tribe sponsors "reservation workshops," where members can learn about the Tribe's political history in relation to reservation issues.

Today, the Little River Band of Ottawa Indians is a vital and growing community. It has evolved from historical nineteenth- and twentieth-century communities of Ottawas who lived in villages on the Grand River and later migrated to the Manistee Reservation—within whose boundaries many members still reside today. Although they have been known by many names over the course of their history, the Little River Ottawas have always been a distinct community of individuals, bound

■ Little River Casino and Resort. Casino. Private
collection of Melissa Zelenak-Rubis.

■ The Little River Band of Ottawa Indians Tribal
Council, 2008. *Front, left to right*: Bob Harden-
berg, Pat Ruiter, Kim (née McClellan) Alexander,
Loretta Bacceria. *Back:* Steve Parsons, Don
Koon, Norbert Kelsey, Shannon Crampton. Private
collection of Melissa Zelenak-Rubis.

■ Ogema Larry Romanelli. Private collection of
Melissa Zelenak-Rubis

together by kinship and governed by leaders who build consensus around issues of importance to the whole community. Modern community leaders have accepted and continue to meet the challenges of rebuilding their Tribe, continuing to change and adapt—as their ancestors did—to changed and changing circumstances. They have used the resources at their disposal for the good of their Tribe and the larger community in which they live. They have determined that events of the past will not deter them from building a secure future for their children and grandchildren. The Little River Ottawas will continue to work towards a world that is a safe home for all living things.

Index of Tribal Councils and Ogemuk since Reaffirmation (1994)

Tribal Councilpersons

Kimberly Alexander

Anne Avery

Daniel Bailey

Carol Ann Bennett

Katherine Berentsen

Margaret (née Bailey) Chandler

Shannon Crampton

Charles Fisher

Norbert Kelsey

Kimberly Kequom

Tammy Kleeman-Brown

Don Koon Jr.

Don Koon Sr.

Jerry Koon

Lisa McCatty

Brian Medacco

Pamela Medahko

William Memberto

Stephen Parsons

Elaine Porter

Patricia Ruiter

Janine Sam

Joan Spalding

Israel Stone

Connie (née Sam) Waitner

William Willis

Ogemas

Robert Guenthardt

Larry Romanelli

Jonnie J. Sam II

Lee A. Sprague

Patrick Wilson

Tribal Judges

Daniel Bailey

Ryan Champagne

Ronald Douglas

Stella Gibson

Brenda Hyma

Michael Petoskey

Jonnie J. Sam II

Angela Sherigan

Abbreviations Used in the Notes and References

BBC   Bishop Baraga Collection, Bishop Baraga Archives, Marquette, Michigan

BIA-BAR   Bureau of Indian Affairs, Branch of Acknowledgment and Research, U.S. Department of the Interior

BIA-Durant   Bureau of Indian Affairs, Special Agent Files, Horace B. Durant, U.S. Department of the Interior

CCF   Central Classified Files, Records of the Bureau of Indian Affairs, National Archives and Records Administration, Washington, D.C.

DRO&CA   Documents Relating to Ottawa & Chippewa Allotments, microfilm, Michigan State University Library, East Lansing, Michigan

H. Exec. Doc. House Executive Document

HRSP-LOC   Henry Rowe Schoolcraft Papers, microfilm, Library of Congress, Washington, D.C.

LRMS&MA   Letters Received by the Michigan Superintendency & Mackinac Agency, 1849–1882, Entry 1131, RG 75, Records of the Bureau of Indian Affairs, National Archives and Records Administration, Washington, D.C.

LROIA	Letters Received by the Office of Indian Affairs, 1824–1881, National Archives Microfilms, Series M234, RG 75, Records of the Bureau of Indian Affairs, National Archives and Records Administration, Washington, D.C.
LSMA	Letters Sent by the Mackinac Agency, 1865–1868, 1877–1885, Entry 1133, RG 75, Records of the Bureau of Indian Affairs, National Archives and Records Administration, Washington, D.C.
LSOIA	Letters Sent by the Office of Indian Affairs, 1870–1908, Entry 96, RG 75, Records of the Bureau of Indian Affairs, National Archives and Records Administration, Washington, D.C.
NAM	National Archives Microfilms, National Archives and Records Administration, Washington, D.C.
NAM M1	Records of the Michigan Superintendency, 1814–1851, National Archives Microfilms, Series M1, RG 75, Records of the Bureau of Indian Affairs, National Archives and Records Administration, Washington, D.C.
RFP	Richmond Family Papers, Grand Rapids Public Library, Michigan, and Family History Division, Grand Rapids, Michigan
RG	Record Group
RG 75	Records of the Bureau of Indian Affairs, National Archives and Records Administration, Washington, D.C.
RG 123	Records of the United States Court of Claims, 1835–1958, National Archives and Records Administration, Washington, D.C.
S. Doc.	Senate Document

Notes

Introduction: The Analytical Paradigm

1. A Survey of Indian Groups in the State of Michigan, 1939, by John H. Holst, Supervisor of Indian Schools, ca. 1939, National Archives and Records Administration, Washington, D.C., RG 75, Central Classified Files, 1907–1939, Records of the Bureau of Indian Affairs [hereafter CCF], 1907–1939, General Services, 9634-1936, 066.

   Quoted in this report is Archie Phinney, a Nez Perce Indian who worked for the Bureau of Indian Affairs in 1939. Phinney was a founder of the National Congress of American Indians, of which the Little River Ottawas are now members.

2. During the 1970s and 1980s, a number of ethnohistorical monographs challenged the view of change in Indian life as a loss of culture. For examples of works in this genre, see Anthony F. C. Wallace, *The Death and Rebirth of the Seneca* (New York: Vintage Books, 1969); Bruce G. Trigger, *The Children of Aataentsic: A History of the Huron People to 1660* (Kingston, Ont.: McGill-Queens University Press, 1976); James Axtell, *The European and the Indian: Essays in the Ethnohistory of Colonial North America* (Oxford: Oxford University Press, 1981); and, most recently, Richard White, *The Middle Ground: Indians, Empires, and Republics in the Great Lakes Region, 1650–1815* (Cambridge: Cambridge University Press, 1991).

3. For recent examples of this perspective, see Eleanor Leacock and Richard Lee, eds., *Politics and History in Band Societies* (Cambridge: Cambridge University Press, 1982); and Emiko Ohnuki-Tierney, ed., *Culture through Time: Anthropological Approaches* (Stanford, Calif.: Stanford University Press, 1990).

Chapter 1. When the Europeans Came

1. Beverly Ann Smith, "Systems of Subsistence and Networks of Exchange in the Terminal Woodland and Early Historic Periods in the Upper Great Lakes," PhD diss., Michigan State University, 1996, 93.

2. Swidden agriculture is a type of agriculture that uses a slash-and-burn method of clearing land.

3. The Ottawas are referred to as "middlemen" in the fur trade in the following works, among others: Richard White, *The Middle Ground: Indians, Empires, and Republics in the Great Lakes Region, 1650–1815* (Cambridge: Cambridge University Press, 1991), 106–7; Lyle M. Stone and Donald Chaput, "History of the Upper Great Lakes Area," *Handbook of North American Indians*, vol. 15, *The Northeast*, ed. Bruce Trigger (Washington, D.C.: Smithsonian Institution, 1978), 602–3; Leo Gilbert Waisberg, "The Ottawa: Traders of the Upper Great Lakes, 1615–1700," master's thesis, McMaster University, 1977, 68; Johanna E. Feest and Christian F. Feest, "Ottawa," *Handbook of North American Indians*, vol. 15, *The Northeast*, ed. Bruce Trigger (Washington, D.C.: Smithsonian Institution, 1978), 773–74.

4. The *coureurs de bois* (translated from French as "woods runners" or "runners of the woods") were unlicensed traders under the regime of New France (in Canada) during the fur trade of the seventeenth through nineteenth centuries.

5. It is unlikely that the Grand River population exceeded 1,500 people in the eighteenth century. In the first accurate count of this population, in 1839, the Grand River Ottawas numbered 1,214 persons—only a little more than one half of the number of southern Michigan Ottawas estimated in 1765 (a figure which may have also included Ohio Ottawas as part of the Detroit population). These population estimates are taken from Johanna E. Feest and Christian F. Feest, "Ottawa," *Handbook of North American Indians*, vol. 15, *The Northeast*, ed. Bruce Trigger (Washington, D.C.: Smithsonian Institution, 1978), 774, 780.

Chapter 3. Coexistence and Conquest

1. Fur-trade posts located at Ottawa village sites became cities, often bearing Grand River Ottawa names. Manistee, Muskegon, Grand Haven, Grand Rapids, and Lowell all grew out of Ottawa villages where Louis Campeau had trading posts. Rix Robinson, supervisor of the American Fur Company's Grand River operations, had posts at Grand Haven and Nebawnaygezhick's village at Ada.

2. For a discussion on the Métis, see Jacqueline Peterson and Jennifer S. H. Brown, eds., *The New Peoples: Being and Becoming Métis in North America* (Lincoln: University of Nebraska Press, 1985).

3. This is apparent in many settlers' recollections of meeting the Grand River Ottawas and reporting how the Grand River Bands lived in the early 1830s. Maria Sanford, who arrived at an Ottawa village that would become the city of Ionia, exemplifies this approach in her remembrances of the Ottawas and their ways of life. Sanford notes that the land between the Grand River and the Straits of Mackinac were "full of tribes of Indians who are noted for their treacherous natures." When her traveling party came upon an Ottawa village, she wrote that the Ottawas dashed outside, throwing their "papooses" over their shoulders, to greet the strangers: "They came with red and black bars across one cheek, or a red daub on the forehead, which gave them a most grotesque and hideous appearance. The children were frightened, and clung closely to their mothers saying 'Don't let them get us!' We found it was only their curiosity, a quality they all possessed in a large degree, that brought the Indians out." For Sanford's full account, see "Pioneer Papers," *Ionia (Mich.) Standard*, 9 June 1893.

Chapter 4. The Will of the Grand Council

1. Frederick Baraga to Most Reverend Direction of the Leopoldine Foundation, 26 June 1834, Bishop Baraga Collection, Bishop Baraga Archives, Marquette, Mich. [hereafter BBC].

2. Ibid.

3. Ibid.

4. Isaac McCoy, *History of Baptist Indian Missions: Embracing Remarks on the Former and Present Condition of the Aboriginal Tribes; Their Settlement within the Indian Territory, and Their Future Prospects* (Washington, D.C.: William M. Morrison, 1840), 494.

5. Noahquageshik et al. to Andrew Jackson, 27 January 1836, National Archives and Records Administration, Washington, D.C., National Archives Microfilms [hereafter NAM], Series M234, RG 75, Records of the Bureau of Indian Affairs, Letters Received by the Office of Indian Affairs, 1824–1881 [hereafter LROIA], reel 422, frames 145–47.

6. Isaac McCoy, *History of Baptist Indian Missions: Embracing Remarks on the Former and Present Condition of the Aboriginal Tribes; Their Settlement within the Indian Territory, and Their Future Prospects*, 494.

Chapter 5. "Civilizing" the Ottawas

1. The Michigan Indians who did flee to Canada were primarily Potawatomis.

2. Hemlock bark is rich in tannic acid, a chemical essential for turning raw animal hides into leather.

Chapter 6. "Strong Titles" and the Government "Swan"

1. Nisawakwatt et al. to George Manypenny, 16 January 1855, National Archives and Records Administration, Washington, D.C., National Archives Microfilms [hereafter NAM], Series M234, RG 75, LROIA, reel 404, frames 561–62; Kapimose et al. to George Manypenny, 7 February 1855, National Archives and Records Administration, Washington, D.C., NAM, Series M234, RG 75, LROIA, reel 404, frames 562–63.

2. Ibid.

3. Henry Gilbert to George Manypenny, 6 March 1854, National Archives and Records Administration, Washington, D.C., NAM, Series M234, RG 75, LROIA, reel 404, frames 368–80.

4. Proceedings of a Council with the Chippewas & Ottawas of Michigan Held at the City of Detroit by the Hon. George W. Manypenny & Henry C. Gilbert, Commissioners of the United States, 25 July 1855, National Archives and Records Administration, Washington, D.C., RG 123, Docket 27978, 49.

5. Ibid., 6, 22–23, 29–33, 39–42.

6. Ibid., 7.

7. Proceedings of a Council with the Chippewas & Ottawas of Michigan Held at the City of Detroit by the Hon. George W. Manypenny & Henry C. Gilbert, Commissioners of the United States, 25 July 1855, National Archives and Records Administration, Washington, D.C., RG 123, Docket 27978, 7, 45.

8. Ibid., 73.

9. Charles J. Kappler, comp., "Treaty with the Ottawa and Chippewa, 1855," *Indian Affairs: Laws and Treaties* (Washington, D.C., Government Printing Office, 1904), 2:725–31; James M. McClurken, "We Wish To Be Civilized: Ottawa-American Political Contests on the Michigan Frontier," PhD diss., Michigan State University, 1988.

   Although the treaty would be interpreted differently only years after its ratification, both the Ottawas and federal officials intended that the United States would continue to interact with the Ottawas as a self-governing people. The language of article 5 of the 1855 treaty "dissolving" the "Ottawa and Chippewa Tribes," intended only to separate the Ottawas from the

Chippewas, would later be interpreted as an annulment of the Ottawas' self-governing status. This erroneous interpretation would cause many problems for the Ottawas in future years in their dealings with the United States, which were finally rectified in 1994 when the Little River Band received federal recognition. This was not before, however, the Ottawas endured over a century of dispossession and hardship, through which they relied steadfastly on the culture that had enabled their survival since their first contact with Europeans and Americans. For a detailed history of this story, see James M. McClurken, "We Wish To Be Civilized: Ottawa-American Political Contests on the Michigan Frontier," PhD diss., Michigan State University, 1988; Proceedings of a Council with the Chippewas & Ottawas of Michigan Held at the City of Detroit by the Hon. George W. Manypenny & Henry C. Gilbert, Commissioners of the United States, 25 July 1855, National Archives and Records Administration, Washington, D.C., RG 123, Docket 27978.

Chapter 7. "Not a Tent, a Wigwam, nor a Camp Fire . . ."

1. Andrew Fitch to J. W. Denver, 14 August 1857, National Archives and Records Administration, Washington, D.C., NAM, Series M234, RG 75, LROIA, reel 405, frames 533–36.
2. "The Indians at Pentwater," *Grand Rapids (Mich.) Daily Enquirer and Herald*, 8 June 1858.
3. "Natives," *Grand Rapids (Mich.) Eagle*, 4 October 1858.
4. "The Ottawas in Oceana and Mason Counties," *Grand Rapids (Mich.) Daily Enquirer and Herald*, 19 June 1858.
5. "Lo the Poor Indian," *Grand Rapids (Mich.) Eagle*, 10 May 1859.

   During this era, the popular press used the term "Lo" or "Lo, the Poor Indian" in articles about both individual Indians and collective groups and communities of Indians. This term was taken from the poem "Essay on Man" by Alexander Pope, which lamented the "disappearance" of Native American culture in the United States.

Chapter 8. New Communities, Established Leaders

1. Annuity payrolls, the numerous petitions the ogemuk sent to federal officers, and documents generated during the allotment process provide details about individuals and bring the emerging bands that comprised the distinct reservation communities into focus. Treaties and annuity payrolls are most useful for establishing band identity between 1855 and 1870. At

the treaty signing in 1855, federal agents carefully collected endorsements from every band leader to help avoid any pretext for later disputes. At subsequent annuity payments, the ogemuk played an important role in creating an accurate count of their band—listing heads of each individual band and household for the payroll, witnessing the payment, and attesting the correctness of receipts. Annuity payrolls therefore provide a great deal of useful information.

2. Ottawas & Chippewas 1868 Annuity Payment Roll, ca. 1868, National Archives and Records Administration, Washington, D.C., RG 75, Records of the Bureau of Indian Affairs, Entry 906, Annuity Payment Rolls, 1841–1949; Annuity Pay Roll of the Grand River Band of Ottawas & Chippewas of Michigan, 1870, National Archives and Records Administration, Washington, D.C., RG 75, Records of the Bureau of Indian Affairs, Entry 906, Annuity Payment Rolls, 1841–1949; Bureau of the Census, *Report on Indians Taxed and Indians not Taxed in the United States (Except Alaska) at the Eleventh Census: 1890* (Washington, D.C., 1894), 332–33.

3. Grand River ogemuk in 1865 were Nebawnaygezhick, Shawgwawbawno, Wawbegaykake, Simon Kenewegezhick, Maishkeawshe, Payshawsegay, Paybawme, Chingwashe, Shawbequoung, Cobmoosa, Maishcaw, Kawgay-gawbowe, Metayomeig, Maymeshegawday, Aishquayosay, Kawbayomaw, Paquodush, Joseph Medawis, Penase, and Awkebemosay.

4. In 1870 there were twenty Grand River bands counted: those of Nebawnay-gezhick, Aishkebawgosh, Wawbegaykake, Kenewegezhick, Maishkeawshe, Payshawsegay, Paybawme, Chingwashe, Shawbequoung, Maishcaw, Kawgaygawbowe, Metayomeig, Aishquayosay, Awkebemosay, Paquodush, Joseph Medawis, Penase, Mawbeece, Aken Bell, and Nawgawnequong. These twelve include Kenewegezhick, whose band received their payment among the Traverse bands in 1870.

5. The Michigan Indian Agency Register of Land Grants shows that the northern community included the Ottawas who settled in lower Crystal Township (Oceana County) and Mason County, as well as the indigenous bands already present in Mason and Manistee counties. The southern community comprised the Ottawas who settled at Elbridge (Oceana County) and Muskegon County.

Chapter 9. A "Great Excitement among the Indians"

1. Charles J. Kappler, comp., "Treaty with the Ottawa and Chippewa, 1855," *Indian Affairs: Laws and Treaties* (Washington, D.C.: Government Printing

Office, 1904), 2:725–31; George Betts to Edward Smith, 2 February 1875, National Archives and Records Administration, Washington, D.C., NAM, Series M234, RG 75, LROIA, reel 410, frames 296–98. [Note: This is the last piece of federal correspondence on file that makes mention of "agricultural goods and implements" being delivered to the Ottawas on the Grand River reservations.]

2. Andrew Fitch to Charles Mix, 2 October 1858, National Archives and Records Administration, Washington, D.C., NAM, Series M234, RG 75, LROIA, reel 406, frames 157–58.

3. Provisions of the 1855 Treaty had stipulated that "all lands remaining unappropriated by or unsold to the Indians after the expiration of the last-mentioned term [ten years], may be sold or disposed of by the United States as in the case of all other public lands." This clause had only given the federal government permission to sell 1855 reserve land after the Ottawas had selected their allotments, but the language was interpreted differently by Americans who wanted title to the yet unallotted Ottawa lands. American claimants argued that the treaty authorized the sale after ten years, whether or not the allotment process was completed. Charles J. Kappler, comp., "Treaty with the Ottawa and Chippewa, 1855," *Indian Affairs: Laws and Treaties* (Washington, D.C.: Government Printing Office, 1904), 2:725–31.

4. William Richmond to George Manypenny, 3 September 1855, National Archives and Records Administration, Washington, D.C., NAM, Series M234, RG 75, LROIA, reel 404, frames 950–52.

5. Nathaniel Taylor to Orville Browning, 27 January 1869, National Archives and Records Administration, Washington, D.C., NAM, Series M234, RG 75, LROIA, reel 408, frames 488–97.

6. Richard Smith to Lewis Bogy, 31 January 1867, National Archives and Records Administration, Washington, D.C., NAM, Series M234, RG 75, LROIA, reel 408, frames 214–17.

Chapter 10. Accidents of History

1. Statement of Pay-baw-me et al., 1 August 1866, National Archives and Records Administration, Washington, D.C., NAM, Series M234, RG 75, LROIA, reel 407, frames 982–83.

2. Nebawnagezhick et al. to United States of America, State of Michigan, 17 June 1865, National Archives and Records Administration, Washington, D.C., NAM, Series M234, RG 75, LROIA, reel 407, frames 1037–40.

3. Moses Shawbekoang et al. to Nathaniel Taylor, 8 May 1868, National Archives and Records Administration, Washington, D.C., NAM, Series M234, RG 75, LROIA, reel 408, frames 543–45.

Chapter 11. The Opposite of Intentions

1. The 1855 Treaty of Detroit provided for Ottawa purchases of additional land at $1.25 per acre. Under the 1872 Homestead Act, Ottawas only had to pay the filing fee.

2. *An Act for the Restoration to Market of Certain Lands in Michigan*, 10 June 1872, *Unites States Statutes at Large* 17:381; Department of Interior Circular by Willis Drummond and Columbus Delano, 5 July 1872, National Archives and Records Administration, Washington, D.C., NAM, Series M234, RG 75, LROIA, reel 411, frames 214–15.

    The Homestead Act of 1862 allowed persons over the age of twenty-one to select 160-acre parcels of "free" land from the public domain. Homesteaders were required to live on the land, make improvements (erecting houses and/or buildings, clearing fields, etc.), and farm for a period of at least five years, after which they could "prove up" their claim and receive a patent for the land parcel.

3. *An Act for the Restoration to Market of Certain Lands in Michigan*, 10 June 1872, *Unites States Statutes at Large* 17:381; Department of Interior Circular by Willis Drummond and Columbus Delano, 5 July 1872, National Archives and Records Administration, Washington, D.C., NAM, Series M234, RG 75, LROIA, reel 411, frames 214–15.

4. Moses Shawbekoung et al. to Ulysses Grant, 20 December 1872, National Archives and Records Administration, Washington, D.C., NAM, Series M234, RG 75, LROIA, reel 410, frames 1028–32.

5. A. C. Shaw et al. to the Senate and House of Representatives, 21 February 1874, National Archives and Records Administration, Washington, D.C., NAM, Series M234, RG 75, LROIA, reel 411, frames 216–19.

6. George I. Betts to Edward P. Smith, 5 October 1875, H. Exec. Doc. 1 (44–1) 1680, pp. 795–97.

7. Edwin Brooks to J. A. Williamson, 27 December 1877, National Archives and Records Administration, Washington, D.C., NAM, Series M234, RG 75, LROIA, reel 413, frames 64–103.

8. George Lee to John Smith, 13 January 1877, National Archives and Records Administration, Washington, D.C., NAM, Series M234, RG 75, LROIA, reel 412, frames 142–46.

9. George Lee to John Smith, February 1877, National Archives and Records Administration, Washington, D.C., NAM, Series M234, RG 75, LROIA, reel 412, frames 207–33.

10. Edwin Brooks to Ezra Hayt, 12 January 1878, National Archives and Records Administration, Washington, D.C., NAM, Series M234, RG 75, LROIA, reel 413, frames 104–36.

11. Edwin Brooks to J. A. Williamson, 27 December 1877, National Archives and Records Administration, Washington, D.C., NAM, Series M234, RG 75, LROIA, reel 413, frames 64–103.

12. *History of Oceana County, Michigan with Illustrations and Biographical Sketches of Some of Its Prominent Men and Pioneers* (Chicago: H. R. Page & Co., 1882), 81.

Chapter 12. The Council of Ogemuk

1. Nebawnagezhick et al. to United States of America, State of Michigan, 17 June 1865, National Archives and Records Administration, Washington, D.C., NAM, Series M234, RG 75, LROIA, reel 407, frames 1037–40.

2. Ibid., emphasis in original.

3. Moses Shobcooung to Dewitt Leach, 5 January 1865, National Archives and Records Administration, Washington, D.C., RG 75, Records of the Bureau of Indian Affairs, Entry 1131, Letters Received by the Michigan Superintendency & Mackinac Agency, 1849–1882 [hereafter LRMS&MA].

4. Ibid.

5. Ibid.

6. Nebawnagezhick et al. to United States of America, State of Michigan, 17 June 1865, National Archives and Records Administration, Washington, D.C., NAM, Series M234, RG 75, LROIA, reel 407, frames 1037–40.

7. Ibid.

8. There is, however, no indication in the federal record that the agent or his superiors retracted their appointment of Joseph Medawis as a federally sanctioned ogema. Medawis retained his position—at least in the eyes of the federal government—as a band or community leader, but his authority was no greater among the Indian Town Ottawas than that of the other ogemuk.

9. The successors of Cobmoosa, Mawbeece, Aishkebawgosh, Paybawme, Maishkeawshe, Payshawsegay, Aishquayosay, Wawbegaykake, Nebawnay-gezhick, and Opego's bands.

10. W. T. Howell to John Cox, 5 June 1869, National Archives and Records Administration, Washington, D.C., NAM, Series M234, RG 75, LROIA, reel 408, frames 718–24.

11. Proceedings of a council held at Paybawme, Oceana County State of Michigan, 24 July 1869, National Archives and Records Administration, Washington, D.C., NAM, Series M234, RG 75, LROIA, reel 408, frames 781–808.

12. Ibid.

13. Technically, an Ottawa was not allowed to sell his allotment or its resources, because his lands were held in trust by the federal government. Many Ottawas never received certificates or patents from the United States verifying their allotments or defining their tenure over these lands.

14. Proceedings of a council held at Paybawme, Oceana County State of Michigan, 24 July 1869, National Archives and Records Administration, Washington, D.C., NAM, Series M234, RG 75, LROIA, reel 408, frames 781–808.

Chapter 13. On the Outskirts

1. *History of Mason County, Michigan with Illustrations and Biographical Sketches of Some of Its Prominent Men and Pioneers* (Chicago: H. R. Page & Co., 1882), 8–9.

2. Bureau of the Census, *Report on Indians Taxed and Indians Not Taxed in the United States (Except Alaska) at the Eleventh Census: 1890* (Washington, D.C., 1894), 334.

3. *History of Oceana County, Michigan with Illustrations and Biographical Sketches of Some of Its Prominent Men and Pioneers* (Chicago: H. R. Page & Co., 1882), 81.

4. George Lee to the Commissioner of Indian Affairs, 31 August 1876, H. Exec. Doc. 1 (44–2) 1949, pp. 480–82.

5. George Lee to the Commissioner of Indian Affairs, 1 September 1880, H. Exec. Doc. 1 (46–3) 1959, pp. 223–25.

6. George Lee to the Commissioner of Indian Affairs, 1 September 1879, H. Exec. Doc. 1 (46–2) 1910, pp. 190–92.

7. Edward P. Allen to the Commissioner of Indian Affairs, 16 September 1885, H. Exec. Doc. 1 (49–1) 2379, pp. 339–40.

8. Edwin Brooks to J. A. Williamson, 27 December 1877, National Archives and Records Administration, Washington, D.C., NAM, Series M234, RG 75, LROIA, reel 413, frames 64–103.

9. Bureau of the Census, *Report on Indians Taxed and Indians Not Taxed in the United States (Except Alaska) at the Eleventh Census: 1890* (Washington, D.C., 1894), 334.

Chapter 14. Teaching the Children

1. Chingquashshe et al. to Sir, 24 January 1865, National Archives and Records Administration, Washington, D.C., RG 75, LRMS&MA.

Chapter 15. A Small Victory

1. In 1902, Andrew Waishkey, a Sault Ste. Marie Chippewa, succeeded in getting a government investigation of funds still due to the Ottawas and Chippewas under the 1855 treaty. An examination of accounts revealed that the Ottawas had $9,555 due to them from back annuities, as well as smaller amounts for blacksmith shops and agricultural implements. In effect, the government had carried Ottawa and Chippewa funds in the Treasury for half a century after the treaty—funds that were meant to be used to elevate the Ottawas by providing them with the equipment and provisions they needed to adapt to a "civilized" way of life.

Chapter 16. Community Councils to Business Committees

1. Sampson Robinson to the Various Leading Members of the Ottawa and Chippewa Indians, Residing in Michigan, 24 May 1919, National Archives and Records Administration, Washington, D.C., RG 75, CCF, 1907–1939, Mackinac, 54767-1919, 260.

2. C. F. Hauke to Dan Vincent, 30 August 1919, National Archives and Records Administration, Washington, D.C., RG 75, CCF, 1907–1939, Mackinac, 54767-1919, 260.

3. Sampson Robinson to Robert Aiken, 16 February 1921, National Archives and Records Administration, Washington, D.C., RG 75, CCF, 1907–1939, Mackinac, 54767-1919, 260.

4. By Laws of Michigan Indian Organization, 1923, National Archives and Records Administration, Washington, D.C., RG 75, CCF, 1907–1939, Mt. Pleasant, 25507-1923, 311.

5. Edgar Meritt to R. A. Cochran, 12 April 1923, National Archives and Records Administration, Washington, D.C., RG 75, CCF, 1907–1939, Mt. Pleasant, 59272-1921, 311.

Chapter 17. A Desperate Decade

1. Louise V. Armstrong, *We Too Are the People* (Boston: Little, Brown and Company, 1938), 200.
2. Ibid., 201.
3. Ibid., 201.
4. Ibid., 201–2.
5. Ibid., 204.
6. Ibid., 204–5.
7. Ibid., 206.
8. Ibid., 206–7.
9. Interview with Alex Sams, Anna (née Sams) Lempke, Bonnie (née Lempke) Kenny, Connie (née Lempke) Waitner, Katherine (née Sam) Glocheski, and Rose Sams, by James M. McClurken, 30 July 1990, private collection of James M. McClurken.
10. Louise V. Armstrong, *We Too Are the People* (Boston: Little, Brown and Company, 1938), 208–9.
11. Ibid., 222.

Chapter 18. New Deal, Renewed Hope

1. Frank Christy to W. Carson Ryan, 6 December 1934, National Archives and Records Administration, Washington, D.C., RG 75, CCF, 1907–1939, General Services, 45653-1934, 806.
2. Mark Burns and Frank Christy to John Collier, 4 May 1935, National Archives and Records Administration, Washington, D.C., RG 75, CCF, 1907–1939, Tomah, 34687-1934, 310.
3. The American Legion is a national volunteer-based organization of veterans. Its aims are community service, outreach, and intervention for the social benefit of all Americans. It remains an intact, functioning organization today.
4. Robert Dominic to John Collier, 21 February 1935, National Archives and Records Administration, Washington, D.C., RG 75, CCF, 1907–1939, General Services, 9634-1936, 066.
5. Forty of the forty-four signatures on the petition are legible. According to Ruth Koon, of these forty signatories, two lived in Custer; seven lived in Northport, but were originally from the Indian Village area and were close relatives of other signers; and the remaining thirty-one lived at Indian Village or at Highbridge, about two miles up the Manistee River from Indian Village,

or at a settlement on Coates Highway three miles from Indian Village. Ruth Koon Dean, 19 May 1994, personal communication with author; Interview with James Coon, Beatrice Coon, Viola Wilson, Ruth Smith, Louie Smith, John Smith, Grace Willis, James Coon Jr., by Bea Bailey, 15 October 1975, tape recording, *Native American Oral History Project*, Grand Rapids Public Library, Grand Rapids, Michigan.

6. Arthur Mobey to John Collier, 25 July 1936, National Archives and Records Administration, Washington, D.C., RG 75, CCF, 1907–1939, General Services, 9634-1936, 066.

7. Mark Burns to John Collier, 6 April 1936, National Archives and Records Administration, Washington, D.C., RG 75, CCF, 1907–1939, General Services, 9634-1936, 066.

Chapter 19. No One's Responsibility

1. Emilia Schaub to Eleanor Roosevelt, 30 March 1937, National Archives and Records Administration, Washington, D.C., RG 75, CCF, 1907–1939, General Services, 9634-1936, 066.

2. Frank Christy to John Collier, 16 June 1937, National Archives and Records Administration, Washington, D.C., RG 75, CCF, 1907–1939, General Services, 9634-1936, 066.

3. Richard White, "Ethnohistorical Report on the Grand Traverse Ottawas" (Suttons Bay, Michigan: Grand Traverse Band of Ottawa and Chippewa Indians, 1984), 164.

4. John Collier to Burton Wheeler, 18 April 1938, National Archives and Records Administration, Washington, D.C., RG 75, CCF, 1907–1939, General Services, 9634-1936, 066.

5. Enos Pego to John Collier, 27 May 1938, National Archives and Records Administration, Washington, D.C., RG 75, CCF, 1907–1939, General Services, 9634-1936, 066.

6. Enos Pego to John Collier, 12 December 1938, National Archives and Records Administration, Washington, D.C., RG 75, CCF, 1907–1939, General Services, 9634-1936, 066.

7. Ibid.

8. Fred Daiker to Enos Pego, 2 February 1939, National Archives and Records Administration, Washington, D.C., RG 75, CCF, 1907–1939, General Services, 9634-1936, 066.

Chapter 20. The Whole of the Holst Report

1. A Survey of Indian Groups in the State of Michigan, 1939, by John H. Holst, Supervisor of Indian Schools, ca. 1939, National Archives and Records Administration, Washington, D.C., RG 75, CCF, 1907–1939, General Services, 9634-1936, 066, p. 4.

2. Ibid, 4.

3. Ibid., 13.

4. Ibid., 13.

5. For a discussion of the Ottawa *potagon*, see Gertrude Kurath, Jane Ettawageshick, and Fred Ettawageshick, "Ritual Reconstruction," *Religious Customs of Modern Michigan Algonquians* (Philadelphia: American Philosophical Society, 1955), 4.

6. A Survey of Indian Groups in the State of Michigan, 1939, by John H. Holst, Supervisor of Indian Schools, ca. 1939, National Archives and Records Administration, Washington, D.C., RG 75, CCF, 1907–1939, General Services, 9634-1936, 066, p. 18.

7. Ibid., 21.

8. Peru Farver to John Collier, 1 December 1939, National Archives and Records Administration, Washington, D.C., RG 75, CCF, 1907–1939, General Services, 9634-1936, 066.

Chapter 21. "Indian Problems"

1. Peru Farver to William Brophy, 20 May 1946, National Archives and Records Administration, Washington, D.C., RG 75, CCF, 1940–1957, Tomah, 24930-1943, 800.

2. An Agreement between the U.S. and the Michigan Children's Aid Society, 4 June 1946, National Archives and Records Administration, Washington, D.C., RG 75, CCF, 1940–1957, Tomah, 24930-1943, 800.

3. Peru Farver to William Brophy, 20 May 1946, National Archives and Records Administration, Washington, D.C., RG 75, CCF, 1940–1957, Tomah, 24930-1943, 800.

Chapter 22. "An 'Advocate' and 'Attorney for the People'"

1. Memorandum of Willard Beatty to William Zimmerman Jr., 21 April 1944, National Archives and Records Administration, Washington, D.C., RG 75, CCF, 1940–1957, Tomah, 38443-1943, 855.

2. The Indian Claims Commission was a special body created by Congress to investigate Native land and monetary claims against the United States. All

such claims were handled by the ICC before Native groups could receive clearance to sue the United States in the U.S. Court of Claims.

3. Robert Dominic to Cornelius Bailey, 5 July 1948, Private Collection of Cornelius Bailey.

Chapter 23. Decades of Success and Political Evolution

1. Thornapple Indian Band, By-Laws, 1970, Thornapple Band of Indians.

Chapter 24. Distinct, Separate, and Sovereign

1. Judge Noel Fox ruled against the state's interpretation of the 1855 treaty language that "dissolved" the Ottawas' political relationship with the United States. He ruled in favor of the correct interpretation—that the relationship between the "Ottawa and Chippewa Tribes" was dissolved so that the two tribes could thereafter conduct their business with the United States as the separate entities they truly were.

2. American Indian Policy Review Commission, *Final Report* (Washington, D.C.: Government Printing Office, 1977), 1:461.

3. "Prepared Statement of Daniel Bailey Chairman, Little River Band of Ottawa Indians," *Pokagon Band of Potawatomi Indians Act and the Little Traverse Bay Bands of Odawa Indians and the Little River Band of Ottawa Indians Act: Hearing before the U.S. Senate Committee on Indian Affairs on S.1066 and S.1357*, 10 February 1994, 103rd Congress, 2nd session, pp. 55–57.

Chapter 25. Constructing a New Government

1. Constitution of the Little River Band of Ottawa, 13 May 2004, Tribal Collection of the Little River Band of Ottawa Indians, Manistee, Michigan.

2. Ibid.

3. Ibid.

Chapter 26. An Ancient Community, a New Century

1. Little River Tribal Census Project, 1 July 2002, Tribal Collection of the Little River Band of Ottawa, Manistee, Michigan.

References

Chapter 1. When the Europeans Came

Allen, Robert S. "The British Indian Department and the Frontier in North America, 1755–1830." In *Canadian Historic Sites: Occasional Papers in Archaeology and History*, no. 14. Ottawa, Ont.: National Historic Parks and Sites Branch, Parks Canada, Indian and Northern Affairs, 1975.

Blackbird, Andrew J. *History of the Ottawa and Chippewa Indians of Michigan: A Grammar of Their Language, and a Personal and Family History of the Author.* Ypsilanti, Mich.: The Ypsilanti Job Printing House, 1887.

Blair, Emma H. *The Indian Tribes of the Upper Mississippi Valley and Region of the Great Lakes, as Described by Nicholas Perrot, French Commandant in the Northwest; Bacqueville de la Potherie, French Royal Commissioner to Canada; Morrell Marston, American Army Officer; and Thomas Forsyth, United States Agent at Fort Armstrong.* Vol. 1, *1911–1912*; reprint, Lincoln: University of Nebraska Press, 1996.

Calkins, C. W., to Rebecca Richmond, 4 November 1909. RFP, collection 94, box 5, folder 2.

Edwards, Ninian, to William Eustis, 12 May 1812. NAM, Series M221, RG 107, Records of the Office of the Secretary of War, Letters Received by the Secretary of War, Registered Series, 1801–1870, reel 44, frames E-56.

Feest, Johanna E., and Christian F. Feest. "Ottawa." In *Handbook of North American Indians*, vol. 15, *The Northeast*, ed. Bruce Trigger. Washington, D.C.: Smithsonian Institution, 1978.

Hamilton, Claude T. "Western Michigan History, Colonial Period." *Michigan History Magazine*, no. 13 (1929): 222–26.

Heidenreich, Conrad. "An Analysis of the Seventeenth-Century Map 'Nouvelle France.'" *Cartographica* 25, no. 3 (Winter 1988): 67–111.

Jameson, Anna Brownell. *Winter Studies and Summer Rambles in Canada*. 1838; reprint, Toronto, Ont.: McClelland & Stewart, 1990.

Jenness, Diamond. "The Indians of Canada." *National Museum of Canada Bulletin* 65, Anthropological Series no. 15. Ottawa, Ont.: National Museum of Canada, 1932. Johnson, Ida Amanda. *The Michigan Fur Trade*. 1919; reprint, Grand Rapids, Mich.: Black Letter Press, 1971.

Kinietz, W. Vernon. *The Indians of the Western Great Lakes, 1615–1760*. 1940; reprint, Ann Arbor: University of Michigan Press, 1983.

Lyon, Charles, to Rebecca Richmond, 1909. RFP, collection 94, box 5, folder 6.

Mason, Ronald J. "Rock Island: Historical Indian Archaeology in the Northern Lake Michigan Basin." MCJA Special Paper No. 6. Kent, Ohio: Kent State University Press, 1986.

McClurken, James M. "We Wish To Be Civilized: Ottawa-American Political Contests on the Michigan Frontier." PhD diss., Michigan State University, 1988.

"Payment to Ottawa & Chippewa Indians." 1839. HRSP-LOC, reel 66, frame 41828.

Smith, Beverly Ann. "Systems of Subsistence and Networks of Exchange in the Terminal Woodland and Early Historic Periods in the Upper Great Lakes." PhD diss., Michigan State University, 1996.

Stone, Lyle M., and Donald Chaput. "History of the Upper Great Lakes Area." In *Handbook of North American Indians*, vol. 15, *The Northeast*, ed. Bruce Trigger. Washington, D.C.: Smithsonian Institution, 1978.

Tanner, Helen Hornbeck, ed. *Atlas of Great Lakes Indian History.* Norman: University of Oklahoma Press, 1987.

Waisberg, Leo Gilbert. "The Ottawa: Traders of the Upper Great Lakes, 1615–1700." Master's thesis, McMaster University, 1977.

White, Richard. *The Middle Ground: Indians, Empires, and Republics in the Great Lakes Region, 1650–1815.* Cambridge: Cambridge University Press, 1991.

Chapter 2. Kinsmen and Confederates

Baraga, Frederick, to Most Reverend Direction of the Leopoldine Foundation, 26 June 1834. BBC.

———, to the Leopoldine Foundation, 20 February 1835. BBC.

Callender, Charles. "Social Organization of the Central Algonkian Indians." Milwaukee Public Museum, Publications in Anthropology, no. 7. Milwaukee, Wisc.: The North American Press, 1962.

Dougherty, Peter. "Diaries of Peter Dougherty." *Journal of the Presbyterian Historical Society* 30, no. 2 (1952): 109.

Harris, C. A., to Joel R. Poinsett, 1 December 1837. S. Doc. 1 (25-2) 314, p. 595.

Henry, Alexander. *Travels and Adventures in Canada and the Indian Territories, Between the Years 1760 and 1776.* 1809; reprint, New York: Burt Franklin, 1969.

Jameson, Anna Brownell. *Winter Studies and Summer Rambles in Canada.* 1838; reprint, Toronto: McClelland & Stewart, 1990.

Leacock, Eleanor, and Richard Lee, eds. *Politics and History in Band Societies.* Cambridge: Cambridge University Press, 1982.

McClurken, James M. *Gah-Baeh-Jhagwah-Buk: The Way It Happened.* East Lansing: Michigan State University Museum, 1991.

————. "We Wish To Be Civilized: Ottawa-American Political Contests on the Michigan Frontier." PhD diss., Michigan State University, 1988.

McKenney, Thomas L. *Sketches of a Tour to the Lakes, of the Character and Customs of the Chippewa Indians, and of Incidents Connected with the Treaty of Fond du Lac.* 1827; reprint, Minneapolis: Ross & Haines, 1959.

"Odawa-Ojibwa, No. 7, Sketches." No date. Paul Radin Papers, American Philosophical Society, Philadelphia. "Habitations," p. 41, note 1; p. 45, notes 1 and 2; p. 43, notes 1 and 2, see section titled "Clans."

"Payment to Ottawa & Chippewa Indians." 1839, HRSP-LOC, reel 66, frame 41828.

Dougherty, Peter, to War Department, 21 January 1848, HRSP-LOC, reel 38, frame 22136.

White, Richard. *The Middle Ground: Indians, Empires, and Republics in the Great Lakes Region, 1650–1815.* Cambridge: Cambridge University Press, 1991.

Chapter 3. Coexistence and Conquest

Baraga, Frederick, to George Porter, 5 November 1833. BBC.

————, to Governor of Michigan, 5 November 1833. NAM M1, reel 33, frames 485–99.

————, to Most Reverend Central Direction of the Leopoldine Foundation, 7 March 1834. BBC.

————, to Most Rev. Directors of the Leopoldine Foundation, 24 May 1834. BBC.

Farmer, John. "An Improved Map of the Surveyed Part of the Territory of Michigan by John Farmer." New York: N. Balch and S. Stiles, Engravers, 1831.

Glocheski, Katherine (née Sam), Connie (née Lempke) Waitner, and Rose Sams. Interview by James M. McClurken, 29–30 July 1990. Private collection of James M. McClurken.

"Honor Michigan's Greatest Native Son." *Grand Rapids (Mich.) Herald*, 10 July 1927.

Johnson, Ida Amanda. *The Michigan Fur Trade*. 1919; reprint, Grand Rapids, Mich.: Black Letter Press, 1971.

Lantz, Raymond C. *Ottawa and Chippewa Indians of Michigan, 1870–1909*. Bowie, Md.: Heritage Books, 1991.

McClurken, James M. "We Wish To Be Civilized: Ottawa-American Political Contests on the Michigan Frontier." PhD diss., Michigan State University, 1988.

McCoy, Isaac. *History of Baptist Indian Missions: Embracing Remarks on the Former and Present Condition of the Aboriginal Tribes; Their Settlement within the Indian Territory, and Their Future Prospects*. Washington, D.C.: William M. Morrison, 1840.

Medacco, Steve, and Dorothy Medacco. Interview by James M. McClurken, 22 July 1991. Private collection of James M. McClurken.

"Payment to Ottawa & Chippewa Indians." 1839, HRSP-LOC, reel 66, frame 41828.

Peterson, Jacqueline, and Jennifer S. H. Brown, eds. *The New Peoples: Being and Becoming Métis in North America*. Lincoln: University of Nebraska Press, 1985.

"Pioneer Papers." *Ionia (Mich.) Standard*, 9 June 1893.

Sams, Alex, Anna (née Sams) Lempke, Bonnie (née Lempke) Kenny, Connie (née Lempke) Waitner, Katherine (née Sam) Glocheski, and Rose Sams. Interview by James M. McClurken, 30 July 1990. Private collection of James M. McClurken.

Chapter 4. The Will of the Grand Council

Baraga, Frederick, to Most Reverend Direction of the Leopoldine Foundation, 26 June 1834. BBC.

Kappler, Charles J., comp. "Treaty with the Ottawa, Etc., 1836." *Indian Affairs: Laws and Treaties*, vol. 2. Washington, D.C.: Government Printing Office, 1904.

A Map of the Acting Superintendency of Michigan, 15 September 1837. LROIA, reel 422, frame 746.

McClurken, James M. "We Wish To Be Civilized: Ottawa-American Political Contests on the Michigan Frontier." PhD diss., Michigan State University, 1988.

McCoy, Isaac. *History of Baptist Indian Missions: Embracing Remarks on the Former and Present Condition of the Aboriginal Tribes; Their Settlement within the Indian Territory, and Their Future Prospects*. Washington, D.C.: William M. Morrison, 1840.

Noahquageshik et al. to Andrew Jackson, 27 January 1836. LROIA, reel 422, frames 145–47.

Robinson, Rix, to Henry Schoolcraft, 21 July 1836. NAM M1, reel 41, frame 91.

Schoolcraft, Henry, to Lewis Cass, 18 July 1836. NAM, Series T494, RG 75, Documents Relating to the Negotiation of Ratified and Unratified Treaties with Various Indian Tribes, 1801–1869, reel 3, frames 368–75.

———, to Lewis Cass, 22 July 1836. NAM M1, reel 37, frame 7.

———, to Carey Harris, 27 February 1837. NAM M1, reel 37, frames 168–70.

Chapter 5. "Civilizing" the Ottawas

Blackburn, George M. "Foredoomed to Failure: The Manistee Indian Station." *Michigan History* 53, no. 1 (1969): 39–50.

Clifton, James A. "A Place of Refuge for All Time: Migration of the American Potawatomi into Upper Canada, 1830 to 1850." National Museum of Man Mercury Series: Canadian Ethnology Service Paper No. 26. Ottawa, Ont.: National Museums of Canada, 1975.

Feest, Johanna E., and Christian F. Feest, "Ottawa." *Handbook of North American Indians*, vol. 15, *The Northeast*, ed. Bruce Trigger. Washington, D.C.: Smithsonian Institution, 1978.

Harris, Carey, to Henry Schoolcraft, 27 January 1837, NAM, Series M21, RG 75, LSOIA, reel 20, frames 499–500.

Hickey, Manasseh. "A Missionary among the Indians: Reminiscences of Rev. M. Hickey as a Minister and Missionary of the Michigan Annual Conference of the Methodist Episcopal Church." *Report of the Pioneer Society of the State of Michigan*, vol. 4. Lansing, Mich.: W. S. George & Co. Printers and Binders, 1883.

McClurken, James M. "We Wish To Be Civilized: Ottawa-American Political Contests on the Michigan Frontier." PhD diss., Michigan State University, 1988.

"Payment to Ottawa & Chippewa Indians." 1839, HRSP-LOC, reel 66, frame 41828.

Richmond, William, to T. Hartley Crawford, 20 October 1845, S. Doc. 1 (29-1) 480, pp. 498–501.

Schoolcraft, Henry, to Carey Harris, 8 April 1837. NAM M1, reel 37, frame 190.

Schoolcraft, James, to Carey Harris, 29 August 1838. LROIA, reel 415, frames 636–43.

Stuart, Robert, to T. Hartley Crawford, 18 October 1841. S. Doc. 1 (27-2) 395, pp. 345–48.

Trygg, J. William. "Composite Map of United States Land Surveyors' Original Plats and Field Notes, Michigan Series." Ely, Minn.: J. Wm. Trygg, 1964.

Chapter 6. "Strong Titles" and the Government "Swan"

Acting Commissioner of General Land Office to Alfred B. Greenwood, 30 August 1859. LROIA, reel 406, frames 547–49.

Blackbird, Andrew J. *History of the Ottawa and Chippewa Indians of Michigan: A Grammar of Their Language, and a Personal and Family History of the Author.* Ypsilanti, Mich.: The Ypsilanti Job Printing House, 1887.

Dougherty, Peter, to George Manypenny, 14 August 1855. LROIA, reel 404, frames 577–79.

Elliott, Joseph, et al. to George Manypenny, 29 August 1855. LROIA, reel 404, frames 580–81.

Gilbert, Henry, to George Manypenny, 1 March 1855. LROIA, reel 404, frames 593–96.

———, to George Manypenny, 6 March 1854. LROIA, reel 404, frames 368–80.

———, to George Manypenny, 26 March 1855. LROIA, reel 404, frames 601–2.

———, to George Manypenny, 12 April 1855. LROIA, reel 404, frames 625–27.

———, to George Manypenny, 9 June 1855. LROIA, reel 404, frames 705–7.

Kapimose et al. to George Manypenny, 7 February 1855. LROIA, reel 404, frames 562–63.

Kappler, Charles J., comp. "Treaty with the Ottawa and Chippewa, 1855." *Indian Affairs: Laws and Treaties*, vol. 2. Washington, D.C.: Government Printing Office, 1904.

Kowise et al. to George Manypenny, 28 February 1855. LROIA, reel 404, frames 553–56.

Manypenny, George, to Robert McClelland, 26 November 1853. H. Exec. Doc. 1 (33-1) 710, pp. 243–64.

———, to Robert McClelland, 21 May 1855. LROIA, reel 404, frames 844–51.

Mashcaw and Kahkekaykahbahwe to Ulysses Grant, 14 August 1872. LROIA, reel 410, frames 642–45.

McClurken, James M. "We Wish To Be Civilized: Ottawa-American Political Contests on the Michigan Frontier." PhD diss., Michigan State University, 1988.

Nabunegezick et al. to George Manypenny, 27 February 1855. LROIA, reel 404, frames 557–66.

Nisawakwatt et al. to George Manypenny, 16 January 1855. LROIA, reel 404, frames 561–62.

Petoskey, William, et al. vs. The United States, 27 May 1905. RG 123, docket 27978.

Proceedings of a Council with the Chippewas & Ottawas of Michigan Held at the City of Detroit by the Hon. George W. Manypenny & Henry C. Gilbert, Commissioners of the United States, 25 July 1855. RG 123, docket 27978.

Richmond, William, to George Manypenny, 3 September 1855. LROIA, reel 404, frames 950–52.

Shaquanon et al. to Robert McClelland, 7 June 1855. LROIA, reel 404, frames 663–67.

Wendell, J. A. T., to George Manypenny, 2 April 1855. LROIA, reel 404, frames 988–91.

Chapter 7. "Not a Tent, a Wigwam, nor a Camp Fire . . ."

"Arrival of Indians—Departed for Their New Homes." *Grand Rapids (Mich.) Daily Enquirer and Herald*, 4 June 1859.

Brooks, Edwin, to Ezra Hayt, 12 January 1878. LROIA, reel 413, frames 104–36.

Campau, Antoine, to Robert Stuart, 6 December 1841. NAM M1, reel 51, frame 643.

Chandler, Margaret (née Bailey), and Katherine (née Sam) Glocheski. Personal communication with author, 17 May 1994.

Citizens of Grand River to Robert Stuart, 1841. NAM M1, reel 50, frame 593.

Craker, George, to Rebecca Richmond, 16 January 1909. RFP, collection 94, box 5, folder 2.

Fitch, Andrew, to J. W. Denver, 14 August 1857. LROIA, reel 405, frames 533–36.

———, to J. W. Denver, 14 August 1857. LROIA, reel 405, frames 537–39.

———, to J. W. Denver, 2 November 1857. LROIA, reel 405, frames 557–58.

———, to Alfred B. Greenwood, 21 May 1859. LROIA, reel 406, frame 444.

"Indian Payment." *Grand Rapids (Mich.) Enquirer*, 2 November 1841.

"Indians Departed." *Grand Rapids (Mich.) Daily Enquirer and Herald*, 29 May 1858.

"The Indians at Pentwater." *Grand Rapids (Mich.) Daily Enquirer and Herald*, 8 June 1858.

Johnston, John, to Robert Stuart, 27 December 1841. NAM M1, reel 51, frame 719.

"Lo the Poor Indian." *Grand Rapids (Mich.) Eagle*, 10 May 1859.

Lyon, Charles, to Rebecca Richmond, 1909. RFP, collection 94, box 5, folder 6.

McDonell, John, and John Clark to Carey Harris, 8 June 1837. LROIA, reel 402, frames 356–60.

"More Indians." *Grand Rapids (Mich.) Eagle*, 12 October 1858.

Nabannaygeshik et al. to Great Father, 12 August 1865. LRMS&MA.

"The Natives." *Grand Rapids (Mich.) Eagle*, 28 May 1858.

"Natives." *Grand Rapids (Mich.)* Eagle, 4 October 1858.

"The Ottawas in Oceana and Mason Counties." *Grand Rapids (Mich.) Daily Enquirer and Herald*, 19 June 1858.

"Poems of Alexander Pope." http://www.underthesun.cc/Classics/Pope/ PoemsOfAlexanderPope/

PoemsOfAlexanderPope7.html. Accessed 25 June 2005.

Schoolcraft, Henry, to Carey Harris, 27 February 1837. NAM M1, reel 37, frames 168–70.

Slater, L., to Henry Schoolcraft, 29 March 1837. NAM M1, reel 42, frames 288–89.

Smith, John, to Ely Parker, 26 November 1869. LROIA, reel 408, frames 997–99.

Smith, Sidney, to Lucius Lyons, 13 February 1837. William L. Clements Library, Ann Arbor, Michigan, LLP, box February–August 1837.

Stuart, Robert, to Antoine Campau, 14 December 1841. NAM M1, reel 38, frame 633.

Stuart, Robert, to Rix Robinson, 9 October 1843. NAM M1, reel 39, frame 319.

———, to Rix Robinson, 17 October 1843. NAM M1, reel 39, frame 330.

Chapter 8. New Communities, Established Leaders

Annuity Pay Roll of the Grand River Band of Ottawas & Chippewas of Michigan, 1870. RG 75, Entry 906, Annuity Payment Rolls, 1841–1949.

Bureau of the Census, *Report on Indians Taxed and Indians Not Taxed in the United States (Except Alaska) at the Eleventh Census: 1890*. Washington, D.C.: 1894.

Chingwash, George, to Ely Parker, 2 May 1870. LROIA, reel 409, frames 18–19.

Chingquosh, George, et al. to Edward Smith, 1875. LROIA, reel 411, frames 482–84.

"Copy of Names from Photostat of 1853 Annuity Roll of Grand River Ottawas." No date. Private collection of Robert and Waunetta Dominic.

Cushaway, Joseph, et al. to Hiram Price, 16 January 1882. RG 75, Entry 91, LROIA, 1881–1907, 1157-1882.

Durant Field Notes on the 1870 Annuity Pay Roll of the Grand River Band of Ottawas & Chippewas of Michigan. RG 75, Entry 906, Annuity Payment Rolls, 1841–1949. [*Note:* The Durant field notes are the notations written by Horace B. Durant on the "1870 Annuity Payrolls of the Chippewas and Ottawas of Michigan." Durant's handwritten notes appear in red and blue pencil on the original document, but do not appear on the microfilm.]

Kappler, Charles J., comp. "Treaty with the Ottawa and Chippewa, 1855." *Indian Affairs: Laws and Treaties*, vol. 2. Washington, D.C.: Government Printing Office, 1904.

Nebenaykezhick and George Chingwash to Wilder Foster and Thomas Ferry, 5 February 1873. LROIA, reel 410, frames 946–47.

Ottawas and Chippewas 1868 Annuity Payment Roll, ca. 1868. RG 75, Entry 906, Annuity Payment Rolls, 1841–1949.

Paiseshawsegay et al. to Nathaniel Taylor, 18 November 1868. LROIA, reel 408, frames 816–18.

Shawbequoung, Moses, to Dewitt Leach, 5 January 1865. LRMS&MA.

Statement of Pay-baw-me et al., 1 August 1866. LROIA, reel 407, frames 982–83.

Chapter 9. A "Great Excitement among the Indians"

Alvord, Henry, to Lewis Bogy, 16 November 1866. LROIA, reel 407, frames 852–65.

Bailey, J., to Robert McClelland, 18 March 1856. LROIA, reel 405, frames 12–14.

Bean, Hiram, to Charles Mix, 12 September 1857. LROIA, reel 405, frames 451–55.

Betts, George, to Edward Smith, 30 June 1873. LROIA, reel 410, frames 889–92.

———, to Edward Smith, 2 February 1875. LROIA, reel 410, frames 296–98.

———, to John Smith, 2 February 1876. LROIA, reel 411, frames 654–55.

Browning, Orville, to Commissioner of the General Land Office, 8 May 1868. LROIA, reel 408, frames 464–65.

———, to [Nathaniel Taylor], 14 December 1867. LROIA, reel 408, frames 155–59.

Edmunds, J. M., to James Harlan, 7 June 1866. LROIA, reel 407, frames 1011–20.

Ferry, T. W., to James Harlan, 10 February 1866. LROIA, reel 407, frames 911–14.

Fitch, Andrew, to J. W. Denver, 14 August 1857. LROIA, reel 405, frames 537–39.

———, to Alfred B. Greenwood, 8 June 1859. DRO&CA c1, R.2:65–66.

———, to Charles Mix, 2 October 1858. LROIA, reel 406, frames 157–58.

Gilbert, Henry, to George Manypenny, 25 February 1856. LROIA, reel 405, frames 244–48.

———, to George Manypenny, 14 July 1856. LROIA, reel 405, frames 215–18.

———, to George Manypenny, 7 August 1856. LROIA, reel 405, frames 145–46.

———. Notice to All Persons Having Claims against the Ottawa & Chippewa Indians. 23 October 1856. LROIA, reel 405, frames 178–79.

Gribb, William James. "The Grand Traverse Bands' Land Base: A Cultural Historical Study of Land Transfer in Michigan." PhD diss., Michigan State University, 1981.

Hendricks, Thomas, to George Manypenny, 2 April 1856. LROIA, reel 405, frames 295–97.

———, to George Manypenny, 5 April 1856. LROIA, reel 405, frames 298–300.

———, to George Manypenny, 24 April 1856. LROIA, reel 405, frames 301–2.

———, to Charles Mix, 10 June 1857. LROIA, reel 405, frames 734–36.

Johnston, William, to George Manypenny, 13 January 1856. LROIA, reel 405, frame 230.

Kappler, Charles J., comp. "Treaty with the Ottawa and Chippewa, 1855." *Indian Affairs: Laws and Treaties*, vol. 2. Washington, D.C.: Government Printing Office, 1904.

Knox, John, to F. A. Walker, 8 December 1871. LROIA, reel 409, frames 684–92.

Leach, Dewitt, to William P. Dole, 26 June 1861. LROIA, reel 406, frames 976–78.

———, to William Dole, 12 June 1864. LROIA, reel 407, frames 433–35.

Manypenny, George, to Henry Gilbert, 29 April 1856. LROIA, reel 54, frame 96.

———, to Robert McClelland, 1 March 1856. LROIA, reel 405, frames 242–43.

McClelland, Robert, to Thomas Hendricks, 11 April 1856. NAM, Series M620, RG 48, Records of the Office of the Secretary of the Interior, Letters Sent by the Lands and Railroads Division of the Office of the Secretary of the Interior, 1849–1904, reel 3, frame 214.

———, to George Manypenny, 11 April 1856. NAM, Series M620, RG 48, Records of the Office of the Secretary of the Interior, Letters Sent by the Lands and Railroads Division of the Office of the Secretary of the Interior, 1849–1904, reel 3, frame 215.

———, to George Manypenny, 14 April 1856. LROIA, reel 405, frames 239–41.

———, to George Manypenny, 24 April 1856. LROIA, reel 405, frames 252–54.

Mix, Charles, to Henry Gilbert, 19 March 1856. NAM, Series M21, RG 75LSOIA, 1824–1881, reel 53, frame 234.

Neu, Irene D. "The Building of the Sault Canal, 1852–1855." *Mississippi Valley Historical Review* 40 (June 1953–March 1954): 28, 38, 44.

Powers, C., to Ely Parker, 13 June 1870. LROIA, reel 409, frames 411–18.

Powers, C., et al. to House of Representatives, 1866. LROIA, reel 407, frames 913–14.

Richmond, William, to George Manypenny, 3 September 1855. LROIA, reel 404, frames 950–52.

———, to George Manypenny, 12 October 1855. LROIA, reel 404, frames 953–55.

Smith, Richard, to Lewis Bogy, 31 January 1867. LROIA, reel 408, frames 214–17.

———, to Dennis Cooley, 3 August 1865. LROIA, reel 407, frame 786.

———, to Dennis Cooley, 8 December 1865. LROIA, reel 407, frames 814–15.

———, to Nathaniel Taylor, 13 March 1867. LROIA, reel 408, frames 247–49.

Sprague, Ebenezer, et al. to [T. W. Ferry], 16 December 1865. LROIA, reel 407, frames 648–51.

Taylor, Nathaniel, to Orville Browning, 27 January 1869. LROIA, reel 408, frames 488–97.

Chapter 10. Accidents of History

Aishquaygonaybe et al. to Unknown, 17 May 1866. LROIA, reel 407, frames 833–35.

Dole, William, to J. P. Usher, 12 April 1864. NAM, Series M348, RG 75, Report Books of the Office of Indian Affairs, 1838–1885, reel 13, frame 376.

Foster, David, to Nathaniel Taylor, 26 August 1868. LROIA, reel 408, frames 431–33.

Howell, W. T., to Secretary of the Interior, 4 August 1866. LROIA, reel 407, frames 977–83.

Leach, D. C., to William P. Dole, 17 October 1863, H. Exec. Doc. 1 (38-1) 1182, pp. 494–500.

Leach, Dewitt, to William Dole, 5 April 1864. LROIA, reel 407, frames 464–66.

———, to William Dole, 22 April 1864. LROIA, reel 407, frames 481–82.

———, to William Dole, 10 May 1864. LROIA, reel 407, frames 487–88.

———, to William Dole, 14 June 1864. LROIA, reel 407, frames 516–19.

———, to William Dole, 4 October 1864. LROIA, reel 407, frames 538–40.

MacSauba, Louis, to Ely Parker, 20 May 1869. LROIA, reel 408, frames 911–13.

Nebawnagezhick et al. to United States of America, State of Michigan, 17 June 1865. LROIA, reel 407, frames 1037–40.

Nebawnaygezhick et al. to Unknown, 3 June 1868. LROIA, reel 408, frames 434–35.

Nawwemuscota and Awkowesay to our Great Father, 20 January 1866. LROIA, reel 407, frames 1034–36.

Prucha, Francis Paul, *The Great Father: The United States Government and the American Indians.* Vol. 1. Lincoln: University of Nebraska Press, 1984.

Shawbekoung, Moses, and Joseph Medawis to W. Welsh, 15 August 1871. LROIA, reel 409, frames 1024–25.

Shawbekoang, Moses, et al. to Nathaniel Taylor, 8 May 1868. LROIA, reel 408, frames 543–45.

Shobcooung, Moses, to Dewitt Leach, 5 January 1865. LRMS&MA.

Smith, Richard, to Dennis Cooley, 12 February 1866. LROIA, reel 407, frames 1060–62.

———, to Nathaniel Taylor, 2 December 1867. LROIA, reel 408, frames 323–28.

———, to Nathaniel Taylor, 12 June 1868. LROIA, reel 408, frames 561–62.

———, to Nathaniel Taylor, 29 October 1868. LROIA, reel 408, frames 573–75.

———, to Nathaniel Taylor, 26 January 1869. LROIA, reel 408, frames 944–47.

Statement of Pay-baw-me et al. 1 August 1866. LROIA, reel 407, frames 982–83.

Taylor, Nathaniel, to W. T. Otto, 8 May 1867. LROIA, reel 408, frame 79.

———, to W. T. Otto, 11 May 1867. LROIA, reel 408, frames 810–12.

———, to Richard Smith, 21 October 1868. LROIA, reel 408, frames 813–15.

Chapter 11. The Opposite of Intentions

An Act for the Restoration to Market of Certain Lands in Michigan, 10 June 1872. *United States Statutes at Large*, vol. 17, p. 381.

An Act to Amend the Act Entitled "An Act for the Restoration to Homestead Entry and to Market of Certain Lands in Michigan." Approved June Tenth, Eighteen Hundred and Seventy-Two, and for Other Purposes, 3 March 1875. *United States Statutes at Large*, vol. 18, pt. 3, p. 516.

Bayshaw et al. to Secretary of the Interior, 7 January 1873. LROIA, reel 411, frames 220–22.

Betts, George I., to Edward P. Smith, 5 October 1875. H. Exec. Doc. 1 (44-1) 1680, pp. 795–97.

Blackbird, Andrew J. *History of the Ottawa and Chippewa Indians of Michigan: A Grammar of Their Language, and a Personal and Family History of the Author.* Ypsilanti, Mich.: The Ypsilanti Job Printing House, 1887.

Brooks, Edwin, to J. A. Williamson, 27 December 1877. LROIA, reel 413, frames 64–103.

———, to Ezra Hayt, 4 January 1878. LROIA, reel 413, frames 53–64.

———, to Ezra Hayt, 12 January 1878. LROIA, reel 413, frames 104–36.

Chingwasha et al. to Commissioner of the Land Office, 4 August 1873. LROIA, reel 410, frames 994–96.

Delano, Columbus, to Acting Commissioner of Indian Affairs, 5 March 1873. National Archives Microfilm, M606, Letters Sent by the Indian Division of the Office of the Secretary of the Interior, 1849–1903, reel 11, frames 312–13.

———, to Edward Smith, 12 July 1873. DRO&CA c1, R.2:545–551.

Delano, Columbus, and Willis Drummond. Department of Interior Circular, 5 July 1872. LROIA, reel 411, frames 214–15.

Deputy Auditor General to James Long, 29 September 1869. LROIA, reel 408, frames 858–59.

Gebhart, W. S., and Joe Tonshe to Ely Parker, 20 January 1871. LROIA, reel 409, frames 595–98.

Griswold, George. "Peter Meshkaw." History of Eden and South Custer. No date, newspaper unknown, Rose Hawley Museum, Native American File.

History of Oceana County, Michigan with Illustrations and Biographical Sketches of Some of Its Prominent Men and Pioneers. Chicago: H. R. Page & Co., 1882.

Hubbell, Jay, to Willis Drummond, 24 March 1874. LROIA, reel 411, frame 250.

Kappler, Charles J., comp. "An act to amend the act entitled 'An act for the restoration to homestead-entry and to market of certain lands in Michigan,' approved June tenth, eighteen hundred and seventy-two, and for other purposes." *Indian Affairs: Laws and Treaties*, vol. 1. Washington, D.C.: Government Printing Office, 1904–1911.

———, comp. "An act extending the time within which homestead entries upon certain lands in Michigan may be made." *Indian Affairs: Laws and Treaties*, vol. 1. Washington, D.C.: Government Printing Office, 1904–1911.

Lee, George, to John Smith, 22 August 1876. LROIA, reel 411, frames 906–8.

———, to John Smith, 13 January 1877. LROIA, reel 412, frames 142–46.

———, to John Smith, February 1877. LROIA, reel 412, frames 207–33.

———, to Ezra Hayt, 10 September 1878. LROIA, reel 413, frames 572–75.

———, to the Commissioner of Indian Affairs, 1 February 1880. LROIA, reel 415, frames 123–30.

Long, James, to Ely Parker, 11 November 1869. LROIA, reel 408, frames 874–76.

McClurken, James M. "Wage Labor in Two Michigan Ottawa Communities." *Native Americans and Wage Labor: Ethnohistorical Perspectives*, ed. Alice Littlefield and Martha Knack. Norman: University of Oklahoma Press, 1996.

Nebenaykezhick and George Chingwash to Wilder Foster and Thomas Ferry, 5 February 1873. LROIA, reel 410, frames 946–47.

Proceedings of a Council with the Chippewas & Ottawas of Michigan Held at the City of Detroit by the Hon. George W. Manypenny & Henry C. Gilbert, Commissioners of the United States, 25 July 1855. RG 123, docket 27978.

Shaw, A. C., et al. to the Senate and House of Representatives, 21 February 1874. LROIA, reel 411, frames 216–19.

Shawbekoung, Moses, et al. to Ulysses Grant, 20 December 1872. LROIA, reel 410, frames 1028–32.

Smith, John, to George Lee, 10 January 1877. LROIA, reel 411, frames 976–84.

Chapter 12. The Council of Ogemuk

Ashquagonabe, George, et al. to My Great Father, 20 June 1872. LROIA, reel 410, frames 16–20.

Betts, George, to Francis Walker, 1 August 1872. LROIA, reel 410, frames 328–33.

———, and John Knox to Unknown, December 1871. DRO&CA c1, R.2:445.

Burns, Daniel, et al. to Lewis Cass, 16 March 1860. LROIA, reel 406, frames 601–4.

Chingquashshe et al. to Sir, 24 January 1865. LRMS&MA.

Downing, Denis, to Lewis Bogy, 22 January 1867. LROIA, reel 408, frames 87–89.

Dunbar, Willis F. *Michigan: A History of the Wolverine State*. Grand Rapids, Mich.: William B. Eerdmans Publishing Company, 1965.

Ferry, T. W., to Orville Browning, 5 June 1868. LROIA, reel 408, frames 424–29.

———, to James Harlan, 10 February 1866. LROIA, reel 407, frames 911–14.

———, to Ely Parker, 15 July 1870. LROIA, reel 409, frames 38–40.

———, to Ely Parker, 25 October 1870. LROIA, reel 409, frames 51–53.

———, to Nathaniel Taylor, 10 October 1868. LROIA, reel 408, frames 439–41.

Fitch, Andrew, to Alfred Greenwood, 20 March 1860. LROIA, reel 406, frames 649–55.

Foster, Wilder, to Francis Walker, 6 July 1872. LROIA, reel 410, frames 479–81.

———, to Francis Walker, 6 August 1872. LROIA, reel 410, frames 486–91.

Fox and Rose to Richard Smith, 23 February 1866. LRMS&MA.

Gay, J. H., to Richard Smith, 20 July 1865. LRMS&MA.

Genereau, Louis, to Richard Smith, 20 June 1865. LRMS&MA.

Genereau, Louis, to Richard Smith, 30 June 1865. LRMS&MA.

Howell, W. T., to John Cox, 5 June 1869. LROIA, reel 408, frames 718–24.

Kahgagahbeway et al. to Richard Smith, 15 June 1865. LRMS&MA.

Kahkekakahbahwe et al. to Richard Smith, 4 June 1865. LRMS&MA.

Knox, John, to Francis Walker, 8 December 1871. LROIA, reel 409, frames 684–92.

Long, James, to Ely Parker, 8 November 1870. LROIA, reel 409, frames 303–9.

———, to Ely Parker, 5 August 1869. LROIA, reel 408, frames 772–80.

———, to Ely Parker, 7 June 1870. DRO&CA ci, R.2:360–362.

———, to Ely Parker, 29 January 1871. LROIA, reel 409, frames 699–701.

———, to Ely Parker, 26 March 1871. LROIA, reel 409, frames 751–54.

———, to Ely Parker, 6 May 1871. DRO&CA ci, R.2:439.

Maynard, A. B., to Columbus Delano, 14 September 1871. LROIA, reel 409, frames 634–36.

Medawis, Joseph, et al. to President Ulysses Grant, 4 August 1871. LROIA, reel 410, frames 697–98.

Michigan Legislature Joint Resolution No. 16, 18 February 1869. LROIA, reel 408, frames 416–17.

Nebawnagezhick et al. to United States of America, State of Michigan, 17 June 1865. LROIA, reel 407, frames 1037–40.

Notinnoka et al. to Richard Smith, 5 June 1865. LRMS&MA.

Page, Aaron, to Richard Smith, 1 August 1866. LROIA, reel 407, frames 1190–93.

Pashawega et al. to Dewitt Leach, 24 February 1865. LRMS&MA.

Paykodushk and Bahdeese to Richard Smith, 8 June 1865. LRMS&MA.

Pheatt, N., to Lewis Bogy, 21 January 1867. LROIA, reel 408, frames 191–93.

Powers, C., to T. W. Ferry, 5 June 1870. LROIA, reel 409, frames 221–27.

Proceedings of a Council Held at Paybawme, Oceana County State of Michigan, 24 July 1869. LROIA, reel 408, frames 781–808.

Robinson, Seth, to Richard Smith, 16 May 1865. LRMS&MA.

Sayles, H. S., to Richard Smith, 10 May 1868. LRMS&MA.

Shawbekaung and David Foster to Indian Agent of Michigan, 9 May 1865. LRMS&MA.

Shawbekoung to Richard Smith, 24 June 1865. LRMS&MA.

Shawbakoung et al. to Dennis Cooley, 26 August 1866. LROIA, reel 407, frames 1156–58.

Shawquabunno et al. to William Dole, 24 February 1865. LROIA, reel 407, frames 749–51.

Shobcooung, Moses, to Dewitt Leach, 5 January 1865. LRMS&MA.

Smith, John, to Edward Smith, 26 September 1876. LROIA, reel 411, frames 1000–1006.

Smith, Richard, to Mendoka, 17 June 1865. LSMA.

———, to the Ottawas and Chippewas at Pere Marquette, 14 July 1865. LSMA.

———, to Nathaniel Taylor, 19 March 1869. LROIA, reel 408, frames 966–68.

Payshawsegay et al. to Francis Walker, 16 January 1872. LROIA, reel 410, frames 664–66.

Sprague, Ebenezer, et al. to [T. W. Ferry], 16 December 1865. LROIA, reel 407, frames 648–51.

Statement of Pay-baw-me et al., 1 August 1866. LROIA, reel 407, frames 982–83.

Taylor, Nathaniel, to Orville Browning, 27 January 1869. LROIA, reel 408, frames 488–97.

Withey, S., to James Long, 13 August 1869. LROIA, reel 409, frames 310–13.

Chapter 13. On the Outskirts

Allen, Edward, to the Commissioner of Indian Affairs, 24 August 1883. H. Exec. Doc. 1 (48-1) 2191, pp. 152–53.

Allen, Edward, to the Commissioner of Indian Affairs, 16 September 1885. H. Exec. Doc. 1 (49-1) 2379, pp. 339–40.

Bailey, Elizabeth (née Theodore), and Margaret (née Bailey) Chandler. Interview by James M. McClurken, 13 October 1990. Private collection of James M. McClurken.

Battice, John, et al. to William A. Jones, 4 December 1900. RG 75, Entry 91, LROIA 1881–1907, 59976–1900.

Betts, George I., to Edward P. Smith, 15 September 1873. H. Exec. Doc. 1 (43-1) 1601, pp. 542–44.

Brooks, Edwin, to Ezra Hayt, 12 January 1878. LROIA, reel 413, frames 104–36.

———, to J. A. Williamson, 27 December 1877. LROIA, reel 413, frames 64–103.

Bureau of the Census. *Report on Indians Taxed and Indians Not Taxed in the United States (Except Alaska) at the Eleventh Census: 1890*. Washington, D.C., 1894.

Campeau, Eliza, Benjamin Campeau, Hazel Plato, Myrtle Campeau, and Gregory Bergez. Tape-recorded interview by Bea Bailey, 21 August 1975. *Native American Oral History Project*, Grand Rapids Public Library, Grand Rapids, Michigan.

Coon, James, Beatrice Coon, Viola Wilson, Ruth Koon Smith, Louie Smith, John Smith, Grace Willis, James Coon Jr. Tape-recorded interview by Bea Bailey, 15 October 1975. *Native American Oral History Project*, Grand Rapids Public Library, Grand Rapids, Michigan.

Cushaway, Joseph, et al. to Hiram Price, 16 January 1882. RG 75, Entry 91, LROIA 1881–1907, 1157–1882.

Durant Field Notes on the 1870 Annuity Pay Roll of the Grand River Band of Ottawas & Chippewas of Michigan. RG 75, Entry 906, Annuity Payment Rolls, 1841–1949.

Gay, J. H., to Richard Smith, 3 July 1866. LRMS&MA.

Gay, James, to Richard Smith, 12 February 1866. LRMS&MA.

History of Manistee County, Michigan with Illustrations and Biographical Sketches of Some of Its Prominent Men and Pioneers. Chicago: H. R. Page & Co., 1882.

History of Mason County, Michigan with Illustrations and Biographical Sketches of Some of Its Prominent Men and Pioneers. Chicago: H. R. Page & Co., 1882.

History of Oceana County, Michigan with Illustrations and Biographical Sketches of Some of Its Prominent Men and Pioneers. Chicago: H. R. Page & Co., 1882.

Lee, George, to the Commissioner of Indian Affairs, 31 August 1876. H. Exec. Doc. 1 (44-2) 1749, pp. 480–82.

———, to the Commissioner of Indian Affairs, 1 September 1879. H. Exec. Doc. 1 (46-2) 1910, pp. 190–92.

————, to the Commissioner of Indian Affairs, 1 September 1880. H. Exec. Doc. 1 (46-3) 1959, pp. 223–25.

————, to Roland Trowbridge, August 1880. LROIA, reel 415, frames 397–402.

Lee, George W., to the Commissioner of Indian Affairs, 28 August 1877. H. Exec. Doc. 1 (45-2) 1800, pp. 517–20.

————, to the Commissioner of Indian Affairs, 1 September 1881. H. Exec. Doc. 1 (49-1) 2379, pp. 190–92.

Lempke, Anna (née Sams), Bonnie (née Lempke) Kenny, Connie (née Lempke) Waitner, and Katherine (née Sam) Glocheski. Interview by James M. McClurken, 29 July 1990. Private collection of James M. McClurken.

"Living Descendants of Peter 'Indian Pete' Espiew." *Mason Memories* 3, special issue (Summer 1979).

McClurken, James M. "Wage Labor in Two Michigan Ottawa Communities." *Native Americans and Wage Labor: Ethnohistorical Perspectives*, ed. Alice Littlefield and Martha Knack. Norman: University of Oklahoma Press, 1996.

Medacco, Steve, and Dorothy Medacco. Interview by James M. McClurken, 22 July 1991. Private collection of James M. McClurken.

Micko, Charity, Theresa Micko, Joe John, and Hazel John. Tape-recorded interview by Bea Bailey and Lee Cohen, 12 September 1975. *Native American Oral History Project*, Grand Rapids Public Library, Grand Rapids, Michigan.

Micko, Charity, Theresa Micko, Joe John, and Hazel John. Interview by James M. MClurken, 30 July 1990. Private collection of James M. McClurken.

Reuter, Dorothy. *Methodist Indian Ministries in Michigan 1830–1990*. Grand Rapids, Michigan: Eerdmans Printing Co., 1993.

Sams, Alex, Anna (née Sams) Lempke, Bonnie (née Lempke) Kenny, Connie (née Lempke) Waitner, Katherine (née Sam) Glocheski, and Rose Sams. Interview by James M. McClurken, 30 July 1990. Private collection of James M. McClurken.

Sayles, Henry, to Richard Smith, 10 May 1868. LRMS&MA.

Shawbekoung to Richard Smith, 24 June 1865. LRMS&MA.

Smith, Richard, to Nathaniel Taylor, 12 June 1868. LROIA, reel 408, frames 561–62.

Valentine, Robert, to Richard Ballinger, 25 January 1910. BIA-Durant.

Wasaquam Pierce, Dorothy, and Andrew Wasaquam. Interview by James M. McClurken, 20 April 1991. Private collection of James M. McClurken.

Chapter 14. Teaching the Children

Altmicks, Servatius, to T. J. Morgan, 16 August 1890. RG 75, Entry 91, LROIA 1881–1907, 25524-1890.

Bailey, Elizabeth (née Theodore), and Margaret (née Bailey) Chandler. Interview by James M. McClurken, 13 October 1990. Private collection of James M. McClurken.

Bailey, Mary, Viola Wilson, George Lawrence, and Joe Lawrence. Tape-recorded interview by Bea Bailey, 20 August 1975. *Native American Oral History Project*, Grand Rapids Public Library, Grand Rapids, Michigan.

Baker, William. "Schools." *Harbor Springs: A Collection of Essays*, ed. Jan Morley. Harbor Springs, Mich.: Harbor Springs Historical Commission, 1981.

Betts, George I., to F. A. Walker, 30 September 1872. H. Exec. Doc. 1 (42-3) 1560, pp. 586–87.

Browning, D. M., to the Secretary of the Interior, 14 September 1894. H. Exec. Doc. 1 (53-3) 3306, pp. 3–92.

Cadotte, Delia Lewis, and Viola Wilson. Tape-recorded interview by Bea Bailey and Lee Cohen, 16 September 1975. *Native American Oral History Project*, Grand Rapids Public Library, Grand Rapids, Michigan.

Chingquashshe et al. to Sir, 24 January 1865. LRMS&MA.

Cochran, R. A., to Peter James, 2 November 1908. CCF, 1907–1939, Mt. Pleasant.

Cochran, R. A., to Mary Tallman, 11 August 1922. CCF, 1907–1939, Mt. Pleasant.

Griswold, George. "Resseguie." History of Eden and South Custer, 29 November 1960, newspaper unknown, Rose Hawley Museum, Native American File.

"Indiantown: The Ottawa-Chippewa Reservation in Michigan," by Dawn Dornbos, 1975, Rose Hawley Museum, Native American File.

Leach, D. C., to William P. Dole, 17 October 1863. H. Exec. Doc. 1 (38-1) 1182, pp. 494–500.

Lee, George, to Hiram Price, 1 July 1881. RG 75, Entry 91, LROIA 1881–1907, 12613-1881.

———, to Hiram Price, 12 August 1881. RG 75, Entry 91, LROIA 1881–1907, 14253-1881.

———, to Roland Trowbridge, 1 October 1880. LROIA, reel 415, frames 428–37.

Lee, George W., to the Commissioner of Indian Affairs, 1 September 1878. H. Exec. Doc. 1 (45-3) 1850, pp. 570–72.

Padgett, Ora, to Edgar Meritt, 30 June 1925. CCF, 1907-1939, Mt. Pleasant.

Paybawme and Aishquayosay to Richard Smith, 20 May 1865. LRMS&MA.

Peters, Mary, Isaac Peters, and Renee Peters. Tape-recorded interview by Bea Bailey, 4 February 1976. *Native American Oral History Project*, Grand Rapids Public Library, Grand Rapids, Michigan.

Prucha, Francis Paul, *The Great Father: The United States Government and the American Indians*. Vol. 2. Lincoln: University of Nebraska Press, 1984.

Smith, Richard M., to N. G. Taylor, 28 August 1867. H. Exec. Doc. 1 (40-2) 1326, pp. 335–40.

Tallman, Mary, to R. A. Cochran, 9 August 1922. CCF, Mt. Pleasant Indian School and Agency, 1892–1946.

Chapter 15. A Small Victory

Acting Commissioner of Indian Affairs to Charles McNichols, 3 November 1905. LSOIA, A268:194.

Acting Commissioner of Indian Affairs to Charles McNichols, 4 November 1905. LSOIA, A286:219.

Ashkebyneka et al. to William Jones, 11 July 1900. RG 75, Entry 91, LROIA 1881–1907, 33159-1900.

Battice, John, et al. to William Jones, 4 December 1900. RG 75, Entry 91, LROIA 1881–1907, 59976-1900.

Dickson, Charles, to Robert Valentine, 20 June 1910. BIA-Durant, 45533-1908, 053.

Durant, Horace, to Robert Valentine, 13 July 1909. BIA-Durant, 45533-1908, 053.

Hauke, C. F., to Charles Dickson, 25 June 1910. BIA-Durant, 45533-1908, 053.

Kijigobenese, Simon, et al. to William Jones, 2 June 1900. RG 75, Entry 91, LROIA 1881–1907, 26720-1900.

Larrabee, Charles, to Horace Durant, 23 July 1908. BIA-Durant, 45533-1908, 053.

———, to Ethan Hitchcock, 10 November 1905. LSOIA, C268:438.

———, to Charles McNichols, 17 November 1905. LSOIA, A268:152.

McNichols, Charles, to Francis Leupp, 5 November 1905. RG 75, Entry 91, LROIA 1881–1907, 89634-1905.

———, to Francis Leupp, 10 November 1905. RG 75, Entry 91, LROIA 1881–1907, 90738-1905.

Pashawsaquay to Francis Walker, 25 January 1872. LROIA, reel 410, frames 667–69.

Paybawme, Joseph, and Moses Shawbequoung, to Ely Parker, 4 February 1870. LROIA, reel 409, frames 373–75.

Petoskey, William, et al. vs. The United States, 27 May 1905. RG 123, docket 27,978.

Tracewell, Robert, to George Cortelyou, 21 November 1907. CCF, 1907-1939, Mackinac, 98005-1920, 170.

Valentine, Robert, to Richard Ballinger, 25 January 1910. BIA-Durant, 45533-1908, 053.

———, to Charles Dickson, 18 May 1910. BIA-Durant, 45533-1908, 053.

White, Richard. "Ethnohistorical Report on the Grand Traverse Ottawas." Suttons Bay, Mich.: Grand Traverse Band of Ottawa and Chippewa Indians, 1984.

Chapter 16. Community Councils to Business Committees

Allen, George, to Cato Sells, 12 June 1920. CCF, 1907-1939, Mackinac, 54767-1919, 260.

Buckland, Romulus, to Robert Valentine, 27 May 1910. CCF, 1907-1939, Mackinac, 14737-1910, 056.

"By Laws of Michigan Indian Organization." 1923. CCF, 1907-1939, Mt. Pleasant, 25507-1923, 311.

Clifton, James A. *The Pokagons, 1683–1983: Catholic Potawatomi Indians of the St. Joseph River Valley*. Lanham, Md.: University Press of America, 1984.

Cobmoosa, Jacob, to Woodrow Wilson, 31 May 1920. CCF, 1907-1939, General Services, 96000-1919, 013.

Cobmoosa, Jacob Walker, to The President of the United States, 9 June 1921. CCF, 1907-1939, General Services, 96000-1919, 013.

———, to Your Honor Sir, 10 July 1918. CCF, 1907-1939, Mackinac, 58250-1918, 052.

Cochran, R. A., to Cato Sells, 16 February 1915. CCF, 1907-1939, Mt. Pleasant, 10088-1915, 300.

"Emmet Indians Organized." *Emmet County (Mich.) Graphic*, 19 April 1934.

Fall, Albert, to Charles Curtis, 15 June 1921. CCF, 1907-1939, General Services, 96000-1919, 013.

Finney, E. C., to James McLaughlin, 27 January 1923. CCF, 1907-1939, General Services, 96000-1919, 013.

———, to Homer Snyder, 7 February 1922. CCF, 1907-1939, General Services, 96000-1919, 013.

Hauke, C. F., to Romulus Buckland, 11 March 1910. CCF, 1907-1939, Mackinac, 14737-1910, 056.

Hauke, C. F., to William Hinman, 6 March 1915. CCF, 1907-1939, Mt. Pleasant, 10088-1915, 300.

———, to Dan Vincent, 30 August 1919. CCF, 1907-1939, Mackinac, 54767-1919, 260.

Hinman, William, to Sir, 25 January 1915. CCF, 1907-1939, Mt. Pleasant, 10088-1915, 300.

House Committee on Indian Affairs. *Report Authorizing the Ottawa and Chippewa Tribes of Indians of Michigan to Submit Claims to the Court of Claims.* 66th Cong., 3d sess., 21 February 1921, H. Rpt. 1344.

H.R. 10010. 67th Cong., 2d sess., 19 January 1922. CCF, 1907-1939, General Services, 96000-1919, 013.

H.R. 10188. 66th Cong., 1st sess., 25 October 1919. *Congressional Record,* vol. 58, pt. 8, p. 7539.

Meritt, Edgar, to R. A. Cochran, 12 April 1923. CCF, 1907-1939, Mt. Pleasant, 59272-1921, 311.

———, to Albert Shananquet, 12 April 1923. CCF, 1907-1939, Mt. Pleasant, 59272-1921, 311.

———, to Jacob Walker Cobmoosa, 8 August 1918. CCF, 1907-1939, Mackinac, 58250-1918, 052.

Vincent, Dan, to Sir, 28 July 1919. CCF, 1907-1939, Mackinac, 54767-1919, 260.

Vogelsang, Alexander, to Charles Curtis, 19 November 1919. CCF, 1907-1939, General Services, 96000-1919, 013.

McLaughlin, James, to Charles Burke, 15 January 1923. CCF, 1907-1939, General Services, 96000-1919, 013.

———, to Cornelius Bailey, 8 January 1916. Private collection of Cornelius Bailey.

———, to Henry Bailey, 21 July 1914. Private collection of Cornelius Bailey.

———, to Henry Bailey, 18 December 1915. Private collection of Cornelius Bailey.

Power of Attorney by Sampson Robinson et al. to Henry Bailey, 18 March 1911. Private collection of Cornelius Bailey.

Robinson, Sampson, to Robert Aiken, 16 February 1921. CCF, 1907-1939, Mackinac, 54767-1919, 260.

———, to the Various Leading Members of the Ottawa and Chippewa Indians, Residing in Michigan, 24 May 1919. CCF, 1907-1939, Mackinac, 54767-1919, 260.

S. 3307. 66th Cong., 1st sess., 25 October 1919. *Congressional Record,* vol. 58, pt. 8, p. 7505.

S. 92. 67th Cong., 1st sess., 12 April 1921. *Congressional Record*, vol. 61, pt. 1, p. 143.

Senate Joint Resolution 141. 67th Cong., 2d sess., 12 December 1921. CCF, 1907-1939, Mt. Pleasant, 59272-1921, 311.

Chapter 17. A Desperate Decade

Armstrong, Louise V. *We Too Are the People*. Boston: Little, Brown and Company, 1938.

Bruchac, Joseph. *The Native American Sweat Lodge: History and Legends*. Freedom, Calif.: Crossing Press, 1993.

Chandler, Margaret (née Bailey), and Katherine (née Sam) Glocheski. Personal communication with author, 17 May 1994.

Chisholm, John A. (Lex). "The Chisholm Trail." 22 April 1967, newspaper unknown, Rose Hawley Museum, Native American File.

Dunifon, Ed. "Some History of Michigan Hunting and Fishing and Their Licenses." Lansing: State Library of Michigan, 1993, p. 48.

Hoffman, W. J. "The Midewiwin or 'Grand Medicine Society' of the Ojibwa." *Seventh Annual Report of the Bureau of American Ethnology, 1885–1886*, vol. 7. Washington, D.C.: Government Printing Office, 1891.

Kurath, Gertrude, Jane Ettawageshick, and Fred Ettawageshick. "Ritual Reconstruction." *Religious Customs of Modern Michigan Algonquians*. Philadelphia: American Philosophical Society, 1955.

Micko, Albert, and Chuck Bailey. Tape-recorded interview by Bea Bailey, 8 January 1976. *Native American Oral History Project*, Grand Rapids Public Library, Grand Rapids, Michigan.

Nelson, Maude, Ben Cogswell, and Viola Wilson. Tape-recorded interview by Bea Bailey, 18 February 1976. *Native American Oral History Project*, Grand Rapids Public Library, Grand Rapids, Michigan.

Olson, Edwardine, to Director of Indian Reservation, 12 November 1928. CCF, 1907-1939, Mt. Pleasant, 55390-1928, 115.

Pamossigay, Cohen, to Charles Burke, 8 June 1923. CCF, 1907-1939, Consolidated Chippewa, 44729-1923, 115.

Prucha, Francis Paul. *Atlas of American Indian Affairs*. Lincoln: University of Nebraska Press, 1990.

Sams, Alex, Anna (née Sams) Lempke, Bonnie (née Lempke) Kenny, Connie (née Lempke) Waitner, Katherine (née Sam) Glocheski, and Rose Sams. Interview by James M. McClurken, 30 July 1990. Private collection of James M. McClurken.

Waymegwans, John, et al. to Commissioner of Indian Affairs, 7 December 1928. CCF, 1907-1939, Mt. Pleasant, 55390-1928, 115.

A Survey of Indian Groups in the State of Michigan, 1939, by John H. Holst, Supervisor of Indian Schools, ca. 1939. CCF, 1907-1939, General Services, 9634-1936, 066, pp. 7, 12–13.

Troufs, Tim, ed. "Spiritual Doctoring, Tipi-Shaking and Bone-Swallowing Specialists." *When Everybody Called me* Gah-bay-bi-nayss: *'Forever-Flying-Bird,'* http://www.d.umn.edu/cla/faculty/troufs/Buffalo.PB32.html, chapter 32. Accessed 1 September 2005.

Chapter 18. New Deal, Renewed Hope

Burns, Mark, and Frank Christy to John Collier, 4 May 1935. CCF, 1907-1939, Tomah, 34687-1934, 310.

———, to John Collier, 6 April 1936. CCF, 1907-1939, General Services, 9634-1936, 066.

———, to John Collier, 16 June 1936. CCF, 1907-1939, General Services, 9634-1936, 066.

Christy, Frank, to W. Carson Ryan, 6 December 1934. CCF, 1907-1939, General Services, 45653-1934, 806.

Coon, James, Beatrice Coon, Viola Wilson, Ruth (née Koon) Smith, Louie Smith, John Smith, Grace Willis, James Coon Jr. Tape-recorded interview by Bea Bailey, 15 October 1975. *Native American Oral History Project*, Grand Rapids Public Library, Grand Rapids, Michigan.

Dean, Ruth (née Koon). Personal communication with author, 19 May 1994.

Dominic, Robert, to John Collier, 21 February 1935. CCF, 1907-1939, General Services, 9634-1936, 066.

Engel, Albert, to John Collier, enclosing petitions to John Collier, 21 September 1935. CCF, 1907-1939, General Services, 45653-1934, 806.

Harper, Allan, to Fred Daiker, memorandum, 14 May 1937. CCF, 1907-1939, Great Lakes, 9592-1936, 066.

Kelly, Lawrence C. "The Indian Reorganization Act: The Dream and the Reality." *Pacific Historical Review* 44, no. 3 (1975): 293–309.

Langdon, Frank, to Roy Woodruff, 4 June 1935. CCF, 1907-1939, General Services, 9634-1936, 066.

Members of the Michigan Ottawa and Chippewa Tribes to John Collier, 29 March 1935. CCF, 1907-1939, General Services, 9634-1936, 066.

Members of the Ottawa Indians of Cross Village, County of Emmet, State of Michigan to the Office of Indian Affairs, 18 February 1935. CCF, 1907-1939, General Services, 9634-1936, 066.

Michigan Indians Defense Association. Meeting minutes, 21 March 1936. CCF, 1907-1939, General Services, 9634-1936, 066.

Mikatebinesi, William, et al. to Office of Indian Affairs, 3 July 1934. CCF, 1907-1939, Tomah, 35574-1934, 310.

Mobey, Arthur, to John Collier, 25 July 1936. CCF, 1907-1939, General Services, 9634-1936, 066.

Ottawa and Chippewa Indians of Michigan petition to John Collier, 20 August 1934. CCF, 1907-1939, Consolidated Chippewa, 57082-1934, 059.

Pego, Enos, to John Collier, 25 October 1935. CCF, 1907-1939, General Services, 96000-1919, 013.

Petition from Edward Francis et al. to John Collier, 22 August 1934. CCF, 1907-1939, General Services, 45653-1934, 806.

Petition from Fred Kishego et al. to John Collier, 13 May 1935. CCF, 1907-1939, Great Lakes, 9592-1936, 066.

Petition from Joseph Shomin et al. to John Collier, 10 May 1935. CCF, 1907-1939, Great Lakes, 9592-1936, 066.

Petition from Michigan Indians, 1934. CCF, 1907-1939, Consolidated Chippewa, 57082-1934, 059.

Petition from Simon Keway et al. to John Collier, 10 May 1935. CCF, 1907-1939, Great Lakes, 9592-1936, 066.

Petition from the Indians of Michigan to Secretary of the Interior, 14 November 1934. CCF, 1907-1939, Consolidated Chippewa, 57082-1934, 059.

Ryan, W. Carson, to Frank Christy, 19 January 1935. CCF, 1907-1939, General Services, 45653-1934, 806.

Ryan, W. Carson, Jr. to Mr. Monahan, memorandum, 15 December 1934. CCF, 1907-1939, General Services, 45653-1934, 806.

White, Richard. "Ethnohistorical Report on the Grand Traverse Ottawas." Suttons Bay, Mich.: Grand Traverse Band of Ottawa and Chippewa Indians, 1984.

Chapter 19. No One's Responsibility

Burns, Mark, to John Collier, 6 April 1936. CCF, 1907-1939, General Services, 9634-1936, 066.

Christy, Frank, to John Collier, 16 June 1937. CCF, 1907-1939, General Services, 9634-1936, 066.

Collier, John, to Burton Wheeler, 18 April 1938. CCF, 1907-1939, General Services, 9634-1936, 066.

Daiker, Fred, to Enos Pego, 2 February 1939. CCF, 1907-1939, General Services, 9634-1936, 066.

Farver, Peru, to A. L. Hook, 11 April 1938. CCF, 1907-1939, Tomah, 17413–1938, 310.

Farver, Peru, to John Collier, 3 May 1938. CCF, 1907-1939, General Services, 9634-1936, 066.

Kelly, Lawrence C. "The Indian Reorganization Act: The Dream and the Reality." *Pacific Historical Review* 44, no. 3 (1975): 306.

McClellan, Levi, to Peru Farver, 9 April 1938. CCF, 1907-1939, Tomah, 17413-1938, 310.

Meekel, H. Scudder. "Report on the Michigan Indians." Washington, D.C.: U.S. Department of Interior Library, 1937.

Pego, Enos, and Peter Stone to Senator Wheeler, 29 March 1938. CCF, 1907-1939, General Services, 9634-1936, 066.

———, to John Collier, 27 May 1938. CCF, 1907-1939, General Services, 9634-1936, 066.

———, to John Collier, 3 June 1938. CCF, 1907-1939, General Services, 9634-1936, 066.

———, to John Collier, 12 December 1938. CCF, 1907-1939, General Services, 9634-1936, 066.

Phinney, Archie. "A Proposed Role for the Federal Government in the Rehabilitation of the Michigan Indians." 1938. CCF, 1907-1939, General Services, 9634-1936, 066.

Schaub, Emilia, to Eleanor Roosevelt, 30 March 1937. CCF, 1907-1939, General Services, 9634-1936, 066.

White, Richard. "Ethnohistorical Report on the Grand Traverse Ottawas." Suttons Bay, Mich.: Grand Traverse Band of Ottawa and Chippewa Indians, 1984.

Zimmerman, William, Jr., to Emelia Schaub, 4 June 1937. CCF, 1907-1939, General Services, 9634-1936, 066.

———, to Prentiss Brown, 11 May 1938. CCF, 1907-1939, Tomah, 17413-1938, 310.

Chapter 20. The Whole of the Holst Report

Collier, John, to Jesse Cavill et al., 29 May 1940. CCF, 1907-1939, General Services, 9634-1936, 066.

Farver, Peru, to John Collier, 1 December 1939. CCF, 1907-1939, General Services, 9634-1936, 066.

Kurath, Gertrude, Jane Ettawageshick and Fred Ettawageshick. "Ritual Reconstruction." *Religious Customs of Modern Michigan Algonquians*. Philadelphia: American Philosophical Society, 1955.

A Survey of Indian Groups in the State of Michigan, 1939, by John H. Holst, Supervisor of Indian Schools, ca. 1939. CCF, 1907-1939, General Services, 9634-1936, 066.

Chapter 21. "Indian Problems"

An Agreement between the U.S. and the Michigan Children's Aid Society, 4 June 1946. CCF, 1940-1957, Tomah, 24930-1943, 800.

Beatty, Willard, to A. B. Caldwell, 26 September 1945. CCF, 1940-1957, Tomah, 37951-1945, 1602.

———, to William Zimmerman Jr., memorandum, 21 April 1944. CCF, 1940-1957, Tomah, 38443-1943, 855.

Caldwell, A. B., to William Brophy, 14 September 1945. CCF, 1940-1957, Tomah, 37951-1945, 1602.

Farver, Peru, to William Brophy, 20 May 1946. CCF, 1940-1957, Tomah, 24930-1943, 800.

Lewis, Henry, George Pego, and Bill Stone. Interview by James M. McClurken, 15 August 1995. Private collection of James M. McClurken.

Memorandum for William Zimmerman Jr., 24 March 1944. CCF, 1940-1957, Tomah, 38443-1943, 855.

Sands, O. R., to Peru Farver, 1 July 1946. CCF, 1940-1957, Tomah, 24930-1943, 800.

Zimmerman, William, Jr. to Willard Beatty, 8 April 1944. CCF, 1940-1957, Tomah, 38443-1943, 855.

Chapter 22. "An 'Advocate' and 'Attorney for the People'"

Agreement with the Northern Michigan Ottawa Association, 1948. Private collection of Cornelius Bailey.

Beatty, Willard, to William Zimmerman Jr., memorandum, 21 April 1944. CCF, 1940-1957, Tomah, 38443-1943, 855.

Chandler, Margaret (née Bailey). Notes on Northern Michigan Ottawa Association Meetings, 28 December 1957, 15 March 1958, 12 April 1958, 17 May 1958, 3 January 1959, 14 February 1959, 14 March 1959, April 1959, June 1959, 12 December 1959, 1960, 5 March 1960, 7 May 1960, June 1960,

28 September 1960, 22 October 1960. Private collection of Margaret (née Bailey) Chandler.

Dominic, Robert, to Charles Rogers, 7 January 1948. Private collection of Robert and Waunetta Dominic.

————, to Cornelius Bailey, 5 July 1948. Private collection of Cornelius Bailey.

————, to Roland Miller, 14 April 1948. Private collection of Robert and Waunetta Dominic.

————, to Roland Miller, 21 January 1949. Private collection of Robert and Waunetta Dominic.

Hawley, Rose D. "Chicken Dinner at Bailey Home." 25 July 1956, newspaper unknown, Rose Hawley Museum, Native American File.

————. "West State Ottawa Indians Organize in Meeting Here." 12 December 1953, newspaper unknown, Rose Hawley Museum, Native American File.

Lempke, Anna (née Sams), Bonnie (née Lempke) Kenny, Connie (née Lempke) Waitner, and Katherine (née Sam) Glocheski. Interview by James M. McClurken, 29 July 1990. Private collection of James M. McClurken.

Memorandum for William Zimmerman Jr., 24 March 1944. CCF, 1940-1957, Tomah, 38443-1943, 855.

Miller, Roland, to All Ottawa Indians, 26 April 1948. BIA-BAR.

Northern Michigan Ottawa Association. Meeting minutes, 21 June 1952. Private collection of Robert and Waunetta Dominic.

Provinse, John, to Robert Dominic, 8 April 1948. CCF, 1940-1957, Tomah, 5207-1948, 066.

White, Richard. "Ethnohistorical Report on the Grand Traverse Ottawas." Suttons Bay, Mich.: Grand Traverse Band of Ottawa and Chippewa Indians, 1984.

Zimmerman, William, Jr. to Willard Beatty, 8 April 1944. CCF, 1940-1957, Tomah, 38443-1943, 855.

Chapter 23. Decades of Success and Political Evolution

Assistant Secretary of the Interior Cohen to Guy Vander Jagt, 8 June 1976. Private collection of Emily Smith.

"Bob and Waunetta Dominic." *Petoskey (Mich.) News Review*, 23 December 1981.

Chandler, Margaret (née Bailey). Notes on Northern Michigan Ottawa Association Meetings, 24 June 1965. Private collection of Margaret (née Bailey) Chandler.

Code of Ethics Adopted at Northern Michigan Ottawa Association Meeting, 4 August 1971. Thornapple Band of Indians.

Cross, William, and David Dominic to Thomas Kleppe, 23 March 1976. Private collection of William Cross.

Dominic, Robert, to E. J. Riley, 15 January 1962. Private collection of Robert and Waunetta Dominic.

———, to E. J. Riley, 16 February 1962. Private collection of Robert and Waunetta Dominic.

———, to Rogers Morton, 5 May 1975. Private collection of Robert and Waunetta Dominic.

Hillman, James R. *The Minutes of the Michigan Commission on Indian Affairs, 1956–1977*. Vol. 1. Canal Fulton, Ohio: Hillman, 1990.

Indian Youth Development Program Proposal, 20 August 1970. Thornapple Band of Indians.

"Indian-State Hunting Tiff to Begin in Court Feb. 14." *Grand Rapids (Mich.) Press*, 6 February 1983.

Meeds, Lloyd, to Morris Thompson, copied to Donald Riegle and Guy Vander Jagt, 3 May 1976. Private collection of Emily Smith.

Minutes from a Business Meeting of the Northern Michigan Ottawa Association, 17 March 1962. Private collection of Robert and Waunetta Dominic.

Minutes of the Northern Michigan Ottawa Association Meeting Enclosing Resolutions 001A, 002A, and 003A, 20 January 1973. Private collection of Margaret (née Bailey) Chandler.

Moran, Homer, to Georgianna Smith, 1 May 1972. Private collection of Linda (née Shagonaby) Andre.

Northern Michigan Ottawa Association. Executive Board meeting minutes, 23 November 1985. Private collection of Sally (née Pego) Jobes.

Northern Michigan Ottawa Association. Meeting minutes, 12 June 1971. Private collection of Margaret (née Bailey) Chandler.

Northern Michigan Ottawa Association: Meeting of Indian Commercial Fishermen, 4 August 1971. Thornapple Band of Indians.

Notes from a Northern Michigan Ottawa Association Meeting, 7 August 1965. Private collection of Margaret (née Bailey) Chandler.

Page from the *Congressional Record* concerning S. 11175, 19 July 1972. Private collection of Margaret (née Bailey) Chandler.

A Proposed Code of Ethics signed by Warren Petoskey, 28 July 1971. Thornapple Band of Indians.

A Resolution by Tribal Members, 17 March 1962. Private collection of Robert and Waunetta Dominic.

Riley, E. J., to Robert Dominic, 15 February 1962. Private collection of Robert and Waunetta Dominic.

———, to Robert Dominic, 9 January 1962. Private collection of Robert and Waunetta Dominic.

———, to Robert Dominic, 24 January 1962. Private collection of Robert and Waunetta Dominic.

———, to Robert Dominic, 23 June 1969. Private collection of Robert and Waunetta Dominic.

"Robert Dominic Dies at Age 63." *Petoskey (Mich.) News Review*, 1 March 1976.

Seneca, Martin, Jr. to George Goodwin, 4 May 1976. Private collection of William Cross.

Thompson, Morris, to George Goodwin, 3 March 1976. BIA-BAR.

Thornapple Band of Indians. Articles of Incorporation, 23 February 1971. Thornapple Band of Indians.

Thornapple Indian Band. By-Laws, 1970. Thornapple Band of Indians.

Vander Jagt, Guy, to Emily Robles, 22 June 1976. Private collection of Emily Smith.

———, to Emily Robles, 4 June 1976. Private collection of Emily Smith.

White, Richard, *Ethnohistorical Report on the Grand Traverse Ottawas*. Suttons Bay, Mich.: Grand Traverse Band of Ottawa and Chippewa Indians, 1984.

Chapter 24. Distinct, Separate, and Sovereign

American Indian Policy Review Commission. *Final Report*. Vål. 1. Washington, D.C.: Government Printing Office, 1977.

Chandler, Margaret (née Bailey), to Department of Treasury, 16 September 1981. Thornapple Band of Indians.

"Death Takes President of Indian Association." *Detroit (Mich.) News*, 23 December 1981.

Kelley, Frank, to Thornapple Band of Indians, 30 July 1981. Thornapple Band of Indians.

Levin, Carl, to Bud Shapard, 20 July 1979. BIA-BAR.

Northern Michigan Ottawa Association. Notice of Thirty-first Annual Council Meeting, 5 June 1979. Private collection of Robert and Waunetta Dominic.

Notes from Review Committee Meeting, 27 January 2007. Little River Band of Ottawa Indians, Manistee, Michigan.

"Prepared Statement of Daniel Bailey Chairman, Little River Band of Ottawa Indians." *Pokagon Band of Potawatomi Indians Act and the Little Traverse*

Bay Bands of Odawa Indians and the Little River Band of Ottawa Indians Act: Hearing before the U.S. Senate Committee on Indian Affairs on S.1066 and S.1357. 103rd Cong., 2d sess., 10 February 1994, pp. 55–57.

Reed, Todd. "Indian Netters Meet Hostility." 16 April 1982, newspaper unknown, Rose Hawley Museum, Native American File.

Shapard, John, to Waunetta Dominic, 13 August 1979. BIA-BAR.

United States v. State of Michigan, 7 May 1979, No. M26–73 C.A., 471 Fed. Supp. 192 (W.D. Michigan, N.D., 1979).

Waitner, Connie (née Lempke). Personal communication with author, 18 March 1994.

Chapter 25. Constructing a New Government

Constitution of the Little River Band of Ottawa, 13 May 2004. Tribal collection of the Little River Band of Ottawa, Manistee, Michigan.

Little River Tribal Census Project, 1 July 2002. Tribal collection of the Little River Band of Ottawa, Manistee, Michigan.

Notes from Review Committee Meeting, 27 January 2007. Little River Band of Ottawa Indians, Manistee, Michigan.

Index